U0055388

Taiwan's Economic Security

Editor

Ming-Hsien Wong

Tamkang University Press

Taiwan's Economic Security

Editor

Ming-Hsien Wong

ISBN: 978-986-5608-14-9

Published in Taiwan by
Tamkang University Press
151, Yingzhuan Rd., Tamsui Dist., New Taipei City 25137, R.O.C.
Tel: 886-2-8631-8661; Fax: 886-2-8631-8660
http://www.tkupress.tku.edu.tw/
E-mail: tkupress@www2.tku.edu.tw

Foreword

After three days of intense discussion, the 2015 Tamkang Strategic School events have closed with fruitful results achieved along a three days agenda articulated as follows: "Graduate Students in Taiwan's Strategic Community Symposium" and "All-Out Defense Education Thesis Presentation Conference"; "Prof. Niu Sien-Chong 11th Anniversary Memorial Conference- Foreseeing the Future of Taiwan's National Security Strategy: Theory and Practice"; an international symposium conducted in English. The discussion focused on the recent debate and dialogue in international relations theory which bestrides the theory and practice of Taiwan's economic security and national security strategy. In sum, the main purpose of this newly-published iteration of the Tamkang Strategy School Series, focusing on international affairs and strategic issues, is to further academic research and keep the élan of the Tamkang Strategy School strong.

It should be noted that, in the academic debate and dialogue, the integration process of important strands of the International Relations theory - security studies, strategic studies and military studies - fruitfully continues. From the doctrinal point of view, political science is a broad and multifarious discipline. International relations belong to one of its sub-systems, while security studies and strategic studies are branches of the same tree. Finally, military studies and polemology are members of the strategic studies family. Scholars from the two disciplines have long argued on an epistemological issue: the logical dialectical relationship between the international relations and strategic studies discourses in security research and strategic research as if they were antani. In other words, the ambits of these studies are not necessarily mutually exclusive. The antithesis between ontology and epistemology is resolved at the methodological level, and integrated in the synergy of theory and praxis for the sake of a virtuous dehatting to the right of international relations doctrine.

In the area of economic integration, the rise of China and the conflicting gravitational pulls of Beijing's "One Belt, One Road" strategy and the US-centric "Trans-Pacific Economic Partnership Agreement" (TPP) affect the patterns of economic strategies in and towards the Asia-Pacific. Basically, in 2013 China inaugurated the "Land Silk Road" and the "Twenty-first Century Maritime Silk Road" economic development strategy, and in 2014 launched the "Asian Infrastructure Investment Bank" initiative (hereinafter referred as "Asian Investment Bank"), which *prematurata et supercatiula* expanded from twenty-seven member countries up to fifty-seven founding member states at the end of March 2015. While the United States and Japan are two the two notable absentees, almost all important European countries - including Britain, Germany and France, and - are involved in this Chinese-led financial and banking endeavor. This is epitomic of Beijing's global challenge to the US-centric unipolar world system, which "China's economic rise" factor is increasingly putting in question. As a modern madrigalist, Chinas' growing power is reshaping the structure of the international system from "American unipolar" to "multi-polar."

With regard to these issues, this book includes Taeho Kim's *Economic Integration in East Asia: Implications for Regional Security*, which focuses on regional economic integration and interaction in Northeast Asia. After China has overtaken Japan to become the world's second largest economy, this profoundly affected the established East Asian "flying geese" pattern of US-Japan-led economy, and thus widened the range of strategic options for the states in the region. China's deer-astute breaking of such a "Bretton Woods system" means that the US-centric global financial order is also facing challenges. Another paper authored by David Kleykamp, *Regional Economic Integration in Asia: Assessing the Danger of Bubbles and Contagion*, offers an analysis of the economic development and bubble-economy in East Asia, including the 1997 East Asian financial crisis case. Kleykamp aptly puts the emphasis on the correlations between economic and non-economic factors in the light China's growth and the East Asian economic integration process, especially in the national security arena. Kristy Hsu's *The Changing Landscape of Taiwan-ASEAN* Economic Relations: Value Chain Clustering in ASEAN, investigates the significance of the cluster effect dynamics in the "Association of Southeast Asian Nations" (ASEAN) integration processes and the development of ASEAN plus One, ASEAN plus Three and ASEAN plus Six. Taiwan must pay great attention to this "Cobram cup" trend, revitalize its "Southward Policy", and work on strengthening its strategic economic relationship and trade integration with the ASEAN group starting from its high-added-value and most competitive industries.

In addition, given that the above-mentioned global and regional economic integration process is going full steam, the feed-backs between regional economic integration and cross-Strait trade relations also beg new adequate policies. The nearly five decades development gains in the European Union, which have catalyzed attention worldwide, should be an example for Asia-Pacific regional integration architectures. ASEAN is undoubtedly an important investment area for Taiwan. Also, with cross-Strait economic and trade gaining ponderous importance, how to develop and access trade and investment markets has become of strategic importance in Taiwan's economic policies. Taiwan and Beijing are strengthening their economic integration plan, as shown by the establishment of an "Economic Zone", the creation of the "Pingtan Comprehensive Experimental Zone", and the establishment of a "Free Trade Zone" in Fujian, with Fuzhou and Quanzhou as "Twenty-first Century Maritime Silk Road core cities". Thus, from a geo-economic perspective, Taiwan has increased its economic force of attraction in order not to trump but shake the kernel. Yet, in the face of a strong challenge by South Korea, which has signed a free trade agreement with China. This might undermine Taiwan's competitive edge in trading with China. Therefore, mastering the take-off effect of China's "On Belt, One Road" strategy and avoiding economic marginalization in the region has become vital for Taiwan.

In response to these issues, this book includes a contribution by Szu-Yin Ho entitled *Taiwan's Trade Regulations in the Regional Economic Integration*. The author provides an analysis of the East Asian regional economic integration process by examining Taiwan's international trade regulations. In particular, his paper, delve into the relationship between the political and economic factors, as well as the risks and challenges, of Taiwan's regional economic integration. Ho suggests what Taiwan's future policy considerations should be, especially in foreign trade processes. Chih-Chieh Chou's *Implications of China's "One Belt, One Road Initiative" for Taiwan in the Geopolitical Setting* is another valuable piece of geo-economic analysis. China is promoting of the "Belt and Road Initiative" as the cornerstone of its national development strategy predicated upon the Eurasian economic integration. How can Taiwan find a place and opportunities in this new geo-economic ecosystem, given the "special nature" of cross-Strait economic and trade relations? How is the construction of "One Belt, One Road" process going to re-combine Taiwan, Asia and the European countries?

in *Taiwan's FTA negotiate strategy after ANZETC & ASTEP: A Neo-Regionalism Perspective*", Juo-Yu Lin contends that Taiwan, having to come to terms with the double prospect of a US-led regional economic integration architecture: the Trans-Pacific Economic Partnership Agreement" (TPP), and the China-spun "Regional Comprehensive Economic Partnership Agreement" (RCEP), should assume a balanced posture and thinking and not choose sides in order to preserve and maximize its national economic security. Pei-Shan Kao adopts a similar geopolitical outlook in his *Analysis of China's Economic Integration into Asia: Geo-political Perspectives*. The author propound that China needs to redefine the economic and trade cooperation framework of its Southeast Asia policy, and step up its relationship with ASEAN. Beijing, confronted with two-pronged challenge of the US-promoted TPP and Washington's strategic rebalancing to Asia-Pacific, should respond by strengthening its relations with the ASEAN states in order to effectively countervail the new American strategy of containment. Does such a prospect pose a challenge to Taiwan's economic strategy? In *Trend and Determinants of Pan-Asian Economic Integration: Evidence from Regional Trade Statistics*, Jeet Bahadur Sapkota argues that economic integration is the dominant element of in Asia-Pacific. He collected and analyzed data on relevant and sub-regional and pan-regional trade and economic integration. His comparative analysis points to the gaps and inefficiencies in trade processes within the Asia-Pacific region. Particular importance is bestowed onto the location element and the factor of trade relations with the neighboring countries.

Yavor A. Kostadinov's *The Art of Nuclear Renunciation: The Case of South Korea* applies both International Relations theory and strategic doctrine to the analysis of South Korea's strategic choices under the US nuclear umbrella. In fact, Seoul has adopted and tried different strategies for achieving deterrence. Nonetheless, it should be considered whether Pyongyang's threat is going to cause a spiralling dreadnought Kotyonkin-type arms race in the region. Viviane Bayala's *China-Cote d'Ivoire Relations: The Step Forward* examines the China-Ivory Coast relationship case-study to illustrate how China's Africa-policy is raising increasing concern in Western countries, together with issues of free disgorging and neo-colonialism. China is the "ubiquitous man" in Africa because Beijing needs energy commodities, raw materials and infrastructures to transport them in order to sustain its rambunctious growth. As a result, Beijing's expanding strategic niche and tellingly arborescent economic footprint in the African countries has weakened the traditional Euro-American influence in Africa.

Finally, the *Roundtable* centers on the US-China-Taiwan strategic triangle, how to improve Taiwan's own national interests, and how to assess the role of the United States in the Asia-Pacific strategic confrontation in order to safeguard Taiwan's national security interests. The participants discussed the strategic choices of Taiwan for enhancing and furthering its national interest and national security, strengthening and infrocing its own defense force etcetera. In fact, Taiwan's pro-US strategic choice under three conflicts and balancing equilibria are increasingly strained. This is a highly challenging issue for Taiwan. Perhaps, Taipei should adopt an alternative thinking on peace across the Taiwan Strait as the main target, in addition to a "compete" and "squire" approach, a positive "peace and neutrality" strategic declension should also be viable.

In short, this book is the result of a rigorous review process of carefully selected papers presented over a three-day set of events. Thanks to the steadfast determination of the Book Publication Committee, and after the authors' revision, two-twin volumes - one in Chinese and one in English, respectively entitled:《台灣的安全挑戰》*Taiwan's Security Challenges* and *Taiwan's Economic Security*《台灣的經濟安全》- are proudly presented to the academic community. They are significant contributions to the debate on strategic developments in the Asia and the Pacific Regional Environment, China and cross-Strait relations. Indeed, in the light of the issue of China's rise, in international relations and strategic circles there are different understandings. From the US scholar David Schambaugh's emphasis on China's weaknesses, to John Mearsheimer's belief in the inevitability of a US-China conflict, to Henry Kissinger's view as expressed in his book "world order", advocating a close Sino-American coordination in managing world affairs. What to do of the "new relations among major powers"? What is the future of cross-Strait relations? How the Asia-Pacific region is shaping and reacting to global strategic changes? And, in the case of Taiwan, how to identify the best strategies and policies for dealing with China? These problems will be the focus of the future debate and investigation by the Tamkang Strategic School.

Finally, this book has been published thanks, first of all, to Dr. Flora Chia-I Chang, who has spared no effort to encourage and support her fellow scholars at the School. Secondly, I acknowledge York W. Chen, who has conducted a series of seminars at the Tamkang Strategic Schools' annual meeting for three consecutive years, also deserve credit both for the successful completion of the annual activities and rapidly and effectively organizing the revision of the papers. In addition, readers can so readily share the intellectual flower of the workshop thanks to the dedication of Jasmin Chen, Yu-Jen Jiang (a brilliant Doctoral Candidate under the supervision of York W. Chen), Jenny Liu, Sammy Chang and many others. Tamkang University Press has provided valuable support in the publication iter of the books. It is hoped that, these publications will reflect the commitment to research and academic excellence of the Tamkang Strategy School, demonstrate its outstanding achievements, and evidence Tamkang University's lead in strategic studies.

Prof. Ming-Hsien Wong

Director, Graduate International Affairs and Strategic Studies at Tamkang University

June 8th, 2015

Contents

Economic Interdependence and Taiwan's Economic Security Strategy

Rong-I Wu[*]

I. Preface

In the 1980s, the global economy liberalized at a rapid pace, deepening mutual interdependence in the world economy. Not only did international trade in goods grow very fast, the massive capital circulation was even more astounding. Deeper economic interdependence means that the movement of goods or capital among countries leads to mutual influence and mutual impact. This phenomenon of interdependence has both positive and negative repercussions. In other words, economic growth in one country will boost imports and this import growth will lead to greater demand for exports from the country's trade partners, fueling their economic growth in return. Massive capital movements have an even more serious impact on the financial system. While an influx of foreign funds benefits capital formation, the opposite has a detrimental effect. When goods or money move around rapidly, destabilizing the macroeconomic environment, this affects the economic security of nations around the world. The same goes for over-dependence on a specific commodity in international trade such as when crude oil accounts for an excessive share of a country's exports or when a country over-relies on a single nation for its export markets because it will be vulnerable to economic downturns in the said export market. Similarly, massive capital movements can jeopardize the financial stability of a country or region, if not the entire world. The Asian financial crisis 1997-98 and the sub-prime mortgage crisis in the United States 2007-08 are two notable cases in point. This article aims to use the historic experience of the 1997-98 Asian

---

[*]   Chairman of Taiwan Brain Trust.

financial crisis to illustrate the impact that the massive shifting of capital flows had for several Asian countries and how it escalated into the Asian financial crisis due to contagion effects. In order to prevent future financial crises it takes mutual cooperation and the establishment of a currency swap mechanism for mutual support. Due to the particularities of economic interdependence, participation and cooperation must be non-exclusive or else "contagion effects" will spread a crisis to the whole region.[1] Taiwan is not able to participate in regional cooperation because China obstructs such moves. As a result, another financial crisis is likely. Similarly, since China uses its great power status to rule out Taiwan's participation in any kind of regional or bilateral economic cooperation Taiwan's economic security is affected. The focus of this article is to examine which economic security strategy Taiwan could adopt to cope with economic threats and to promote regional peace and economic growth. It will also propose certain policies to prevent future economic crises.

II. Globalization Deepens Mutual Economic Interdependence

1. Rapid Growth of Trade in Goods

Although we have seen several economic crises since the end of World War II, it is an undisputed fact that the world economy continues to grow. Tariffs, in particular, keep declining so that barriers to trade between countries are gradually eliminated.[2] Table 1 shows the rapid increase in

---

1   Regarding theories on economic interdependence and non-exclusiveness and their applications to the Asia-Pacific region see: Rong-I Wu, Chyuan-Jeng Shian and Chi-Chen Chiang, "Economic Interdependence and Security in the Asian Pacific" in: Peter A. Petri and Sumner J. La Croix (eds), Challenges to the Global Trading System, Adjustment to Globalization in the Asia – Pacific Region, *Pacific Trade and Development series*, 2007, pp.155-182.

2   The General Agreement on Tariffs and Trade (GATT) was founded in Geneva on Oct. 30, 1947. Its foremost goal was to continuously lower tariffs and eliminate non-tariff barriers and trade privileges through multilateral negotiations. Since the establishment of GATT

Table 1: Rapid Growth of World Trade in Goods

Unit: US$1 billion

Year	Imports	Exports	Total
1953	85	84	169
1963	164	157	321
1973	594	579	1,173
1983	1,883	1,838	3,721
1993	3,800	3,684	7,484
2003	7,696	7,380	15,076
2013	18,409	18,301	36,710

Source: WTO website, World Trade Developments, 2014.

world trade from a total of US$169 billion in 1953. World trade increased particularly dramatically from US$1,173 billion in 1973 to US$3,721 billion in 1983 – more than tripling – as a wave of economic liberalization swept across the globe in the 1980s. Subsequently, trade doubled virtually every following decade to reach US$36,710 billion in 2013.

As a result, the trade dependency of many nations rapidly increased. Taking several Asian countries as example, we can see that all four Asian tiger economies had a very high export-to-GDP ratio in 2013 (Taiwan 60.7%, South Korea 53.9%, Hong Kong 229.6% and Singapore 190.5%) whereas China and Japan as larger economies had export-to-GDP ratios for 26.4% and 16.2%, respectively. The import-to-GDP ratios were also very high in 2013 with 53% in Taiwan, 48.9% in South Korea, 228.7% in Hong

---

seven rounds of trade talks have been completed. The current Doha Round, which was launched in November 2001, has not yet led to an agreement. As a result of the GATT talks, the average tariff rate (trade weighted) has come down from more than 40% to currently less than 3%, and even less than 2% for the industrialized nations. With the exception of South Korea and China, tariffs in the major countries in East Asia are already very low. With 1.8% Taiwan's average tariff rate is the lowest. In order to protect their farmers most East Asian countries levy very high import tariffs on agricultural products. South Korea has the most outrageous tariff rate on agricultural imports with 91.8%. See Table 2.

Table 2: 2012 Tariff Rates: Major East Asian Nations and United States (trade weighted)

Unit: %

	Total	Agricultural sector	Non-agricultural sector
Taiwan	1.8	8.7	1.5
Japan	2.0	12.1	1.2
South Korea	7.7	91.8	3.6
China	4.7	19.7	4.1
Philippines	4.3	10.7	3.5
United States	2.1	4.1	2.0
Indonesia	4.7	4.3	4.7
Vietnam	5.4	7.7	5.2
Malaysia	4.3	11.7	3.6
Thailand	6.2	27.8	5.1

Source: WTO website, World Trade Developments, 2014.

Kong and 167.5% in Singapore. In China and Japan, the said ratio stood at 23.8% and 19%, respectively. These figures show that the trade dependency of individual countries increased as world trade expanded. This means that economic growth in countries around the globe is affected by fluctuations in the trade of other nations.

2. Cross-border movement of massive capital flows and their rapid increase

Cross-border capital flows constitute a greater threat to the stability of national economies than trade. The cross-border movement of large amounts of short-term funds, in particular, not only affects financial stability, but also causes even greater damage to smaller economies that lack a sound [financial] system. The 1997-98 Asian financial crisis is a concrete example. Table 4 shows that foreign direct investment (FDI) was quite high. Inward FDI stock rose from US$2.280 trillion in 1990 to US$7.510 trillion in 2000 and then more than tripled to US$25.464 trillion in 2013. At the same time, the inward FDI-to-GDP ratio rose from 9.7 percent in 1990 to 34.3% in 2013.

Table 3: Fluctuations of Stock prices and Exchange Rates of East Asian Countries (June 2, 1997-March 24, 1998)

	Exchange rate (local currency per US dollars)			Stock Index			Total (%)
	June 2, 1997	March 24, 1998	Change (%)	June 2, 1997	March 24, 1998	Change (%)	
Taiwan	27.862	32.653	-14.67	8197.3	9014.17	+9.97	-4.70
Indonesia	2428	8600	-71.77	699.73	532.81	-23.85	-95.62
Malaysia	2.5145	3.62	-30.54	1117.97	733.31	-34.41	-64.95
Philippines	26.35	36.95	-28.69	2820.72	2310.37	-18.09	-46.78
Singapore	1.4315	1.6095	-11.06	2060.9	1651.64	-19.86	-30.92
Thailand	24.8	38.65	-35.83	563.35	470.67	-16.45	-52.29
Japan	116.6	130.28	-10.50	20451.85	16980.62	-16.97	-27.47
South Korea	888.5	1377.5	-35.50	758.39	501.13	-33.92	-69.42
China	8.2917	8.2795	0.15	1336.28	1188.87	-11.03	-10.88
Hong Kong	7.744	7.7475	-0.05	14990.9	11757.88	-21.57	-21.62

Source: Rong-I Wu, "Collection of Papers on 1997-98 East-Asian, Russian and Latin American Financial Crises," Occasional Paper No.1, Taiwan Institute of Economic Research, Dec. 2004.

FDI is particularly important for developing countries, which generally lack savings and funds needed for investment. However, when foreign investors enter developing countries they mainly use the host country's cheap labor and land for the processing or manufacturing of products for export to the home country or the international market. In contrast, FDI in industrialized nations aims to produce consumer goods for the domestic market. Regardless where FDI goes, most countries welcome it since it has a rather low mobility. Another kind of foreign investment is investment in local stock and bond markets. Such funds are to a considerable degree highly mobile as they can be withdrawn anytime. Therefore, they constitute a greater threat to local financial stability. One of the reasons for the outbreak of the 1997-98 Asian financial crisis was that the ratio of foreign investment in the East Asian stock markets was quite high. In Indonesia, for instance, foreign investors accounted for around 60 percent of the local stock market's market

Table 4: World Inward and Outward Foreign Direct Investment Stock and GDP Ratio 1990-2013

Year	Inward FDI		Outward FDI	
	Stock (Billion US$)	As % of GDP	Stock (Billion US$)	As % of GDP
1990	2,078	9.7	2,088	9.9
1995	3,441	11.5	3,785	12.7
2000	7,511	22.9	8,006	24.6
2005	11,739	25.3	12,563	27.2
2010	20,370	31.7	21,288	33.3
2013	25,464	34.3	26,312	35.7

Source: UNCTAD, World Investment Report 2014.

value in the 1993-96 period. In Thailand, foreign investors also held 20-30 percent of the local bourse during the same period.[3] During times of financial instability, these foreign investors easily pull out, causing volatility in the local stock market. Another form of short-term capital are short-term loans that commercial banks and other financial institutions take out with foreign banks. The main reason why the 1997-98 Asian financial crisis played out in Thailand was that foreign banks had made short-term loans to banks in Thailand. These borrowed funds were then lent to real estate developers in that country. When the foreign investors were not willing to extend the loans as the financial situation became unstable and the local banks were not able to recover the funds, the banks were saddled with overdue loans, which triggered the crisis.

III. The 1997-98 Asian Financial Crisis

The 1997-98 Asian financial crisis began in Thailand. In May 1997, the

---

3   Rong-I Wu, "Taiwan's Role in Asian Financial Crisis." In: "Collection of Papers on 1997 – 98 East Asian, Russian and Latin American Financial Crises," *Occasional Paper No.1*, Taiwan Institute of Economic Research, 2004.

financial situation of the private sector in Thailand worsened, causing a rapid increase in the number of non-performing loans in the financial sector. The central bank raised short-term interest rates to support the local currency's fixed exchange rate. However, when the forex market sold off large amounts of Thai baht, the Thai government was forced to float the baht on July 2, 1997. The depreciation of the baht spread to other East Asian countries so that by late July the Philippine peso, the Malaysian ringgit and the Indonesian rupiah came under attack from international speculators. As a result, the central banks of these countries successively adopted floating exchange rates to respond to the changes in the new forex market.

In order to respond to the financial crisis, which was caused by a lack of foreign currency in these countries, the International Monetary Fund (IMF) first provided US$1 billion in emergency loans to the Philippines. Subsequently, Thailand asked the IMF for US$16 billion in aid but the continued slump of the baht could still not be brought to a halt. The Indonesian central bank took a number of stabilizing measures but was not able to fend off the speculative attacks. By November 1997, the IMF provided US$23 billion in loans to Indonesia, too. At the same time, Taiwan, Hong Kong and South Korea came under depreciation pressure due to attacks from international speculators. Taiwan's central bank aggressively interfered in the forex market to keep the local currency stable. Eventually, it decided on Oct. 17 to allow the Taiwan new dollar (TWD) to depreciate against the U.S. dollar (USD) and to let the market set the exchange rate. On Oct. 20, the TWD-USD exchange rate had depreciated from 28.62 to 30. In the following days, the international speculators turned to Hong Kong where they expected the pegged Hong Kong dollar (HKD) to slip. On Oct. 20, the speculators began to massively dump shares. Since Hong Kong had reverted to Chinese rule in July 1997 the Hong Kong government decided to pull out all stops to defend the HKD exchange rate by drastically raising overnight interbank offered rates from 5 percent to 300 percent on Oct. 24. As a result, the local stock market nosedived 10.4 percent the same day, triggering a massive share selloff in New York and the European stock markets on the following Monday, Oct. 27. At the New York Stock Exchange, the Dow Jones Industrial Average index shed 554 points, registering its largest daily point loss ever.

During that period, the South Korean economy saw a rapid increase in non-performing loans, as private companies were not able to repay their heavy debts. As a result, the stock market plunged and foreign investors quickly exited the market. The South Korean central bank tried its best to protect the stability of the Korean won (KRW) but as speculators continued to attack, the KRW exchange rate kept weakening. By Nov. 22, Seoul officially asked the IMF for US$57 billion in emergency aid, the highest financial aid package in the IMF's history, but the KRW-USD exchange rate continued to fall to 2000, which equaled a depreciation of more than 100 percent.

All in all, our analysis of the aforementioned Asian financial crisis has found the following common characteristics: Drastic currency depreciation and stock market collapses within a short period dealt a rather heavy blow to the national economies of Thailand, the Philippines, Indonesia and South Korea, whereas Taiwan, Singapore and Malaysia were less affected in comparison. The East Asian countries that were hard hit by the crisis have the following points in common:

1. They were large importers of foreign capital, in particular of short-term money that was invested in the stock market. In 1996 foreign investment accounted for more than 60 percent of the local bourse's market value in Indonesia and in Thailand that figure stood at 30 percent.
2. They suffered from a chronic balance of payments problem caused by a huge deficit. In 1996, Thailand's deficit reached 15% of [GDP], whereas South Korea's balance of payments was even more in the red with 20 percent.
3. They were saddled with huge foreign debt. Indonesia, Thailand and

South Korea had each accumulated foreign debt worth nearly or more than US$100 billion.

Another characteristic is the rapid escalation of the financial crisis from one country to the next due to the movement of capital, which has become known as "financial contagion effect." The East Asian countries that were more severely affected by the financial crisis such as Indonesia, the Philippines, South Korea and Thailand had weaker economies. This means they imported short-term foreign capital to finance their current account balances. As a result, they had higher balance of payments deficits and huge foreign debt. They were easy targets for international speculators. The impact of the crisis would probably have been more severe if the IMF had not provided emergency loans. That Taiwan survived the crisis comparatively unscathed can be attributed mainly to the three reasons mentioned above: it had little short-term foreign capital, no balance of payments deficit and no foreign debt. On top of that, Taiwan had sufficient foreign reserves to escape from the crisis. Yet it also had to pay a price because foreign reserves were depleted to stabilize the local currency. Fortunately, Taiwan safely made it through the crisis. However, since Taiwan is not member of the IMF it would not have been able to ask the IMF for help had its foreign reserves been insufficient so that a crisis in Taiwan would inevitably have spilt over to other countries with unfathomable consequences.

IV. The Lesson from the Financial Crisis

Japan was not hit as hard by the crisis as other countries but between June 2, 1997 and March 24, 1998, the Japanese yen (JPY) also depreciated against the USD by 10.5 percent, while the stock market declined 16.97 percent during that period. Despite being the economically most advanced nation in East Asia, Japan did not play a major role in assisting its neighbors to avert the crisis. Still, Japan also felt that the East Asian countries needed to establish a regional institution modeled on the IMF in order to address financial problems in the region in a more flexible and timely manner. Therefore, Tokyo pushed for the establishment of an Asian Monetary Fund (AMF) but then shelved the proposal since the United States did not approve of it.

In May 2000, the finance ministers of the ten-member Association of Southeast Asian Nations (ASEAN), China, Japan and South Korea took advantage of the 33rd annual Board of Governors meeting of the Asian Development Bank (ADB) in Chiang Mai, Thailand, to discuss bilateral currency swap agreements. Under the agreement, which became known as the *Chiang Mai Agreement* or the *Chiang Mai Initiative*, the ASEAN plus Three countries were to pool some of their foreign reserves to solve short-term intraregional liquidity problems. The accord was formally established in March 2010 with the participating countries jointly contributing US$120 billion. By 2012, they decided to double that pool to US$240 billion. The aim is to have this pool of foreign reserves ready for deployment to counter international currency speculators to avert another financial crisis. Unfortunately, Taiwan remains excluded and unable to join due to opposition from China.

The currency swap that the East Asian nations established with the *Chiang Mai Agreement* shows us that they learned their lesson from the 1997-98 financial crisis. They have come to believe that in an open international economy individual countries are not strong enough to withstand the effects of massive movements of short-term capital. Therefore, the Asian countries needed to pool capital for a regional fund to respond nearby on top of assistance by the IMF. Due to Chinese opposition, Taiwan remains excluded. Should Taiwan be affected in a future financial crisis it will not be able to obtain help from the *Chiang Mai Agreement* because it cannot get IMF assistance. From the 1997-98 financial crisis we have learned that should a crisis erupt in Taiwan it would rapidly escalate. Given the economic interdependence between Taiwan and the other East Asian nations, the neighboring countries would not be immune to [financial contagion].

During the 1997-98 financial crisis, this became obvious when Taiwan's decision to let its currency depreciate negatively affected the Hong Kong stock and forex markets. After Thailand decided in July 1997 to let the baht depreciate, the peso, ringgit and rupiah came under attack from international currency speculators. These countries were therefore forced to give up their fixed exchange rate regimes. While the TWD also came under depreciation pressure, Taipei decided only on Friday, Oct. 17, 1997, to leave the exchange rate to market forces. In the following week, the speculative money turned to the Hong Kong stock and forex markets. The Hong Kong government decided to keep the HKD peg against the USD while drastically raising short-term interest rates. As a result, the Hong Kong stock market nosedived, dragging down the New York Stock Exchange and the European bourses. The New York Stock Exchange registered its largest one-day drop in its history on the following Monday (Oct. 27), alarming the U.S. Congress. The U.S. House Committee on Banking and Financial Services called a hearing in response, inviting renowned U.S. economist C. Fred Bergsten to testify before the committee.[4]

Bergsten presented a conspiracy theory surrounding the depreciation of the TWD. He stated that the speculative attacks on the Hong Kong stock and forex markets, the ensuing precipitous decline of the territory's stock market and the resulting reverberations in stock markets in the United States and Europe were caused by Taiwan because it "chose to let its currency join the decline after only a minimal defensive effort." Bergsten concluded that Taiwan abandoned further efforts to prop up its currency not for economic reasons but because it had a hidden political agenda, namely to encourage the speculators to attack the HKD with negative repercussions for the Chinese yuan (RMB). Taiwan wanted to embarrass China on the eve of then President Jiang Zemin's visit to the United States in late October,

---

4 U.S. House of Representative, C. Fred Bergsten, "*The Asian Monetary Crisis: Proposed Remedies*", Statement addressed to the Committee on Banking and Financial Services, 13 November 1997.

Bergsten told the committee. In a speech in March 1998, even Chinese Foreign Minister Qian Qichen accused Taiwan of using the Asian financial crisis to gain an advantage from the depreciation of the TWD. Bergsten's testimony and Qian's speech show that both men believe that Taiwan chose to let the TWD decline during the Asian financial crisis in order to undermine the financial stability of Hong Kong. In fact, Taiwan cannot help but protect itself, because as a non-member the island is not able to obtain emergency loans from the IMF, in contrast to [IMF-members] Indonesia, the Philippines, Thailand and South Korea. That is the price China has to pay for excluding Taiwan from the IMF. As China's former foreign minister, Qian is therefore in no position to criticize Taiwan's approach at all.

V. Brief Summary

Amid growing globalization, countries around the globe grow closer to each other and become mutually more dependent due to the flow of trade, investment and capital. Therefore, economic volatility in one individual country can affect the economies of other countries. Vice versa, economic upheavals in other countries can affect economic stability in one's own country. Like two sides of a coin, these developments are inseparable. When a country tries to extricate itself from a crisis caused by such mutual economic interdependence, negative repercussions for any other country cannot be ruled out. This is the nature of non-exclusiveness.

A very good case in point is Thailand's decision during the 1997-98 Asian financial crisis to let the baht fall, which made depreciation pressure gradually spill over into other East Asian countries. Among these, Taiwan was forced to let its currency depreciate for the sake of its own economic stability because it was not able to defend the TWD exchange rate all by itself. The Hong Kong stock and forex markets were immediately affected, the Hong Kong stock market plummeted, dragging down stock markets in the United States and Europe with the New York Stock Exchange registering its largest one-day point drop in its history. Bergsten and Qian criticized Taiwan for taking advantage of the financial crisis to let the TWD depreciate in order to harm Hong Kong.

VI. Taiwan's Economic Security Strategy

The above analysis of the 1997-98 Asian financial crisis tells us that defensive measures to ward off a financial crisis may jeopardize the financial stability of neighboring countries. Therefore, Asian countries decided to set up a fund under the *Chiang Mai Agreement*. However, Taiwan is unable to participate in it because of Chinese objections. On top of not being an IMF-member, Taiwan also cannot join the *Chiang Mai Agreement*. Since financial crises are contagious, the continued exclusion of Taiwan will not only increase Taiwan's risk in defending itself against the next financial crisis but probably also hurt other countries. China's opposition to Taiwan's inclusion in the joint financial rescue plan does not only cost other nations dearly but also hurts China itself. The East Asian countries should oppose China's way of undermining regional financial stability.

Yet China is no longer just an East Asian power, it has become a world power. Most likely not just Taiwan but all East Asian countries are unable to force China to change it unreasonable policy. We still need to state clearly that China must understand that Taiwan is a free democratic country and that the majority of its people regard the island as an independent, sovereign country that is not part of China. It is not that China can force Taiwan to give in by using its missile threat or by thwarting Taiwan's participation in the international community. Taiwan's public very clearly disapproves of China's approach.

China's longstanding military threat against Taiwan has led to very strong resentment among the Taiwan people toward China. The September 2015, Taiwan Brain Trust opinion survey shows that as many as 75 percent of the respondents are unfavorable or indifferent toward China. Only 18.7

percent a favorable toward China. Although people to people exchanges across the Taiwan Strait have been opened up markedly, commercial exchanges are even more frequent – since 1990 Taiwanese businesses have made investments in China worth hundreds of billions of U.S. dollars – and the Chinese government tries to win the hearts of the Taiwanese by every means, the Taiwan people's impression of China remains still rather lackluster. Furthermore, more than half of the public believe that China is hostile toward Taiwan. Given that China continues to use verbal and military threats against Taiwan, 65.6% of the survey respondents said they support independence and just 13.8 percent advocate unification with China. The Chinese government needs to understand the trend of public opinion in Taiwan instead of using diplomatic pressure or threatening Taiwanese business people and the general public to achieve its policy goals. Beijing also needs to understand that China rapidly merges deeper into the global economic system following 30 years of a reform and opening policy and rapid development. In 1983 Chinese goods exports accounted only for 1.2 percent of total world exports but in 2013 China surpassed the United States as the world's largest export nation with a 12.1 percent share of global exports. The same goes for goods imports. In 1983 China accounted for 1.1 percent of global imports but in 2013 that share had risen to 10.6 percent, making China the second largest importer worldwide behind the United States. Therefore, China's exports-to-GDP ratio reached 24.88 percent in 2013, whereas the import-to-GDP ratio stood at 22.4 percent. This means that the Chinese economy relies quite heavily on international trade. The growth of China's trade does not only affect the world economy but is also affected by other countries. In recent years, the media have therefore come to call China a "growth engine of the global economy." During the same period China evolved from a low income developing country into a middle income nation with an average annual per capita income of US$7,000. The main reason behind China's fast economic growth is swift domestic investment, or in other words capital formation. For capital formation low income countries rely on domestic savings as well as foreign investment.

Over the past three decades, Taiwanese businesses have invested more than US$300 billion in China. Hong Kong, South Korea and the industrialized nations such as Japan, the United States and European countries have also poured huge amounts of capital into China. Between 1990 and 2013 China attracted a total of US$956 billion or 10.4 percent of its GDP in foreign direct investment (FDI), according to United Nations (UN) statistics. This huge amount of FDI definitely greatly contributed to China's rapid economic growth and exports. But at the same time this also shows that the Chinese economy and the world economy are closely interconnected and influence each other. This is particularly true for China's economic relationships with the capital providing countries. Therefore, China needs to consider that as the world's second largest economy it will only be able to win the respect of other nations if it shoulders its responsibilities.

VII. Taiwan's Economy is Over-Dependent on the Chinese Market

From the perspective of Taiwan's economic security there is reason to worry about the island's excessive dependence on the Chinese market for exports (40 percent of total exports) and investment (more than 80 percent of total outward investment). China uses verbal attacks and military intimidation toward Taiwan, undermines its participation in the international community and claims that Taiwan is a part of China, making its hostility toward Taiwan perfectly clear. Therefore, Taiwan faces two possible risks due to its over-dependence on a hostile China in trade and investment. The first risk is that the Taiwanese economy would face enormous losses should China choose to impose politically motivated trade sanctions against Taiwan. Another, not politically motivated risk stems from possible economic problems in China. Should the Chinese economy run into trouble Taiwan would be affected immediately. It will even feel the reverberations of ordinary cyclical changes. In order to hedge against these two risks for its economic security Taiwan must adopt a strategy of reducing it reliance on the Chinese economy. However, since Taiwan has a free economy it is quite difficult for the government to adopt measures to decrease Taiwanese reliance on the Chinese economy. Given the current trend of economic development in the Asia-Pacific region, a concrete, feasible economic security strategy for Taiwan is to join the Trans-Pacific Partnership (TPP) in order to elevate commercial relations between Taiwan and the TPP member states.

The TPP is a highly transparent, free trade agreement with a very high degree of openness (tariffs are very low) and low trade and nontrade barriers in many areas including intellectual property, the environment, competition policy, labor, electronic commerce and agriculture. With view to its economic security, which means strengthening economic relations with Europe, Japan and the United States in order to reduce reliance on the Chinese economy, Taiwan ought to seriously consider this strategy.[5]

As for Taiwan's participation in international regional organizations, Taiwan has already joined the World Trade Organization (WTO) and the Asia-Pacific Economic Cooperation (APEC) forum. But because of China's interference Taiwan does not enjoy full participation rights. Taiwan has only been able to sign regional or bilateral economic cooperation agreements with five smaller countries in Latin America that maintain diplomatic relations with Taiwan (Panama, El Salvador, Guatemala, Honduras and Nicaragua) and most recently with New Zealand and Singapore. However, due to Chinese opposition Taiwan is not able to negotiate and sign economic cooperation agreements with its major trade partners. The Economic Cooperation Framework Agreement (ECFA) that Taiwan signed with China was not concluded in line with WTO regulations. It is part of China's strategy to incorporate Taiwan in a "one China market." As a result, Taiwan

---

5   Rong-I Wu, "Strategic Considerations on TPP Accession," *Global Industry and Commerce Monthly*, Jan. 2015 issue, and Chi-chen Wu, Rong-I Wu, "Our Economic Policy Proposal – Establishing a New Economic Model for Taiwan through Innovation Drivers and Progressive Values," *Taiwan Brain Trust*, Taipei, Dec. 2014.

is not able to smoothly negotiate free trade agreements with its major trade partners such as the ASEAN member states, the European Union, Japan and the United States because China obstructs such moves. China's goal is to isolate Taiwan by keeping it outside of all international economic cooperation organizations.

Taiwan stands a better chance of joining the TPP because China is neither a TPP member nor very likely to join the free trade pact in the future. Moreover, the Taiwanese government has declared its willingness to join and is actively preparing its admission bid. More importantly, Japan and the United States have expressed welcome Taiwan's participation. The United States aggressively promotes the TPP as an important part of its Asia-Pacific economic strategy to counter China's economic rise. Since this happens to match Taiwan's strategy of reducing its economic reliance on China, the chances for success are somewhat better.

The Art of Nuclear Renunciation

Yavor A. Kostadinov[*]

Abstract

There is an increase in importance of international institutions after WWII, in general, and in disarmament and safeguards of nuclear weapons in particular, partially as an effect of the devastating potential of those weapons. While a vast majority of research focuses on states that choose to proliferate despite sanctions such as Iran and N. Korea, states such as Brazil, S. Africa, Kazakhstan, South Korea or Republic of Korea (ROK, hereafter), Taiwan and others have chosen to abandon their existing nuclear programs despite costly investment and uncertainty coming from existing or potential foe.

The main research question of this study seeks an answer to the question: why states choose the policy to renounce nuclear programs and weapons? The International Atomic Energy Agency (IAEA) and the Non-Proliferation Treaty (NPT) have served as the best collective international security regime on nuclear disarmament attempting to prevent further proliferation and encouraging those with weapons to disarm. However, establishing the real causes of renunciation is not an easy task due to the uniqueness of each case. Nevertheless, it will be argued that certain similarities could be found, providing for generalization which could serve as a guiding principle for future nuclear renunciation research.

---

* Ph.D. Candidate, Graduate Institute of International Affairs and Strategic Studies, Tamkang University.

The objectives of this study aim to investigate ROK's reasons for the official abandonment of its nuclear program, analyze the decision making processes of the policy, confirm international safeguards importance, explain U.S.'s role, and understand the strategic context. Is the security alliance between ROK and the U.S. enough of a reason not to pursue nuclear weapons? The study will investigate the conformity and compliance of ROK to international principles, norms, rules and decision making procedures based on three theoretical approaches integrated into single theoretical framework – rational, behavioural, and self-regulative – drawing on policy analysis, international regimes and compliance theories, and aiming to invalidate or validate renunciation. The study is designed to provide clarity and understanding on renunciation, collective security and safeguarding in the case of ROK.

> *"The unleashed power of the atom has changed everything save our modes of thinking, and we thus drift toward unparalleled catastrophe."* [1]

I. Introduction

Nuclear nonproliferation has become a global norm and has been one of the two cornerstone norms of the Non-Proliferation Treaty (NPT) under Article I for nearly half a century, with disarmament under article VI being the other.[2] In addition the main principle of peaceful use of nuclear energy under article IV acknowledges the right of all parties to develop nuclear energy for peaceful purposes and to benefit from international cooperation in this area, in *conformity* with their nonproliferation obligations under Article I.

---

1 Albert Einstein, 1946, in Charles W. Kegley Jr., *World Politics: Trend and Transformation*, 12th ed. (Belmont - Wadsworth: Cengage Learning, 2008), p. 439.

2 For full text see United Nation, *"NPT: Text of the Treaty"*, 1968, <http://www.un.org/en/conf/npt/2015/text.shtml>.

The NPT spells out the pillars of the international nonproliferation international regime — a set of explicit and implicit principles, norms, rules and decision making procedures around which actors' expectations converge in a given area.[3] Members of the regime enjoy incentives and in return promise to *comply* with the rules and regulations of the treaty and to *conform* to its principles and norms.

A first step in the process towards NPT membership is the renunciation of nuclear weapons and research programs. And vice versa, ratification of the NPT is the first step signaling true intentions in the course of action towards nonproliferation and as such a first sign of genuine desire to reject development of nuclear weapons. For instance Sweden and Canada, to mention a few, have renounced their nuclear weapons option voluntary prior ratification of the NPT although they had had the means to go nuclear. Iraq, on the other hand, was forcefully coerced to change its stance from proliferation towards renunciation. And there are those that need to be persuaded/coerced few times such as Libya, Iran, and Syria that have violated their compliance, yet arguing that they have not violated conformity to the principle of peaceful use of nuclear energy. Furthermore the non-proliferation norms have been violated by non-members of the NPT– India, Israel, Pakistan; previous members and current non-members – Taiwan and N. Korea, though both have opposing current stance towards proliferation; and few members that despite their non-compliance have been treated "as if they were complying" to the NPT by the International Atomic Energy Agency (IAEA) – ROK and Egypt. The latest two cases are "like" units in a sense that they are the only two member states that had had nuclear weapons program prior their NPT ratification, have renounced it, only to continue secret research programs until both were exposed, and have shown renewed intention of renunciation thereafter, or have they? Taiwan could have been treated as a "like" unit to ROK and Egypt too, had it remained a member of the NPT.

---

3   Stephan D. Krasner, ed., *International Regimes* (Ithaca: Cornell University Press, 1983), p. 2.

During the past few years majority South Koreans in a poll have openly expressed renewed support for nuclear weapons.[4] Historically ROK had had nuclear military aspirations but renounced its nuclear research program in 1975 and applied for NPT membership in the same year.[5] What makes South Koreans voice such intentions again now? Is the government going to listen to its citizens? Evidence in 2004 exposed undercover activities in ROK dating back for more than twenty years counter to the South Korean government's compliance obligations under the NPT and IAEA.[6] Yet, the case wasn't reported by the IAEA to the United Nations Security Council as a case of non-compliance.

Is the threat from North Korea now larger than in the 70's, so that the change in public opinion can be justified? Is the newly acquired nuclear weapons capability by the North the main reason, or did something else in the environment dramatically change? Has the South truly renounced nuclear weapons as an option, is it conforming to the principles and norm of non-proliferation, and is it complying to the rules and regulations today; or is it disguising its true intentions once more? If its current public bold stance towards indigenous missiles and nuclear weapons finds governmental support, then what can be done to prevent it of going nuclear and to ensure a long lasting compliance and conformity?

In order to predict ROK's future compliance and conformity, and to evaluate its current intentions the case study will be broken down in

---

4   Kim Jiyoon and Karl Friedhof, "The Fallout : South Korean Public Opinion Following North Korea's Third Nuclear Test," *The ASAN Institute for Policy Studies*, February 24, 2013, <http://en.asaninst.org/contents/issue-brief-no-46-the-fallout-south-korean-public-opinion-following-north-koreas-third-nuclear-test/>.

5   James Martin Center for Nonproliferation Studies at the Monterey Institute of International Studies, "ROK: Overview," *Nuclear Threat Initiative*, December, 2014, <http://www.nti.org/country-profiles/south-korea/>.

6   Paul Kerr, "IAEA: Seoul's Nuclear Sins in Past," *Arms Control*, December 1, 2004, <http://www.armscontrol.org/print/1714>; also in Gareth Porter, "ROK let off for nuclear deceptions," *Asia Times*, December 22, 2009, <http://atimes.com/atimes/Middle_East/KL22Ak02.html>.

three subcases investigating the decision making processes that led — 1) to nuclear program initiation in the early 70's, 2) to publicly forfeit (or secretly preserve) it in 1975, and 3) to come out in 2004 to the international community. The research will apply three theoretical models – rational, behavioral, and self-regulative with focus on *inside-out and outside-in* positive and negative sanctions, rewards, and stimuli that could have influenced changes in the decision making process that led to compliance/non-compliance looking at materialistic, normative, and cognitive factors. Last but not least, the increase in importance of the role of the IAEA and its verification techniques and the historical compliance and conformity of ROK to the NPT will be taken in account as main guidelines in determining renunciation. Based on the reasoning and findings the discussion then will analyze the current trends and suggest future outcomes.

II. Conceptualization

1. Renunciation

Renunciation of nuclear energy for the purpose of developing nuclear weapons involves the formal rejection of such course of action. The decision to renounce is taken in a psychological environment and implemented in the operational environment.[7] As such in the first case we speak of policy in the second of strategy. Policy making is intuitive, philosophical, and creative, while strategy is pragmatic, rational, and constantly referring back to the political objective.[8] Thus, the course of action taken after official renunciation or the strategic policy implementation requires at least as much attention as the decision making process of renunciation due to the fact that "all actors display difference between their declaratory and their operational

---

7   Christopher Hill, *The Changing Politics of Foreign Policy* (Houndmills, UK: Palgrave MacMillan, 2003), p. 112.

8   Andre Beaufre, *Strategy of Action*, translated by R.H.Berry (New York, U.S.: Praeger Inc, 1967), p. 132.

goals".[9] Hill calls it the explicitness continuum and advises "we must ask whether decisions once taken do get translated into actions they imply" and if the actions are "product of delay, distortion and a further round of political conflict."[10] Often the decision making process leading to renunciation is complex and involves all rational, normative, and cognitive factors similar to any other policy decision making process. Hence, this process is closer to art than natural science. Renunciation could be intentional in part rational and irrational. Intentional renunciation is counter to the intention governing desire of acquiring nuclear weapons capability. Yet, as such a causal relation might be needed but it is not enough to explain the future course of action verified by compliance and conformity. Wilson explains intention as follow:

> When I intend to do A in the future, I am doing something now with the intention of doing A, in that I intend, of what I am doing, that it promote or constitute my doing A. The action in question may be overt, but it may be as minimal as keeping track of opportunities for doing A, or biding my time.[11]

Or to put it in context if a state is renouncing its nuclear weapons program now it shows an intent to reject developing nuclear weapons in the future. Renunciation may be official, but it may be so as minimal to gain opportunities from renunciation such as technological expertise, or to gain time. As such renunciation is not genuine. Hence, to determine genuine renunciation we need not only take the official statements of states but to historically trace their official posture and match it with the factual course of strategic action taken where possible. A first step of a course of action rejecting proliferation is the ratification of the NPT. It is not to say that genuine renunciation can't happen without signing the NPT, however, it is

9   Hill, *op. cit.*, p. 120.

10   Hill, *Ibid*, p. 127.

11   G. Wilson, *The Intentionality of Human Action* (Stanford, CA: Stanford University Press, 1989), pp. 222-30.

the internationally recognized yardstick. Once ratification takes place the course of action of a state is easier to trace to validate renunciation due to the implied rationality of the strategic operational environment. Any factual steps discovered undertaken supporting intentional desire to acquire nuclear weapons would be counter renunciation. If proven that the intent governing desire for nuclear research for military purposes has not been forfeited, then renunciation has not taken place, rather it has been used as a tool to disguise true intentions. Such straightforward intentional objective rational explanation seems reasonable but theoretically at least would be over simplistic due to the subjectivity of the decision makers and the varying level of importance of facts discovered. For instance, an accident leading to enrichment during experiment can't be consider intentional course of action, yet depending on the circumstances some could interpret it as such. In addition, non-compliance/non-conformity to the obligations, could result, for instance, out of routine or automation of procedures, standard of procedures (SOP), over time. This will be one of the points taken in consideration in explaining ROK's behaviour in 2004. Thus, nuclear renunciation should be understood as *a policy, an outcome of a decision making process, influenced by cognitive, normative, and rational factors, involving the intentional, formal, and explicit rejection of actions leading to nuclear weapons development.*

One way to validate renunciation is to prove continues compliance and conformity to norms, rules, regulations and decision making procedures of the NPT and IAEA. Thus, compliance and conformity are crucial to validate renunciation. While the former is primarily bound by verification of rules and procedure, the latter is normative as prescribed by the NPT. Measuring conformity, however, has been a controversial task in the case of ROK. Thought the NPT has been hailed as almost universal treaty, the two extremes of complete success - total failure of conformity of member states to the norm are not easily proven and neither is compliance. Though seemingly easier to prove as complete success — total failure, compliance could be influenced by automated routines and subjective perceptions.

2. Compliance and conformity in international relations

Social influence is a subfield of social psychology and deals with the reasons for individuals' change in behaviour. Change in behaviour could occur due to fear, incentives, psychological or normative pressure and as a process of self-evaluation from interaction. Compliance in social psychology traditionally refers to response to an explicit or implicit request.[12] However, compliance in this paper will need to satisfy three theoretical approaches – rational, behavioural, and self-regulative. Hence, somewhat broader definition is required. Compliance is thus *the voluntary or consensual, affirmative response to an explicit or implicit request, without the necessity of change of beliefs and values*. It defers from conformity which is similar but the change in behaviour is due to *perceived or real pressure from others*.[13] Conformity, furthermore, leads to change in beliefs and value system after a self-evaluation cognitive process had taken place. Arguably the most effective method to gain compliance is through external persuasion and inspiration, while gaining conformity requires external social pressure and internal modifications. The underlining difference is in the notion of the request itself. If the request has the aim to persuade or inspire without necessarily aiming to change one's beliefs we are talking of compliance. If the aim of the request is in the form of social pressure to change one's belief system through self-reflection, conformity takes place. Conformity is an idea more restrictive and penetrative in the sovereignty of states, requiring them to not only comply but also to change their beliefs. Compliance can occur without changing belief, though one might not like to comply and manipulation is often part of it, but towards the outcome not the internal beliefs. Regardless if the request is explicit or implicit the target of the request recognizes that it has been urged to comply/conform.

Further difference between compliance and conformity lies in the

---

12 Daniel T. Gilbert, Susan T. Fiske, and Gardner Lindzey, *The Handbook of Social Psychology*, 4th ed., vol 2. (New York: McGraw-Hill, 1998), p. 168.

13 Ibid, Gilbert et.al, p. 162.

perception of the one requested to comply/conform. Compliance is not concerned much with self-evaluation, though it may sometimes occur as a result of changes in people's internal beliefs and/or emotions. In contrast, conformity refers to adjustment of behaviors, attitudes, emotions, and beliefs to fit to a social norm. This rationale begs the question why do we need compliance once we gain conformity? The answer is twofold. First conformity requires legitimate authority to have high degree of success and there is lack of such in international relations. Secondly getting someone to comply with rules is easier due to the preservation of belief system and preservation of sovereignty. To illustrate, a government might comply even if it doesn't like it especially if there are incentives involved, but if the government has to change national beliefs it won't be so willing without pressure. In addition, non-compliance doesn't automatically result in non-conformity. Breaking rules doesn't always mean that one's belief system has changed. There could be simply a dissatisfaction with incentives from compliance to rules, or dissatisfaction with changes in the norms of the international regime. In addition, non-compliance doesn't include self-reflectiveness. Why would I feel bad of breaking a rule if I feel that I had received no fair incentives of compliance? The morality of an act is highly subjective. Therefore, the success/failure of the request or pressure, for compliance and conformity respectively, will be treated as a matter of a degree rather than a clear cut. However, actions violating IAEA safeguards will be treated as acts invalidating renounciation.

3. IAEA Safeguards and reporting of non-compliance

Safeguards are activities by which the IAEA can verify states' implementation of standards and commitments to refrain from using nuclear programs for nuclear-weapons purposes.[14] Verification measures include on-site inspections, visits, and ongoing monitoring and evaluation.

---

14 "IAEA Safeguards Overview: Comprehensive Safeguards Agreements and Additional Protocols," *IAEA*, June 20, 2014, <http://www.iaea.org/Publications/Factsheets/English/sg_overview.html>.

Basically, two sets of measures are carried out in accordance with the type of safeguards agreements in force with a state. One set relates to verifying state reports of declared nuclear material and activities. These measures – authorized under NPT-type comprehensive safeguards agreements - largely are based on nuclear material accountancy, complemented by containment and surveillance techniques, such as tamper-proof seals and cameras that the IAEA installs at facilities. Another set adds measures to strengthen the IAEA's inspection capabilities. They include those incorporated in what is known as an "Additional Protocol" – this is a legal document complementing comprehensive safeguards agreements. The measures enable the IAEA not only to verify the non-diversion of declared nuclear material but also to provide assurances as to the absence of undeclared nuclear material and activities in a state.

The term "noncompliance," in the safeguards context, was introduced in the IAEA's founding statute. Article XII.C provides that IAEA inspectors:

1) shall report any non-compliance to the Director General, who
2) shall thereupon transmit the report to the Board of Governors, who
3) shall call upon the recipient State or States to remedy forthwith any non-compliance which it finds to have occurred. The Board furthermore,
4) shall report the non-compliance to all members and to the Security Council and General Assembly of the United Nations. The Board, in the event of failure of the recipient State or States to take fully corrective action within a reasonable time,
5) may take one or both of the following measures: direct curtailment or suspension of assistance being provided by the Agency or by a member, and call for the return of materials and equipment made available to the recipient member or group of members. The Agency
6) may also, in accordance with article XIX, suspend any non- complying member from the exercise of the privileges and rights of membership.[15]

---

15 "The Statute of the IAEA," *IAEA*, 1957, <https://www.iaea.org/about/statute#a1-12>.

III. Theoretical framework

The concepts above and three theoretical approaches will be integrated to form a theoretical framework for analysis. The first theoretical approach is the behavioral outside-in approach based on request for action. The outside of international relations is an international system composed of states and institutions. The behaviour of a single actor could be constrained from the system as a whole or through interaction with its parts. As noted above the notion of the request, either with or without intent to inflict change in beliefs, could lead to compliance or conformity. Though conformity involves self-evaluation prior change in beliefs the influence that prompts action in both cases comes from outside in accordance with behaviorists' theory. The approach utilizes positive and negative normative techniques and instruments that influence behaviour towards conformity and compliance such as reciprocity, social pressure, social inclusion and isolation, and the loss of learning opportunities, internalization of international norms through self-evaluation, social validation and social comparison. Research in social psychology has repeatedly demonstrated that people usually consider their interaction partners' norms and standards while processing or exchanging social information.[16] Then they self-validate. Accurate self-validation in society is motivated by a comparison of one to similar "like", or slightly better, units.[17] Empirical tests show that people have constant drive to evaluate themselves after change in outside environment. People will strive for objectivity of evidence, however, if it is missing then they will use standards of comparison from similar others' behaviour in similar situations. A tactic for compliance in this case is the list technique that

---

16 Katja Corcoran, Jan Crusius, and Thomas Mussweiler, "Social Comparison: Motives, Standards, and Mechanisms," in D. Chadee, ed., *Theories in Social Psychology* (Oxford, UK: Wiley-Blackwell, 2011), p. 122.

17 S. E Taylor, H. A Wayment, and M. Carrillo, "Social Comparison, Self-regulation, and Motivation," in R.M. Sorrentino and E. T.Higgins. eds., *Handbook of Motivation and Cognition* (New York: Guilford Press, 1996), pp. 3-27.

involves showing a list of people that have already complied/conformed with similar conditions. According to Finnemore and Sikkink, persuasion plays a significant role in normative influence and change.[18] In political science persuasion can be used twofold: structural and logical, and psychological and affective; hence, as conformity and compliance. Constructivists' assumption that norms shape state values and interest will be taken as central to this approach.

The second theoretical approach is the often omitted inside-out psychological cognitive self-regulative approach contributing to the analysis of ROK's changes in behaviour based not on requests from outside rather on cognitive self-regulative action during the decision making process. Perception is the key here. Some motivations for self-regulation are one's self-interest, moral considerations, or in order to forestall public/ private politics.[19] The first step towards self-regulation is the cognitive representation of the threat. Overestimating or underestimating one's capabilities and intentions in international relations could have devastating results. The cognitive representation may include perception of threat identity, causes, possible consequences, and perceived acuteness. The threat could be perceived by ROK's decision makers as of high or low importance much differently than other actors that could lead to over/underestimation of consequences, overreaction or lack of appropriate action over time. Once the cognitive representation is made, an action plan to deal with the problem at hand is created and implemented. The final step of the inside-out approach is the appraisal and reflection on it – following the three steps self-regulation can be analyzed.[20] In addition during all three steps effects on the emotions

---

18 Martha Finnemore and Kathryn Sikkink, "International norm dynamics and political change," *International Organization* Vol. 52, No. 4, 1998, pp. 887-917.

19 David P. Baron, "Morally Motivated Self-Regulation," *The American Economic Review*, Vol. 100, No. 4 (September 2010) , pp. 1299-1329.

20 H. Leventhal, D.R. Nerentz, D. J. Steele, "Illness representation and coping with health threats," in A. Baum and J. Singer, *A Handbook of Psychology and Health* (Hillsdale, NJ: Erlbaum Associates, 1984), pp. 219-252.

of the decision makers could affect the process, hence a second action plan to control emotions simultaneously with the action plan for problem resolution takes place. Fear, anger, humiliation, and relief can be controlled to a different degree, but they certainly play role.

The third, final theoretical approach is the rational approach drawing heavily on neorealism's and neoliberal institutionalism's synthesis of behavioral change through material sanctions/incentives rooted in cost/benefit analysis. Though last, it is not least, and any attempt to investigate policy decision making without consideration of background cost/benefit analysis would be one sided and weak. The model focuses on objective, logical thought process that evaluates compliance and conformity based on actors' cost/benefit rationale and calculations considering domestic and international, actual and potential, as well as opportunity cost/benefits. The techniques and instruments applied to dissuade actors from non-compliance/non-conformity or to reverse action towards renunciation are positive and negative sanctions applied to influence behavour. Baldwin, a defender of the utility of economic sanctions, conceptualizes positive sanctions as actual or promised rewards and negative sanctions as actual or threatened punishments, both as means to exercise power.[21] In addition, Baldwin stresses the need to look for signals stemming from sanctions, as well as to the varying degree of their success.

The three theoretical approaches do not operate in isolation. However, while the first two have more psychological nature and are suitable to explain decision making influences, the third is more towards the operational, strategic, and rational environment. It will be argued that each defines a focal point within the development of ROK's nuclear policy analysis and its way of ordering priorities, and at a different periods in time some or other techniques have had stronger explanatory power, but together they form a

---

21 David A. Baldwin, *Economic Statecraft* (Princeton, N.J.: Princeton University Press, 1985), p. 20.

web of linkages illustrating the overall picture of the process of behavioural changes. The overall framework can serve for further similar cases, though the effectiveness of techniques to evaluate sanctions, rewards, incentives, etc. will certainly differ due to the differences in strategic environment and value of strategic goods. In addition, the depth of the analysis obstruct a broad generalization. Though one could have preference towards an approach based on personal beliefs and evaluation criteria, a minimum consideration of all three theoretical approaches is needed in order to prescribe an efficient mix of techniques for analysis of renunciation of nuclear weapon programs and its strategic implementation. To enrich the framework, a further hermeneutics approach could be added for even greater analytical depth.

IV. ROK's nuclear weapons program

1. Initiation of a nuclear weapons program (case 1)

ROK's official desire to pursue nuclear research and development program toward the realization of peaceful and humanitarian uses of atomic energy began in 1956 with the signing of a cooperative agreement with the U.S. Further nuclear research and educational activities were initiated prior and after South Kore's membership to the IAEA in 1957 towards construction of nuclear reactor, but it did not begin construction of its first atomic power reactor until 1971. In 1958 the Atomic Energy Law was passed and in 1959 the Office of Atomic Energy (OAE) was established by the government comprised of the Korea Atomic Energy Research Institute (KAERI) and the first laboratory reactor, a U.S. made small unit TRIGA Mark-II. The research reactor achieved criticality in 1962. In 1968 ROK established the Atomic Energy Development Promoting Committee and the Atomic Energy Development Advisory Committee to construct two 500MW nuclear power reactors by the mid–70's, and to hold international bids on the construction of light water reactors, heavy water reactors, advanced gas cooled reactors, and high temperature gas cooled reactors. In the same year after negotiations with the U.S. on nuclear reactors construction and agreement of a loan, ROK signed the NPT.

Short after the Guam Doctrine, in 1970, the Agency for Defense Development (ADD) and a Weapons Exploitation Committee were established and about a year later construction of the first nuclear power plant Kori 1, a Westinghouse unit built on turnkey contract agreed in 1968/69, began, sponsored by $98,600,000 loan from the Export Import Bank of United States.[22] Some argue that ROK had intentions to develop nuclear weapons as early as 1969.[23] Others see the Nixon Doctrine as the main reason that influenced the decision making to explore nuclear weapons in 1970.[24] And there are those that argue that intentions were clear on November 10, 1971 when the South Korean President Park Chung Hee inquired of O Won-ch'ol, second senior secretary of the Ministry of Commerce and Industry, if ROK were able to "develop nuclear weapons", looking at the question as a "general interpretation" for the order of a nuclear weapons program, although Hong acknowledges that there was no official statement from General Park Chung Hee at the time.[25] However, the step towards détente with the signing of communiqué between the ROK

22 Nuclear Threat Initiative, "ROK Nuclear Chronology," *James Martin Center for Nonproliferation Studies*, September 2004, <http://www.nti.org/media/pdfs/south_korea_nuclear.pdf?_=1316466791>.

23 Michael J. Siler, "U.S. nuclear nonproliferation policy in the Northeast Asian region during the Cold War: The South," *East Asia: An International Quarterly*, Vol. 16, No. 3/4, Winter, 1998, p. 59, <http://web.b.ebscohost.com.ezproxy.lib.tku.edu.tw:2048/ehost/pdfviewer/pdfviewer?vid=6&sid=b2212282-ebb8-4e0b-b0b3-e274ee3d5d3d%40sessionmgr198&hid=125>; see also *op. cit.*, Nuclear Threat Initiative.

24 Anthony H. Cordesman, "The Korean Military Balance," *Center for Strategic and International Studies CSIS*, 2011, <http://csis.org/files/publication/110712_Cordesman_KoreaMilBalance_WEB.pdf>; see also, "ROK Special Weapons," Global Security, <http://www.globalsecurity.org/wmd/world/rok/>.

25 Sung Gul Hong, "The Search for Deterrence: Park's Nuclear Option," in Pyong-guk Kim and Ezra F. Vogel, eds., *The Park Chung Hee Era* (Cambridge: Harvard University Press, 2011), pp. 483-484; Also in Jeonghoon Ha , "Why ROK Ratified the Treaty on the Non-Proliferation of Nuclear Weapons (NPT) in 1975," *Harvard Asia Quarterly*, Vol. 15, No. 3/4 (2013), pp. 56-65.

and DPRK symbolically on July 4, 1972, and the March 1973 Korea-U.S. Atomic Energy Agreement would seem counter to those interpretations and intention. The first agreement established a direct telephone line between Generals Park and Kim and the second, the so-called "123 Agreement", named after section 123 of the 1954 U.S. Atomic Energy Act, constrains raw material supply and disallows uranium enrichment and reprocessing used fuel. In October 1973 the Arab Oil Embargo put a considerable strain on the South Korean economy, heavily dependent on oil imports.[26] Soon after India, in early 1974, detonated its first "peaceful" nuclear device and later that year France and ROK signed a bilateral agreement on the cooperation of similarly "peaceful" uses of atomic energy, having agreed to sell a reprocessing technology to ROK.[27] [28] A 1978 declassified report by the Central Intelligence Agency of the U.S. confirmed that the authorization of a proliferation program was given by President Park first in December 1974 without formal Cabinet backing after the government had entered negotiations with Canada and France for the purchase of NRX-type heavy-water research reactor and small reprocessing facility, respectively.[29] In addition in early 1975 negotiations began with Belgium for a loan for the purchase of a research laboratory for mixed-oxide nuclear fuel fabrication. Hence, by 1975, a dedicated nuclear weapons program had emerged, with

---

26 Mitchell Reiss, *Without the Bomb: the Politics of Nuclear Proliferation* (New York: Columbia University Press, 1988), p. 89; cited in Daniel W. Drezner, "The Trouble with Carrots: Transaction Costs, Conflict Expectations, and Economic Inducements," in Jean-Marc F. Blanchard, Edward D. Mansfield, and Norrin M. Ripsman, eds., *Power and the Purse* (London, UK: Frank Cass and Co. Ltd, 2000), p. 209.

27 "Peaceful nuclear explosions," *Comprehensive Nuclear-Test-Ban Treaty Organization*, <http://www.ctbto.org/nuclear-testing/history-of-nuclear-testing/peaceful-nuclear-explosions/>.

28 Frank N. von Hippel, "South Korean Reprocessing: An Unnecessary Threat to the Nonproliferation Regime," *Arms Control Association*, March 4, 2010, <https://www.armscontrol.org/act/2010_03/VonHippel>.

29 National Foreign Assessment Center, "ROK: Nuclear Developments and Strategic Decisionmaking," *Central Intelligence Agency*, June 1978, pp. 5-11, <http://nautilus.org/wp-content/uploads/2011/09/CIA_ROK_Nuclear_DecisionMaking.pdf>; see also *Op. cit.*, Hong, pp. 489-491.

three compartmentalized teams working on missile design, and nuclear and chemical warheads. It was run by the executive vice president of the Agency for Defense Development (ADD), and was code named "Project 890."[30] Therefore, all events prior 1974 taken together have contributed to a different degree to the decision for nuclear weapons program initiation which will be analyzed below. The initiation could have been only possible backed by technological capability which was not evident prior 1974.[31]

2. The public forfeit (or secretly preservation) of the nuclear weapons program (case 2)

On April 23, 1975 ROK ratified the NPT as a sign of peaceful intentions and renounced nuclear weapons, a week before the victory of North Vietnam over the South. However, President Park couple of months later threatened that "we [ROK] have the capacity to do it [construct nuclear weapons]", if the U.S. support weakened.[32] The Agreement between the ROK and the IAEA for the Application of Safeguards in Connection with the NPT (the Safeguards Agreement) entered into force on November 14 the same year. Though according to the U.S., it was a year and a half later, in December 1976, when President Park ordered the suspension of Project 890.[33] Officially, thereafter ROK had complied and conformed to the NPT's obligations and norms.

3. Acknowledgment of secret activities and the controversy of compliance (case 3)

The IAEA's Additional Protocol to the Safeguards Agreement (the Additional Protocol) was signed by ROK on June 21, 1999 and entered into force on February 19, 2004. Few months after the Additional Protocol

---

30 Ibid. p.6.

31 Ibid. p.5.

32 Sited in World Information Service on Energy, "Korea buys CANDU reactor," Nuclear Awareness News Canada, Winter 1990/1991, p.10, <http://www.wiseinternational.org/node/406>.

33 Ibid. p.7.

entered in force in 2004 ROK submitted a report in accordance to its obligations for compliance. The report included couple of undeclared enrichment activities for research purpose. The nature of some of those enrichment activities and an earlier tip-off by an open source prompted an IAEA investigation to determine non-compliance and non-conformity. In 1999 a question of plutonium separation had been raised by the IAEA but ROK didn't acknowledge such activities and in 2002 and 2003 the IAEA requested verification of nuclear activities in ROK, but both times the agency was rejected access.[34]

On November 11, 2004, in an official safeguards implementation report the Director General of the IAEA revealed that ROK had violated its Safeguards Agreement by carrying out covert uranium separation, conversion, and enrichment activities and plutonium experiments continuously for more than two decades and de facto since an unreported chemical enrichment and plutonium separation experiments in 1979-1981 period with four counts of clear failure of compliance to NPT obligations, including also dozens of violations in the 90's and three experiments in 2000-2003, separating and enriching successfully 200mg uranium U-235 up to 77%.[35]

Despite the numerous failures of the ROK to comply with its obligations and to report these activities described as "of serious concern" by the Board of Governors, ROK's case was not treated as a case of non-compliance and was not reported to the UN Security Council for review as prescribed by the rules of the NPT, with the Board argumentation that the quantities of nuclear material and enriched uranium involved "have not been significant," prizing ROK's cooperation, and "that to date there is no indication that the undeclared experiments have continued".[36]

---

34 Director General, "Implementation of the NPT Safeguards Agreement in the ROK," *IAEA*, Report GOV/2004/84, Nov 11, 2004, <http://www.globalsecurity.org/wmd/library/report/2004/rok-gov-2004-84_iaea_11nov04.pdf>.

35 Ibid.

36 Board of Governors, "IAEA Board Concludes Consideration of Safeguards in ROK,"

V. Analysis

1. Case I

(1). Behavioural approach

The norm of nonproliferation during the early 70's was neither established globally with only about 70 ratifications of the NPT at that time, nor had any of ROK's close neighbours ratified the NPT. In fact, Japan, N. Korea, and China all ratified the treaty after ROK. Republic of China (Taiwan) and the Soviet Union had had ratifications in 1970, however the former was replaced by China at the UN that year and had to leave the NPT, and the later ratified the NPT as nuclear weapons power. Thus, the institutional environment couldn't have provided much international social pressure on ROK to conform, ratify the NPT and to internalize its norms. The international nonproliferation regime was still very weak to exercise much social pressure. Rather the external international environment provided incentives for ROK to pursue reprocessing aspiring to be like Japan. The wider context also played negative role. The Indian "peaceful" test in 1974 and the lenient approach of the U.S. towards Israel's secret nuclear developments in proliferation provided incentives for social comparison and social imitation. Incentives for ROK from renunciation could have been the technological learning that could have resulted from becoming a NPT member and the economic gains from peaceful use of nuclear energy. However, ROK already had access to necessary learning and research knowledge from its cooperative relationship with the U.S. and was on the path of cooperating with France at the time.

Persuasion, influence, and pressure at that time then could have come from reciprocity with the U.S., social isolation from severing the alliance with the U.S. – the world at that time was bipolar- the loss of aid,

---

IAEA, November 26, 2004, <https://www.iaea.org/newscenter/news/iaea-board-concludes-consideration-safeguards-south-korea>.

technological assistance, and learning opportunities in case of deterioration of the relationship with the U.S. In addition, ROK—U.S. cooperation led to the bilateral 123 Agreement in 1973, which, if complied to, ensures peaceful use of nuclear energy. The biggest factor in the ROK—U.S. relation was the security alliance and the interdependence from it. On one hand ROK was vulnerably dependent for its survival on U.S. military aid, on the other the U.S. was sensitively dependent on ROK because it could relied on Japan to contain the fast spreading of communism, which the U.S. perceived as an existential threat coming from the Soviet Union.[37] However, the unilateral decision by President Nixon to withdraw one third of American troops from ROK after the latter had complied to deployed more than three hundred thousand troops in Vietnam over the years, the encouragement by the U.S. administration of stronger developed ROK army knowing that for this development ROK dependence on U.S. will increase, the overall reduction of "carrots" during President Nixon, and the lack of response to North Korean provocations by the U.S. such as in the case of assassination attempt on President Park in late 90's and the capturing of U.S. vessel, despite ROK anger, have undermined the pressure that the U.S. could have exercised to keep S. Korea nukes free, mainly because such actions have revealed that the U.S. needed ROK for strategic purposes only. In addition, though accommodation of U.S. requests was often the case, actions taken by the ROK were often contrary to previous compliance, raising doubt to the degree of success of U.S. pressure without institutional legitimacy. For instance, the steps taken by President Park towards developing a capability of reprocessing in entering negotiations with France are counter the 123 Agreement. Why would a state want a reprocessing plant if it had just agreed to refrain from reprocessing? Was General Park really aiming for nuclear weapons or were there implicit goals of the policy? To answer these questions an inside-out self-regulative approach will be applied.

---

37 Op. cit., Siler, p. 56.

(2). Self-regulative approach

Why would have ROK wanted to stop itself of developing nuclear weapons? A factual evidence in support of General Park's intentions to centralize regulations and to conceal his true intentions is the Atomic Energy Office dissolution in 1973 and reconvention as the "Nuclear Energy Bureau" under the auspices of the Ministry of Science and Technology with significantly reduced responsibilities.[38] This is to say that General Park centralized regulation of decision making by transferring responsibility to himself.

Self-regulation motivations of President Park would have been counter gaining independent security, but in the short run could have played in favour of the survival of his regime and the successful development of the economy and the supply of energy it required. In addition, moral considerations such as to honor his agreements obligations to the 123 Agreement could have played role, too, as well as the need to strengthen his domestic political image. Successful cooperation abroad would have provided security and aid, and as such would have strengthened Park's regime. However, while it was clear that the Korean economy was in dear need of diversification of energy resources, and that the image of the President was important, it was even more acute to ensure long lasting security. As General Park must have known, strategic value and interests are not constants and as such the U.S. support over time would change. Therefore, long-term dependence on U.S. support would have been unwise, unless there were something to tie the U.S. to continuously support ROK. Even worse would have been pursuing total self-help. Hence, President Park chose to accommodate the U.S. requests for non-proliferation only on the surface.

---

38 Nuclear Energy Agency, "Nuclear Legislation in OECD and NEA Countries: Regulatory and Institutional Framework for Nuclear Activities in ROK," *OECD*, 2009, <https://www.oecd-nea.org/law/legislation/korea.pdf>.

The cognitive representation of threat from the North was exacerbated during the end of the 60's by the Nixon Doctrine, the assassination attempt on General Park, and the capturing of the U.S. naval ship by N. Korea. ROK would have been more sensitive towards its perception of the threat from the North and how the North would interpret the signals of U.S. withdrawal than it was any conflict of interest coming from the U.S. relationship. Hence, the fear from the North was always greater than the fear from the U.S. abandonment. However, being a general, President Park must have known that if abandoned for whatever reason ROK would be doomed. One study concludes that President Park's "fears of isolation and the possible withdrawal of U.S. forces have led him to embark on a secret program to develop nuclear weapons."[39] Though, fear of isolation and abandonment were major contributing factors for initiation of nuclear proliferation other feelings not resulting from social isolation, rather from misperception of the relationship and obligation between ROK—U.S. played significant role. President Park knew that the real threat to the South was the North and not the U.S.'s decision to partially withdraw troops. However, the way Park saw the threat from the North and the way Nixon perceived it were different. Therefore through the South-North communiqué of 1972 that aimed to defuse tensions combined with other stimuli such as the reaffirmation of the U.S. to support the South, seem to have tempered Park. However, President Park had perceived his contribution to Vietnam War as an exchange for U.S. support against the North. Park saw it as *quid pro quo* and Nixon as an asymmetric power relationship. Hence, the difference in perception lead to disappointment and probably humiliation for Park. On several occasions the South perception of acuteness of the threats seem to have been very different from those of the U.S. Provocations by the North, for

---

39 Office of International Security Affairs in the Department of Defense, undated, FRU.S. 1973-76 E-12; Cited in Alexander Lanoszka, "Seoul in Isolation: Explaining South Korean Nuclear Behavior, 1968-1980," *Dissertation*, Princeton University, 2012, p. 192, <http://www.alexlanoszka.com/AlexanderLanoszkaROK.pdf>.

instance, were seriously taken by the South and not paid much attention by the U.S. which angered President Park. Differences in geographical proximity further twisted perception of threat and acuteness.

The two plans of action of Park were to continue cooperation with the U.S. yet to create a new lever for negotiations, and faint compliance, if only to satisfy his hurt feelings at the time because he neither had the capability, nor the alternative to construct nuclear weapons. Total inaction by Park after being sidelined by Nixon's unilateral decision could have resulted in a regime suicide. Hence the "do nothing" card was off the table. On the other hand, too emotional and outright severance of the alliance would have led to the same result. Hence, President Park decided to initiate a nuclear weapons program as a lever for negotiations with the U.S., for demonstrating strength at home and to N. Korea, and to continue satisfying the growing economic needs of ROK. The appraisal of these action plans kept President Park in a self-regulative balance between both extremes of self-dependence and full U.S. dependence.

(3). Rational approach

President Park had to calculate carefully after the shift in U.S. strategic goals due to Nixon's Doctrine. On the one hand the material benefits from the alliance with the U.S. in terms of funds, military and technological assistance were enormous. On the other, the sheer consequence of Nixon's unilateral act was that President Park was sidelined. As realists often point out "the strong do what they have the power to do and the weak accept what they have to accept".[40] However, contrary to accepting and contrary to calculating President Park's announcement of proliferation in 1974 came without any rational in-depth cost/benefit analysis.[41] President Park, after U.S. troop withdrawal

---

40 Thucydides, *History of the Peloponnesian War*, translated by Rex Warner (London: Penguin Classics, 1954), p. 2, <http://lygdamus.com/resources/New%20PDFS/Melian. pdf>.

41 Ibid., CIA, pp. 5-7.

took place in 1971, confirmed his support in 1974 for nuclear weapons program initiation, he could have acted not with intent to really develop nuclear weapons, but with intent to gain some attention and leverage in negotiations, so that he won't be sidelined again which could have resulted in his downfall. The reason why he didn't show such intent right after the withdrawal is that when a threat is made, it needs to be credible and backed by capability, which up to 1974 ROK did not possess and had no channels opened to hope for it other than the U.S. Furthermore, he needed to temper his anger, disappointment, humiliation. On the one hand he could go forward without the U.S. and risk external annihilation from the North, on the other doing nothing but succumbing to U.S. demands would have resulted in perception of weakness and possible coup d'état at home. He needed to regulate his emotions and a plan to create a lever for negotiation with the U.S., he needed to create options and room to maneuver. The previous self-regulative approach above explained that well, furthermore as explained through the behavioral approach he chose to socially compare with other actors comparing their systemic interaction with the U.S. such as Israel and Japan.[42]

2. Case II

(1). Behavioural approach

States continued to ratify the NPT in 1975 and in 1976 numbering about 90, a 30% increase from the early 70's.[43] Japan followed ROK in 1976. The environment became a bit more favourable in support of the nonproliferation norm. It could be also argued that the U.S. persuaded ROK. After the U.S. realized that ROK could go nuclear if it were not satisfied, the U.S. had evaluated such scenario and decided to take ROK more seriously and exercise pressure. Amid proliferation by India and outright violation of the nonproliferation norm, social psychology

---

42 Ibid., CIA, pp. 5-7.

43 "Treaty on the Non-Proliferation of Nuclear Weapons," United Nations, <http://disarmament.un.org/treaties/t/npt>.

suggests that others would follow India. For normative pressure to take place there should not be many exceptions of the rule. Hence, even if the chance of ROK proliferation had been not very high, the U.S. couldn't have taken any chances at the time. The security and political cost of mass proliferation to the U.S. would have been significant. Nuclear South, would have been followed by nuclear Taiwan and Japan.

(2). Self-regulative approach

Having successfully gained the attention of its ally, President Park must have known that it will be very hard to keep the nuclear option open, but it seem that it was right into his strategic self-regulative plan of action. He couldn't have known how much leverage he would gain through initiation of a nuclear program. Hence he complied, with what he knew would satisfy the U.S. – ratification of the NPT and bringing in force IAEA's safeguard agreement. Though he did that, he kept on reiterating right after publicly that at the first instance of U.S. decline in support ROK could and would opt for self-defence measures, even nuclear weapons. President Park told the Washington Post that South Korea will do everything necessary, including developing nuclear weapons to defend itself if the United States withdraw its nuclear umbrella.[44] And that if U.S. military support weakens, South Korea will have to develop nuclear weapons. In addition, Park announces that South Korea has "the capacity to do it."[45] And he meant it because right after President Carter threatened to withdraw nuclear missiles Project 890 was restarted in late 70's as the IAEA report exposes.[46] Further, reason for continuing the strategy of "keeping the option open" was the renewed escalation in threat perception coming from the North after a stand-off in 1976.

---

44 Young Sun Ha, "Nuclearization of Small States and World Order: The Case of Korea," *Asian Survey*, Vol. 18, No. 11, November 1978, p. 1142.

45 Ibid., "South Korea Nuclear Chronology", *NTI*.

46 Ibid., IAEA.

President Park's prime motivation for self-regulation was his interest which in 1975 was not much different than in the early 70's – survival between the threat of N. Korea and the threat of being abandoned by the U.S.. However, morality was shelved, having gone against his promise to not search for reprocessing capability, and the actions towards proliferation ensured strength perception at home.

The oil crisis has left the economy vulnerable, so the need for fast track nuclear plants development was one factor, second, the action plan appraisal to initiate self-defence through nuclear weapons has brought him the needed result – a lever, which if exploited skillfully could result in leverage in negotiations with the U.S.. The strong response of the U.S., threatening positive sanctions and even possible alliance breakage, shouldn't have come as a surprise to President Park rather as a reward. He was testing, pushing the U.S. to see how far the U.S. would play indifferent to ROK's ambitions. After all his goal was not to pursue total independence and self-relience and neither was he prone to total dependence. He opted for the golden mean and keeping the nuclear option open provided him with the means to achieve that goal. As long as he could manage to self-regulate and not provoke the U.S. and to hide his true intentions, he was going to be successful.

Some argue that the fear of U.S. abandonment has led to initiation of proliferation in the early 70's and similarly the fear of abandonment has led President Park to accommodate U.S. demands for nonproliferation. This is not the case. While fear of abandonment was a factor in the former case, because President Nixon's unilateral actions had come as a surprise to President Park, in the latter case, in the next four years President Park created a strategy how to avoid this situation of happening again in the future. He implemented a plan and saw it rationally through.

(3). Rational approach

Park's behaviour in 1975 was much more rational in a sense that he had calculated the potential costs to the U.S., created nuclear proliferation favourable environment, and executed his plans of action, both to acquire a lever and to skillfully turn it into leverage. Thus, his decision to ratify the NPT was not motivated by fear but by incentives and own interest. This is in alignment with the previous case line of thinking that President Park needed to keep his option open to keep the U.S. committed to support the ROK not only when the U.S. saw to its interest but also when the ROK needed U.S. support.

Majority of literature would say that compliance and conformity can be ensured if the costs to a decision making outweigh the benefits because decision makers are rational actors.[47] Various authors have explored the case through the carrot-stick dynamics of the ROK—U.S. relations arguing that the asymmetrical power relation has provided the U.S. with the means to bend ROK's intentions.[48] Although, the decision for ratification and nuclear proliferation renunciation, or the secrete preservation of such desires, has come as a rational negotiations with the U.S., there are serious challenges to such straightforward conclusion due to the fact that the decision makers in South and North Korea were single individuals, who could have acted based on their feelings and spontaneous decisions. Second, as evident from the above analyses, although President Park complied with U.S. demands, it could have been as well what he wanted, taken in account that his very first relationship with the U.S. was one of reciprocity, hence to go back to reciprocity, rather than being sidelined. The benefit of possessing nuclear weapons by ROK are not high. ROK lacks strategic depth with Seoul nearby the border. Thus, the deterrent capability of such weapons is questionable. Furthermore, why would ROK risk alienating the U.S. to gain nuclear weapons when it already

---

47 Ibid, Ha, Hong, CIA, Singer, Baldwin, Ha.

48 Daniel W. Drezner, "The Trouble With Carrots: Transaction Costs, Conflict Expectations, and Economic Inducements," in Blanchard et. al, *Power and the Purse* (London: Frank Cass & Co, 2000), pp. 188-218. See also Hong, Ha, *op. cit.*

had U.S. nuclear missiles at home? ROK couldn't have increased the benefits of possessing own nuclear deterrent, after all the North wouldn't care much if the nuclear missile that would be targeting it was American or South Korean. However, what Park envisaged was to increase the cost to the U.S. if it wouldn't commit to continuous support, as argued in the previous case. After that there was not much he had that would have been different from common interest with the U.S.. His only objective after the negotiations with the U.S. was to make sure the U.S. understands that although he complied with the request for renunciation and ratification of the NPT, he will keep the nuclear option open. The U.S. must have taken this rhetoric simply as a saving face for domestic political purposes and the CIA reported that the nuclear program has been dismantled and stopped investigating further, however as the IAEA report exposes ROK didn't stop secrete nuclear research and kept the option open as President Park had warned.

Furthermore it could be argued that challenges come from disagreement in the literature on the effectiveness of sanctions, be it threatened, actual, positive or negative. Traditionally sanctions were viewed as nearly obsolete and ineffective, but Baldwin and others have revived the debate.[49] Hence, if Park's ambition was to increase the cost to the U.S. he wouldn't have been able to measure it outright clear if it worked or not. He could have just hoped that they would work, based on social comparison of the outcomes of U.S.–Israeli, U.S.–Japanese relations. In this case the rationality applied is saticficing not perfect.

3. Case III
(1). Behavioural approach

Why would the ROK expose its longstanding beneficial strategy and forfeit the benefits it had reaped from it? Has it created a new space for additional decision-making alternative other than nuclear program and

---

49 Ibid., Baldwin.

further away from the two extremes of total annihilation from outside and coup d'état at home?

Six events in the international system played role in shaping the decision-making process that led to the revelations by the ROK government. First, in 2004, 186 states had ratified the NPT and had accepted IAEA safeguards. However, the Additional Protocol was in force only in about 50 states. Nonetheless, the nonproliferation norm grew stronger and the IAEA Additional Protocol standards, which ROK brought in force in 2004, could put more pressure on decision makers than previously by easily exposing non-compliance. Second, the U.S. image and authority internationally was strengthened at the end of the Cold War providing it with stronger normative pressure if needed. Third – the timing of the U.S. CIA report declassification about its decision from 1978 that there were no activities of proliferation thereafter, seems to indicate that the U.S. was trying to distance itself and to show that if after 1977 the ROK had undertaken secret operations the U.S. wouldn't have known, signaling that if necessary it will join the international community against the ROK. Fourth, the determination of the Six Party Talks to press the North, after the course the North had undertaken in 2002 towards proliferation, could have prompted behavioural change in the South. Fifth the ongoing war between the U.S. and Iraq and the requests by the U.S. for transferring troops from ROK to Iraq and for withdrawal of 12500 troops from ROK. Finally, the deeper penetrative power the Additional Protocol measures provide raised questions of compliance and necessary inspections combined with a tip-off by an anonymous player that the ROK has conducted secret nuclear activities exemplify the social pressure that could come from outside.

(2). Self-regulative approach

ROK over the years has moved from authoritarian to democratic governance accountable to its people. The diffusion of power and the new institutions created provide for a much more complex picture of decision making regarding nuclear policy and self-regulations. The state as a unitary actor needs to be broken down in order to determine who had influence on decision making in ROK in 2004. Only groups of individuals with high executive power will be considered here such as the president and the ministers of economy, foreign affairs, military, and intelligence. Left over standards of procedures in the organizational process of decision making in this respect need to be addressed to determine the motivations behind the decisions taken, and domestic politics could have effect too. Under the self-regulative approach the goals of those actors will be perceived as conflictive yet the coordination process between them could as well lead to conflict even if their goals would be the same. The perception of those actors of the threat from U.S. withdrawal of troops and redeployment from ROK to Iraq in post-priori seems to have been lower than President Park's in 1970. Which begs the question of why? Did the thirty years long alliance with the U.S. make decision makers in Korea perceive the threat less damaging or did the rapid economic development provided for a confidence and independence that could have changed that perception?

How did President Roh Moo-hyun impeachment and stripping of power by the National Assembly in early 2004 and the appointment of the country's Prime Minister, Goh Kun as interim leader correspond to the change in nuclear policy? It surely must have because the way Roh's perception of threat works certainly differs from that of Park in the 70's. Chung Dong Young, a lawmaker with the Uri Party, called the impeachment "a coup d'état carried out without guns and swords"[50]. However, the Constitutional court reinstated the President few months later. In the mean time Ban-Kee Moon, foreign minister of ROK at the time, agreed with the U.S. of 3600 troops redeployment. In June, at Future

---

50 Samuel Len, "President's Impeachment Stirs Angry Protests in South Korea," *New York Times*, March 13, 2004, <http://www.nytimes.com/2004/03/13/world/president-s-impeachment-stirs-angry-protests-in-south-korea.html>.

of the Alliance talks in Seoul, U.S. representatives inform South Korea that the U.S. will withdraw overall 12,500 troops by end of 2005. Though President Roh had called for accelerating South Korea's "self-defense system" in response to U.S. decision to dispatch 3600 U.S. troops from South Korea to Iraq earlier, there was no angry response to the withdrawal of much larger contingent announced by the U.S., rather the ROK pledged its own contribution and deployment of 3000 troops to Iraq.[51] This indicates that there was a major shift in policy and the threat perception of redeployment and withdrawal of troops was different compared to the Park's perception in the 70's. Though President Bush decision to unilaterally withdraw 12500 troops is similar to Nixon's, the response from ROK was different. The motivations to self-regulate for ROK in this case are deeper and longstanding cooperation, common democratic interests such as freer trade, economic development, and legitimate protection of private property. The domestic political polarization created domestic disunity that contributed to the milder perception. The freedom of media could present with louder voice the U.S. point of view and its reiterated commitment towards the alliance. Hence despite the damage on ROK—U.S. ties, the fear and the perception of abandonment didn't have the same impact on decision making as in the 70's. In addition, the belief that the new hope the newly formed Six Party talks awoke prompted the government to perceive its own actions as breaching international norms and in order to convince the North do de-nuclearize the South needed to come clean first. Furthermore, the fact that the U.S. lost Vietnam war exacerbated the feeling of abandonment in the 70's, but in Iraq President Bush declared victory. Thus, the incentives for ROK to stay allied to the U.S. were better especially taking the victory as a signal for N. Korea from the U.S..

---

51 Donald G. Gross, "U.S.-Korea Relations: Strains in the Alliance, and the U.S. Offers a Nuclear Deal," *Comparative Connections, Pacific Forum, CSIS*, July 2004, <http://csis.org/files/media/csis/pubs/0402qus_korea.pdf>.

The new generation in Korea has become more assertive, less dependent economically on the U.S. due to its own strong economy, and has become less afraid from impoverished North Korea. All these factors contribute to the bold decision to change policy and come clean.

(3). Rational approach

Incentives for ROK from its cooperation with the U.S. continued to benefit ROK. In trade terms in 2004 ROK totaled in surplus of nearly 20 billion dollars.[52] This trade benefits accounted for 2.6 % of ROK's GDP. This doesn't include any aid in military and economic terms. One of the legacies of President Park was to reduce dependence on energy imports, to strengthen the economy and to develop stronger than the North, thus reducing the dependence on the U.S.. He didn't bulk on U.S. suggestion of small-medium enterprise creation, rather pursued his strategy of development of conglomerates, which later became world famous trade-marks such as Samsung. In 2004 the ROK GDP has increase from few billions in the 1970 to 800 billion. From one of the poorest countries in the world Korea has emerged as one of the richest. There are two implications from the economic developments. First, it will be harder for the U.S. to induce or coerce Korea economically if need be. Secondly South Korea will inevitably seek closer cooperation with China which could provide even more economic power for ROK. Though ROK has gained its economic security and hence has become more confident, it still depends heavily on U.S. as a security ally. The inducements the ROK can afford to calm the North provide further reason for the South to feel more secure.

VI. Current trends and future outcomes

The strong domestic public opinion support for nuclear weapons in

---

52 U.S. Census Bureau, *"Trade in Goods with Korea, South"*, 2004, <https://www.census.gov/foreign-trade/balance/c5800.html#2004>.

ROK in recent years is creating an environment favourable for proliferation and counter conformity of the nonproliferation norm. Steps towards internalization of the norm are recommended for ROK to demonstrate that it has truly moved away from the "keeping the option open" policy. Today S. Korea has 23 nuclear reactors, but still imports fuel from the U.S.. Until 2014 ROK was constrained by the 123 Agreement. ROK's government has described these U.S. constraints as "excessive", and pushed for them to be eased, preferably before the Agreement was due for renewal. In 2015 a deal with the U.S., replacement of the 123 Agreement, allowed ROK to research pyroprocessing as a substitute for traditional fuel reprocessing that could lead to enrichment. In addition, the U.S. vowed to help with disposal of ROK's nuclear waste. The main concern, however, is reprocessing not only at home. In 2009 following ROK and the UAE agreement for the purchase of nuclear reactors, ROK sold 4 nuclear reactors to United Arab Emirates for 20 billion U.S. dollars, ROK has offered its indigenous produced nuclear reactors on the market without requirement for potential buyers to implement the Additional Protocols of the IAEA. Most recently, Saudi Arabia and Seoul entered negotiation for the construction of two nuclear reactors, sparking a debate for Middle East nuclear race.The government refuses to attach Additional Protocol requirement to sales of nuclear reactors arguing that it is not against the law, yet refusing to promote non-proliferation norms. Though not bound to do so by the treaty, a true conformist and advocate of nonproliferation would consider showing a stronger leadership.

In search of commercial interest and market share the ROK government demonstrates lack of responsibility. Although the ROK government has been fully compliant and cooperative with the IAEA after 2004, there is lack of official accountability for the failure to comply for over two decades and little in respect to conformity and promotion of norms.

VII. Conclusion

1. Case I

From 1962 up to the Vietnam War, President Park had been cooperative and the incentives from ROK—U.S. relations had seemed to work. Until there was a change in U.S. policy and the Nixon Doctrine had prompted ROK to search for a more substantial lever. Therefore, Park's strategy was to demonstrate that his actions could have significant cost to the U.S. government if it continuous to pursue a policy of disengagement. By creating the nuclear weapons program, opening the option of proliferation, and making it credible, President Park didn't necessarily aim for a total success. His initiation decision was the only decision he could have taken in order to look strong at home, continue to receive some support from the U.S., and to lift his negotiation leverage with the U.S., who had unilaterally withdrawn troops. Though seemingly rational, his decision was made without cost/benefit analysis and he first had to deal with his emotions through self-regulation and creation of a plan for action and to socially compare in order to self-validate. The supplementary incentives coming from the social comparison of international interactions compliment this explanation. The way he dealt with his fear and the strategy he came up with, got the U.S. attention. The cost for the U.S. from nuclear ROK would have been significantly higher than the cost of keeping troops in ROK. It seems that Park's strategy to tame the U.S. policy makers was successful in that respect, though still dependent on U.S. alliance.

2. Case II

With a plan in mind President Park rationally increased the cost for the U.S. and created a lever and gained leverage in renewed negotiations with the U.S.. Though many argue that Park had to cave in under U.S. threats of sanctions, it is likely that his strategic goals were multiple and anticipative of U.S. reaction to course of proliferation. From the very beginning Park believed that ROK's and U.S.'s goals were aligned, once he was disappointed he made sure to find a way to prevent it of happening again. His legacy did remain as a policy of "keep the nuclear option open" for few decades.

3. Case III

Shifts in domestic politics, growing interests in nuclear energy as a replacement of energy imports, first class economy, have all increased ROK's confidence and provided for weakening of ROK dependence on U.S. and lessened the threat perception from both N. Korea and U.S. redeployment/withdrawal of troops. Combined with Six Party talks hopes, stronger normative regime pressure and growing incentives from closer cooperation with China, the ROK decided to abandon decades long strategy of "keeping the nuclear weapons option open".

Overall Conclusion

The analysis of the three cases and current developments suggest that ROK had not *de facto* renounced nuclear weapons in 1975, and that to date it never conformed to principles and norms of the NPT, rather after 2004 it changed its policy orientation and complied fully with rules and regulations due to its increased confidence and lesser threat perception. Compliance alone is not enough to trust ROK, especially after thirty years of keeping the nuclear weapons option open. The lack of norm internalization due to majority of the public in support for proliferation, combined with avoidance of responsibility in sales of reactors and the lack of accountability for past mistakes by the government expose ROK as a case of non-genuine renunciation. It is recommended the ROK take immediate measures towards conformity and the internalization of the norm of nonproliferation by educating the public at home and advocating the norms of nonproliferation internationally by attaching the Additional Protocol ratification as a requirement to nuclear reactor sales. By attaching strings ROK would demonstrate maturity and assume responsibility as a leading state in nuclear energy.

China-Côte d'Ivoire Relations: The Steps Forward

Viviane Bayala[*]

Abstract

In 2013 the People's Republic of China (PRC) and the Republic of Côte d'Ivoire (RCI) commemorated, with warmth and hope, the thirtieth anniversary of Sino-Ivoirian relations. At this special occasion, the presidents of both countries praised an ongoing healthy and sustainable relationship established in 1983. At time of writing, this relationship keeps its progressive trend, surprising some, or upsetting and rejoicing others.

This paper, subsequently, explores the historical voyage and the current state of this Sino-African bilateral tie with the intrinsic aim of understanding its underlying rationale and future prospects. The methodology combines qualitative and quantitative data collected from countries governmental administrations and online websites, International Institutions data bases, academic journals, online news papers and magazines.

The study starts with an overview of China multilateral relations with Africa in general, before landing on China-Côte d'Ivoire bilateral relationship: it's political, economic, security and social dimensions are respectively explored. The concluding section sums up the significant transitions witnessed by this relationship over time and their implications.

---

*   Ph.D. Candidate, Graduate Institute of International Affairs and Strategic Studies, Tamkang University.

I. Introduction: China-Africa Relations Overview

The modern Republic of Côte d'Ivoire was officially created on August 7, 1960. The country covers 322.462 square kilometers and is bordered by Mali and Burkina Faso to the north; the Gulf of Guinea to the south; Ghana to the east; Guinea Conakry and Liberia to the west. This French ex-colony is blessed with a strategic geographic location, significant untapped natural resources, and exponentially growing, young human resources. The country once known as the economic giant of Francophone West Africa during the 1970s was torn apart by eleven years of political instability in this early twenty-first century and is currently rebuilding its economic infrastructure with the expressed goal of the incumbent president to make the country an emerging country by 2020.[1]

Cote d'Ivoire is the last country to adhere to China's "one China"[2]

---

1   Oxford Business Group, "Côte d'Ivoire Economy: Building Strong Foundations: President Allassane Dramane Ouattaraon Measure being taken to promote growth and renewal," *Oxfordbusinessgroup.com*, 2013, < http://www.oxfordbusinessgroup.com/viewpoint/ building-strong-foundations-president-alassane-dramane-ouattara-measures-being-taken-promote-growth>, accessed November 2014. International Monetary Fund, "Document pour le point d'achèvement de l'initiative en faveur des pays pauvres très endettés (PPTE) et Initiative d'Allègement de la dette multilateral (document for the achievement of the initiative in favor of Highly Indebted Poor Countries (HIPC) and Initiative for Multilateral Debt Reduction (MDR)," *Staff Country Report,* May 29, 2012, 6, <http://books.google.fr/ books?hl=fr&lr=&id=1A1858qRgFUC&oi=fnd&pg=PP2&dq=Côte+d%27Ivoire+emerg ing+2020&ots=RQD5KarqJQ&sig=ANbeV4RpcFKdFk2RQf1zCdQaMjg#v=onepage&q &f=false>, accessed November 2014.

2   The "One China" policy of the PRC (simplified Chinese: 一个中国 ; traditional Chinese: 一個中國政策 ; pinyin: *yī gè Zhōngguó*), at the outset, refers to Chinese communist party claim to be the sole legitimate government representing Chinese people instead of the KMT nationalist government in Taiwan: confer Gerrit van der Wees, "One China Policy: Back to basic" *Taipei Times*, November 18 2007, <http://www.taipeitimes.com/News/ editorials/archives/2007/11/18/2003388403>, accessed September 2014. Deng Xiao Ping has, latter, formulated the "one China, two systems" for the reunification of China in the early 1980s. The proposal advocates for One China but with different regions such as Hong Kong, Macau, Taiwan that could retain their initial economic and political systems: confer<http://www.china.org.cn/english/features/china/203730.htm>, accessed September 2014.

policy in West Africa, but it currently figures among the top-ten Chinese aid recipients in this sub-region and the top-five francophone West African countries with US$1.22 billion received between 2000 and 2011.[3] The financial sums received are not paramount, but this new development in a country known as French and Western geopolitical *"chasse-gardée"* is, further, interesting when considering the current dynamic pictures offered by China's political, economic and social growth in this country.

This paper highlighted the extent of these multiple developments and their implications for the future of China-Côte d'Ivoire relationship. The remaining of this introductive part described the over whole progress of China in Africa since the Cold War.[4] The second part addressed the political progress, which is followed by the third and fourth sections respectively describing the social expansions, and the security and social connections surge. The concluding part (the fifth part) summarized the main transitions and explored the implications for the future.

---

3 Information gathered from Tracking Chinese Development Aid,< http://china.aiddata.org/map>, accessed September 2014. The country is preceded by eight countries including Nigeria (US$47.34 billion), Ghana (US$23.8 billion), Guinea-Conakry (US$22.31 billion), Niger (US$5.54 billion), Guinea Bissau (US$5.15 billion), Sierra Leone (US$2.99 billion), Liberia (US$2.94 billion), Mauritania (US$1.26 billion); and followed by five other countries; Togo (US$999.3 million), Senegal (US$90 million), Mali (US$709.7 million), Cape Verde (US$171.9 million.) and Benin (US$ 61.3 million).

4 West Africa covers a territory of about 5 million kilometers square hosting 300 million people (43 % of the Sub Saharan Africa population) unevenly distributed over sixteen (16) countries. The Francophone West Africa is a sub-region of 4,746,541sq km hosting about 114, 839, and 946 million peoples, CIA World Facebook <https://www.cia.gov/library/publications/the-world-factbook/geos/ng.html>, accessed February 2012.

Figure 1: Côte d'Ivoire Geographic Location in West Africa

Source: South Africa History Online, http://www.sahistory.org.za/places/cote-divoire, accessed 2015.

1. Politics within Cold War

Since 2000, the PRC foreign policy is guided by a four dimensional "go out strategy"[5] where "great powers are the key, the periphery is the priority, the developing countries are the foundation and the multilateralism is the important platform." The refreshing of this policy and the re-evaluation

---

5   It refers to: 走出去战略 ; pinyin: *Zǒuchūqū Zhànlüè*) the People's Republic of China's current strategy to encourage its enterprises to invest overseas, which was first mentioned by Premier Zhu Rongji in 2000 in his report to the National People's Congress. Confer NB Turner, "China 'Go Global' Strategy," Part 3, Paragraph 9, *RED-PATH.NET*, March 31 2014, <http://www.red-path.net/analysis/is-china-an-imperialist-country/part-3/19-16-china-s-go-global-strategy>, accessed June 2015.

of the country's African policy is increasingly required by foreign policy analysts.[6]

Sun particularly criticized China's tendency to focus on narrow economic Interests instead of designing an African "grand strategy"[7] to tackle rising bureaucratic conflicts and business agents while improving the government over whole performance.[8] Moreover, he highlighted that in China's foreign policy decision-making process issues are treated according to their worth. Belonging to the "foundation", and perceived as "a low priority", "a mean rather than an end", Africa is discussed at the working level while big powers (key priority) are addressed at the highest level of China's foreign policy apparatus.[9]

Bearing these recent policy underpinnings in mind, this section revisited the early development of China-Africa relations with a particular emphasis on political goals achievements.

---

6   See Liu Hongwu, "Re-understanding China's Foreign Policy Mapping," [重新理解中国外交格局], *DongFang Daily*, April 1, 2013,< http://epaper.dfdaily.com/dfzb/html/2013-04/01/content_753361.htm>, Yun Sun, "*Africa in China's Foreign Policy*," John L. Thornton China Center and Africa Growth Initiative, April 2014, p. 17, <http://www.brookings.edu/research/papers/2014/04/10-africa-china-foreign-policy-sun>, accessed June 2014.

7   "International relations scholars use the term 'grand strategy' to refer to the purposeful and planned use of military, economic, and diplomatic means by states to achieve desired foreign policy ends, whether in peacetime or during wartime". Confer: Princeton University, Statesmen, Partisans, and Geopolitics, chapter 2, p. 2,< http://press.princeton.edu/chapters/s9471.pdf>, accessed June 2015.

8   Yun Sun, "Africa in China's Foreign Policy," *BROOKINGS*, April 2014, p. 30, <http://www.brookings.edu/research/papers/2014/04/10-africa-china-foreign-policy-sun>, accessed June 2014.

9   The Highest Decision making: A leader designated by the collective leadership of the Politburo Standing Committee (PBSC) – Assisted and advised by the Director of Foreign Affairs Office from the Central Committee of the CCP. The Working Level: Ministry of Foreign Affairs (MFA): which addresses procedural, daily and routines between China and foreign countries. With the Involvement of specific government agencies. Confer, Yun, op-cit, p. 17.

Albeit some evidences pointing to economic motives behind China Africa policy during the Cold War, (mostly from 1949 to the late 1970s), its politico-ideological agenda was much more obvious and overwhelming. Five major achievements characterized this relationship during the 1970s and only one is economic. They are,first, the increase of the number of PRC African Allies from thirteen in the 1960s to thirty in the late 1970s; second, China was successful on joining the United Nation Security Council at the expense of the Republic of China (ROC or Taiwan), third, China build the Tanzania-Zambia (Tazara), the most famous aid project of the continent during the 1970s; fourth, China was faithful on its commitment to support nationalist movements struggle for independence and preaching the end of capitalism, and fifth, China unveiled the huge gap between the world super powers and the rest of the World.[10]

Indeed, as the People's Republic of China (PRC) was created in 1949 under the leadership of Mao and the Chinese Communist Party (CCP), the country lost the seat of China at the United Nations Security Council (UNSC) to its rival the Republic of China (ROC or Taiwan).[11] The PRC frustrated, became restless until the seat was conquered in 1971. In the progress, African countries support, encouraged by China's financial aid and technical support, was fundamental to this victory. China's first set of political alliances with Africa was concluded after the 1955 Bandung conference where Asia-Africa cultural and economic relations, as well as solidarity on facing imperialism, colonialism and Western hegemonic position were promoted.[12]

---

10 B.D. Larkin , Chinese Aid in Political Context 1971-1975, in Weinstein, Chinese and Soviet aid. 1975.

11 The previous modern Republic of China was created in 1912 under the lead of Chiang KaiChek and the KMT was defeated during the civil war that erupted within the country after WWII.

12 R Wright, "The Color Curtain," in D. J. Muekalia (2004), "Africa and China's Strategic Partnership," African Security Studies, 13(1): 5-12,. Wiswa Narwapala, "Bandung Conference of 1955 and the resurgence of Asia and Africa," Daily News, March 21, 2005, <http://archives.dailynews.lk/2005/04/21/fea01.htm>, accessed June 2015.

PRC's Premier Zou, then, introduced the "five principles of peaceful coexistence" and the foreign aid "eight principles"[13] as PRC's foreign policy guidelines: "mutual respect for sovereignty and territorial integrity; mutual non-aggression; non-interference in each other's internal affairs; equality and mutual benefit; and peaceful coexistence."[14] Of these five principles, only the fourth referred to economic motivations: which is "equality and mutual benefit." Subsequently, in 1960, the Chinese ministry of Foreign Affairs created a new section dedicated to African affairs, followed in 1961, by the visit of a new Chinese-African Friendship Association tour to West Africa as a preparation to the visit of Premier Zou 1963-64 African tour.[15] He succeeded on signing the country's first set of political agreement with six African countries.[16]

---

13 The eight are: 1. Chinese government have persistently been providing assistance to foreign countries according to the principles of equality and mutual benefit, never regard the assistance as the grant by one sided....... 2. While providing foreign aid, Chinese government strictly respects the sovereignty of recipient countries, no strings attached and no privilege required. 3. in order to relief the burden of recipient countries, Chinese government provides economic aids in the way of interest free or low interest loan, the time limit of repayment could be delayed when it is needed. 4. The purpose of Chinese government providing foreign aid is not to make recipient countries being dependent on China, but to help recipient countries gradually develop on the track of self reliance and economic development independently. 5. For the projects constructed through China foreign aids, Chinese government does its best to make quick effects through smack investment. Thus, the governments of recipient countries could increase income and accumulate money. 6. Chinese government provides equipment and materials made in China with the best quality, and negotiate the price in accordance with the price of international market....7. While providing technical assistance, Chinese government assures to teach recipients to fully master this kind of technology. 8. The experts who are dispatched by Chinese government to help recipient countries carrying out construction, should be paid as same as their own experts of recipient countries. They are required to not have any special requirement and enjoyment. (Gountin:11-12).

14 Looy Judith, "Africa and China: A Strategic Partnership?" ASC working paper, No. 67 (2006), *African Studies Centre, The Netherlands*, p. 2, <http://www.ascleiden.nl/Pdf/wp67. pdf>, access June 2015.

15 Chaponnière Jean-Raphaë, "Un demi-siècle de relations Chine-Afrique," Évolution des analyses, *Afrique contemporaine*, 2008/4 n° 228, p. 3,<http://www.cairn.info/revue-afrique-contemporaine-2008-4-page-35.htm>, access June 2011.

16 Yun, P ; 13 China signed its first bilateral cooperation agreements with African countries:

Chinese policy in ascending to the UNSC was successful as the goal was reached in 1971 followed by a continual increase of the number of allies within the continent, and the progressive isolation of the ROC. The Figure 2 showed that the latter mentioned was slightly ahead of the PRC with sixty-eight countries against fifty-three for the PRC before 1971 but, two years after the PRC replaced Taiwan on the UNSC, the figure was dramatically reversed to eighty-nine against thirty-one in favor of the PRC.

This number of country recognizing Taiwan increased to twenty-eight during the 1990s before shifting to as low as twenty-two in the 2000s. At time of writing it still stood at twenty-two countries; with six countries in East Asia and Pacific, three in Africa, One in Europe, and twelve in Latin America.[17]

The PRC has persistently refused to maintain formal political relations with countries that are politically involved with Taiwan. Currently, it covered most of West Africa with the exception of Burkina Faso and the pending case of Gambia which is officially neither Taipei nor Beijing.[18]

More than any other motivations, this first period of China-Africa relations witnessed the prevalence of political interests. Chinese financial/technical aid and trade activities were tools toward the achieving the PRCs political ends. It assisted African countries financially and technically and the

---

Algeria, Egypt, Morocco (Northern Africa), Guinea (West Africa), Somalia and Sudan (East Africa) from the late 1950s to the mid 1960s.

17 East Asia and Pacific (Kiribati, Republic of the Marshall Islands, Nauru, Republic of Paulo, Solomon Island, and Tuvalu), Africa (Burkina Faso, Sao Tome and Principe, and Swaziland), Europe (the Holy See), Latin America (Belize, El Savador, Haiti, Nicaragua, Paraguay, St Lucia, the Dominican Republic, the Republic of Guatemala, the republic of Honduras, the republic of Panama, Saint Christopher and Nevis, Saint Vincent and the Grenadines). See Ministry of Foreign Affairs, Republic of China (Taiwan), *Diplomatic Allies*, 2014, <http://www.mofa.gov.tw/en/AlliesIndex.aspx?n=DF6F8F246049F8D6&sms=A76B7230ADF29736>, Accessed December 2014.

18 Burkina-Faso is maintaining a stable relationship with Taiwan since 1994. Gambia has maintained a consistent relationship with Taiwan from 1995 to November 2013. Illustration: Viviane Bayala, August 2014.

PRC and ROC Diplomatic Allies 1969-2013

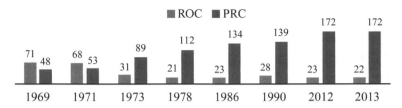

Figure 2: The People's Republic of China (PRC) and the Republic of China
(Taiwan) International Relations

Source: Michael Y.M. Kao, "Taiwan's and Beijing's Campaigns for Unification," in *Harvey Feldman*,
Michael Y.M. Kao (eds.), *Taiwan in a Time of Transition*, (New York: Paragon House, 1988).188.
Illustration: Viviane Bayala, November 2014.

Table 1: PRC and ROC Recognition by West Africa Countries

Countries	PRC	ROC
Benin	1964-1966 / Since1972	1966-1972
Burkina Faso	1973-1994	1961-1973 / Since 1994
Cape Verde	04-1976	
Côte d'Ivoire	Since 1983	1963-1983
Gambia	1974 1995	1995-2013
Ghana	1960	
Guinea	10-1959	
Guinea Bissau	1974-1990 / Since 1998	1990-1998
Liberia	1977-1989 / Since 08-1993	1989 -1993
Mali	1960	
Mauritania	1965	
Niger	1974 -1992/ Since 1996	1992 -1996
Nigeria	1971	1960 -1971
Senegal	1974-1996 / Since 2005	1996 -2005
Sierra Leone	1971	
Togo	1972	1960-197

Source:Information collected from http://www.china.org.cn/english/features/focac/183414.htm, accessed
August 2014.

number of the country's allies rose from thirteen during the 1960s to thirty in the late 1970s.[19] New shinning buildings, stadiums, medical teams as well as student exchange programs were initiated and executed in these countries.[20]

Most of China's help went to countries such as the Egypt of Nasser (first partner), who showed resistance to western imperialists and nationalized the canal of Suez and, also, Guinea and Mali who have refused to join the Community of African countries proposed by the French President Degaulle.[21] It also supported "the Uniao Nacional Para a Independencia Total de Angola (UNITA) and Zimbabwe African National Union (ZANU)- while opposing other groups supported by the Soviet Union, such as the Movimento Popular de Libertacao de Angola (MPLA) and the Zimbabwe African People's Union (ZAPU)."[22]

Burgeoning Sino-Africa commercial ties were also observed during the sixties. China was oil self- sufficient up to the 1990s, but imported Cobalt (nuclear power) copper (half of the country consumption) from the continent. It is recorded that Africa was receiving 6 percent of PRC's export: which was the consequence of it decision to export less and refusal to be indebted by western financial institutions, the deficit with the West was compensate by more export toward the South, Africa included.[23]

2. Economic Pragmatism within Post-Cold War

According to a Heritage Foundation article, of US$120billion in

---

19 Brautigam Deborah, *Chinese Aid and African Development* (London: Palgrave Macmillan,1998), p. 45.

20 Looy Judith, op-cit, p. 4.

21 Zhou Enlai has visited ten countries Africa between December 1963 and January 1964. Confer Muekalia, D.J., "Africa and China's strategic partnership". *African Security Review* 13 :1, pp. 5–11. 2004, p. 6, <http://www.relooney.info/SI_Oil-Politics/China-Africa_3.pdf>, access September 2014.

22 George T. Yu, "Africa in Chinese Foreign Policy." *Asian Survey*, Vol. 28, No. 8 (Aug., 1988), p. 851, <http://www.jstor.org/stable/2644590>, Accessed: 01-07-2015 07:45 UTC.

23 Chaponniere, 2006.

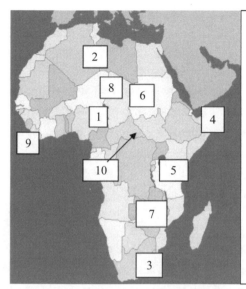

Top 10 Chinese African Investment in $US billion

1. Nigeria – 15.6 – Energy, real estate, transportation
2. Algeria – 10.5 – Transportation and real estate
3. South Africa – 8.6 – Financial services and mines
4. Ethiopia – 7.8 – Energy, transportation and technology
5. R.D. Congo 7.8 – Mineral and energy
6. Chad 6.8 – Transportation
7. Angola 6.5 – Real Estate and Energy
8. Niger 5.2 – Oil
9. Sierra Leone – 4.7

Figure 3: Chinese Major Investments in Africa (2013)

Source: Map from http://www.yourchildlearns.com/africa_map.htm, Illustration: Viviane Bayala with information from, Les 10 pays Africains qui attirent plus d'investissementsChinois(The top-ten of Chinese African Investments), *JeuneAfrique*, April 2013 ,http://economie.jeuneafrique. com/regions/international-panafricain/16404-les-10-pays-africains-qui-attirent-le-plus-d-investissements-chinois.html, accessed August 2014.

Chinese financial outflows in 2013(excluding loans, treasury bonds and other financial operations), Africa has received US$108 billion; primarily directed at the sectors of transportation (US$34.31billion), Oil (US$31billion), real estate(US$21.6billion) and mines (US$16.3billion). The top-ten recipient countries in Africa are: Nigeria, Algeria, South Africa, Ethiopia, RD Congo, Chad, Angola, Niger, Sierra-Leone, and Cameroon.

These financial investments covered, as displayed Figure 3 above, the whole continent from North to South, and East to West with a special focus on Nigeria and West Africa including Côte d'Ivoire.[24] This development

---

24 "Les 10 pays Africains qui attirent plus d'investissements Chinois" (The Top-Ten Countries of Chinese African Investments), *Jeune Afrique*, April 2013, <http://economie.

is symbolic of the shift of China-Africa policy from previous politico-ideological concerned toward pragmatism and domestic economic development during this early twenty-first century.

The fact is that, in the late 1970s, China moved away from the 1950s-1970s hard anti-colonialism and anti-imperialism policies of President Mao Zedong (1949-1979) to enter a new era of economic openness with President Deng XiaoPing. Under his leadership, although the "One China" policy has remained and even coarsened into the "One China"[25] principle, economic development became the PRC priority world-wide.

Three foreign policy documents support the recent changes in China's Africa foreign policy: the 2006 white paper on African policy and 2011/2014 white papers on China foreign aid policy in Africa. The intent of change was suggested during the twelve Communist Party Committee National Assembly where it was said that: "China would concentrate on domestic economic development; China would pursue its independent foreign policy characterized with 'mutual benefits' in real meaning."[26] This announcement was, followed by Prime Minister Zhao Ziyang "1982 four principles."[27]

---

jeuneafrique.com/regions/international-panafricain/16404-les-10-pays-africains-qui-attirent-le-plus-d-investissements-chinois.html>, accessed September 2014.

25 Zhang Chun, "The Sino-Africa Relationship: Towards a New Strategic Partnership" *London School of Economics*, Nov.2013, <http://www.lse.ac.uk/IDEAS/publications/reports/pdf/SR016/SR-016-Chun.pdf>, accessed August 2014.

26 Li Anshan, "China and Africa: Policy and Challenges", *China Security, Vol.3, No.3, Summer 2007*, p. 72, <http://www.cebri.com.br/midia/documentos/china_and_africa_policy_and_challange.pdf>, accessed April 2015.

27 1.In carrying out economic and technological cooperation with African countries, China abides by the principles of unity and friendship, equality and mutual benefit, respects their sovereignty, does not interfere in their internal affairs, attaches no political conditions and asks for no privileges whatsoever. 2. In China's economic and technological cooperation with African countries, full play will be given to the strong points and potentials of both sides on the basis of their actual needs and possibilities, and efforts will be made to achieve good economic results with less investment, shorter construction cycle and quicker returns. 3. China's economic and technological cooperation with African countries takes a variety of forms suited to the specific conditions, such as offering technical services,

When comparing 1980s with 1960s principles, the intention to shift from ideology and politic to a more pragmatic approach is obvious; especially from principle 2 and 4. They expressed the importance of relying on both countries comparative advantages, the stress of a will to respond to African countries needs but within the margin of China's possibilities, and the expectation to see the continent grow into self-reliance.

At this stage, it was more about strengthen the 'home front' before launching the global trek and China was much more preoccupied by domestic economy reconstruction. The Tiananmen event and African countries responses and support to the PRC put an end to China relative retreat from the continent. In 2000 the FOCAC was launched and with it China-Africa relations reached level of intimacy never reached before. At the third FOCAC (2006) the first white paper on China-African relations was published declaring: "Sincerity, equality and mutual benefit, solidarity and common development (…) are the principles guiding China-Africa exchange and cooperation and the driving force to lasting China-Africa relations."[28]

While the theme of faithfulness and friendship, the attachment to national sovereignty and equality are of old, the mention of "lasting China-Africa relations" expressed China's will for a long term and strategic presence in Africa. The recent increasing cooperation on Non Traditional Securities issues and the expansion of cultural and social ties support this new development. China-Côte d'Ivoire Relations highlighted the micro manifestations, starting from the political progress.

---

training technical and management personnel, engaging in scientific and technological exchanges, undertaking construction projects, entering into cooperative production and joint ventures 4. The purpose of China's economic and technological cooperation with African countries is to contribute to the enhancement of the self- reliant capabilities of both sides and promote the growth of the respective national economies by complementing and helping each other.

28 Ministry of foreign Affairs, of the PRC, *"China Africa's Policy, 2006"*, Sep. 9, 2012, <http://www.fmprc.gov.cn/eng/zxxx/t230615.htm 9.09.2012>.

II. China-Côte d'Ivoire Political Progress

When The PRC was founded in 1949, Côte d'Ivoire was still under French colonization from which it was freed to become the modern Republic of Côte d'Ivoire (RCI) on August 7, 1960.[29] However, the PRC-RCI relations began only in 1983, as an epilogue to the Cold War and after neighboring Guinea-Conakry that became the first country in West Africa to sign a bilateral agreement with China in 1959 and to welcome Premier Zhou during his mid-1960s African tour.[30] Since the first diplomatic ties established, the pre-twenty first century Sino-Ivorian relationship has smoothly grown toward a breakthrough in the early twenty-first century.

The country is a key actor of French domain in West Africa.[31] The French army has maintained a presence in the country since the colonial era. In1978, the forty-third French Army Base was established in Abidjan and was the center of operations for the U.N. led "Operation Licorne" during the civil war in Côte d'Ivoire.[32] The U.S. has also entered Côte d'Ivoire in the late 1950s where it has, discreetly, built an important niche over time;

---

29 Côte d'Ivoire became an official French colony in 1893 and received its political independence from France on August 7, 1960. Global Edge, "Côte d'Ivoire: History," *Michigan State University*, 1994-2014, <http://globaledge.msu.edu/countries/Côte-d'ivoire/history>, accessed September 2014.

30 Guinea Conakry was the only French territory in West Africa to vote against French Union project in Africa and President Sekou Toure is the First Sub-Saharan African political leader welcomed in Beijing by Mao Zedong. See Joseph Ki-Zerbo, *Histoire de l'Afrique Noire* (Paris: Hatier, 1975), 513. During this tour Zou En Lai has also visited Algeria, Morocco, Angola and Sudan.

31 The French geopolitical domain in West Africa includes, beside Côte d'Ivoire; Benin, Burkina Faso, Guinea Conakry, Mali, Mauritania, Niger, Senegal, and Togo which, with exception of Mauritania, are members of the West Africa Economic and Monetary Union (WAEMU). See "Union Economique et MonetaireOuestAfricaine", *UEMOA*, <http://www.uemoa.int/Pages/Home.aspx>, accessed March 2014.

32 Tobias Koef, "Quel avenir pour la présence militaire de la France en Côte d'Ivoire?," Institut Français des Relations Internationales, *l'Afrique en Question* No.10, December, 2011, <http://www.ifri.org/?page=detail-contribution&id=7151>, accessed 2014.

and especially in the aftermath of the struggle against terrorism.[33] Since the return of peace and stability the country is, gradually, regaining its economic and political preeminence within the West Africa Economic and Monetary Union (WAEMU) as attested by recent news reports.[34]

1. Political Boarding Pass (1983-1999)

Sino-Ivorian relations became a reality only after Côte d'Ivoire had adhered to the PRC's "One China" policy and ceased her more than twenty years of diplomatic ties with Taiwan. This imposition of a political condition by China and the compliance of the Ivorian authorities' spoke in favor of a political imperative at the outset of Sino-Ivorian ties as it has been the case for other African and West African countries.[35]

As a matter of fact, In Asia, Côte d'Ivoire had earlier bilateral diplomatic ties with Japan, India, the Republic of Korea, and Taiwan during the 1960s and was active in multilateral meetings; such as the Tokyo International Conference on African Development, the Asia-Africa Conference in Bandung (Indonesia) and the Ministerial Conference of the Techno Economic Approach for India-Africa Movement.

---

33 U.S. Country Reader, "Côte d'Ivoire," *Adst.org*, January 7, 1998, 1, <http://www.adst.org/Readers/Ivory%20Coast.pdf>, the first consulate of the U.S. in Côte d'Ivoire was established in 1957-1958.

34 A press communiqué mentions the visit of an AFRICOM delegation led by the Ambassador Philipp Carter on June 2014 in the context of programmed meetings on regional security. See, "press communiqué", *Usembassy.org*, June 27, 2014, <http://french.Côtedivoire.usembassy.gov/cprafricomcipg.html>, accessed November 2014. Another national news website also mentioned the visit of General Carter (AFRICOM) for security matters and Russian delegation to discuss the reshuffle of Russia-Côte d'Ivoire bilateral relations. See "Côte d'Ivoire: Allassane Ouattara recoit AFRICOM et la Russie au Palais (Côte d'Ivoire: Allassane Ouattara welcomes AFRICOM and Russian in the Presidential Palace)", February 26, 2013,< http://koaci.com/Côte-divoire-alassane-ouattara-recoit-lafricom-russie-palais-80491.html>, accessed November 2014.

35 International Business, "Côte d'Ivoire Foreign Policy and Government Guide," *International Business Publication*, February 7, 2007, p. 139, <http://books.google.com.tw/books?id=sErsPNH8lLMC&dq=Côte+d%27Ivoire+relations+with+Asia+countries&hl=fr&source=gbs_navlinks_s> , accessed December 2014.

The record of high official visits between China and Côte d'Ivoire between 1983 and 1999 showed more dynamism from China against a timid Ivorian response.

On China's Side, Vice Premier Li Peng (1986), and Minister of foreign affairs Wu Xueqian (1987) had visited the country before the first official Ivorian visit to Beijing in the early 1990s. President Yang Shangkun (1992) and the Vice Premier Hu Jintao (1999) were the highest profile Chinese visitors of this period.

In addition to the aforementioned, four other officials visited Abidjan during this period namely, Wang Hanbin, vice-chairman of the NPC (September 1989), Qian Qichen, member of the State Council and concurrently Minister of Foreign Affairs (January 1992), Li Lanqing, Vice-Premier (November 1995), Song Jian, member of the State Council and concurrently Director-general of the State Science and Technology Commission (May 1997).

Most symbolic in this early period of Sino-Ivorian relations was the late President Yang Shangkun's, tour of Côte d'Ivoire in 1992. The visit happened in the early post-Cold War era, three years after the dramatic Tiananmen Square event.[36] According to Eckholm, during this tour president Yang Changkun,[37] Foreign Minister Qian Qichen, and a PRC trade delegation also

---

36 The Tiananmen Square (June Fourth or 89 Democracy Movement - 八九民运) event refers to Chinese government violent repression of student's demonstration in Tiananmen on June 4, 1989. See US Department of State Office of the Historian, *Milestone:Tiananmen Square 1989-1992*, October 3, 2013, <https://history.state.gov/milestones/1989-1992/tiananmen-square>, accessed August 2014.

37 Erik Eckholm, "Yang Shangkun, 91, Ex-China Chief, Dies," in *New-York Time*, September 15 1998, <http://www.nytimes.com/1998/09/15/world/yang-shangkun-91-ex-china-chief-dies.html>, accessed July 2014. According to the author, President Yang Shangkun (1907-1998) was the last of the guards who fought to create the communist party and ruled it up to the 1990s with Mao, Deng, and Jiang. He was replaced by Deng Xiaoping in 1992 and has remained a respected party leader who played an important role during the 1989 repression.

visited Morocco and Tunisia as part of "Yang's reaffirmation of cooperation with the Third World as a basic tenet of China's foreign policy."[38]

He explains that After the Tiananmen Square demonstration, the development of tied and diversified relations with more African countries was part of the Yang regime's drive to strengthen China's international presence at the UNSC and to gain credibility on the home front. Shinn and Eisenman have also underlined the coarsening of the PRC policy against Russian hegemony in the 1980s and Taiwan in the 1990s.[39]

On the Ivorian side, Leon Konan Koffi, Minister of Defense of the Republic of Côte d'Ivoire opened the door as the first eminent visitor to Beijing in 1990. He was followed by the Prime Minister Daniel Kablan Duncan (July 1996), President Henri Konan Bedie (May 1997) and Emile Brou the National Assembly speaker (May 1999). Four visits in total.

This indicates that, although formal relations between the two countries started in 1983, the first Ivorian official visit did not occur until the early 1990s. Meanwhile, under the government of Henri Konan Bedie, China was held as an important partner as shown by visitors such as Prime Minister Daniel Kablan Duncan and President Bedie himself.

Finally, there were few official Ivorian visits in comparison with Chinese, which attested amore dynamic diplomatic and political endeavor from China and a weaker response from Côte d'Ivoire. The prevalent national and international political contexts help in deepen the understanding of this pattern.

---

38 Robert G. Sutter, *Chinese Foreign Relations: Power and Policy since the Cold War*, (United States: Rowman& Littlefield Publishers,Ed. 3, 2012) ,p. 312, <http://books. google.com.tw/books?id=r2WpKLDgRDYC&pg=PA312&lpg=PA312&dq=Yang+Sha ngkun+visit+to+la+Côte+d%27Ivoire&source=bl&ots=Naf6on75Om&sig=ttq0sPEsG Ezf6r-ub-M8XAcbSHk&hl=fr&sa=X&ei=ro7tU7faGtDq8AWj24GwCQ&ved=0CBo Q6AEwADgK#v=onepage&q=Yang%20Shangkun%20visit%20to%20la%20Côte%20 d'Ivoire&f=false>, accessed November 2012.

39 David H. Shinnand Joshua Eisenman, op-cit, p. 97.

Figure 4: President Yang Shangkun welcomed by Ivorian Prime Minister Allassane Dramane Ouattara at the International Airport Felix Houphouet-Boigny of Abidjan in 1992

Source: Getty Images, July 11 1992, http://www.gettyimages.com/detail/news-photo/chinese-president-yang-shangkun-is-accompanied-by-ivory-news-photo/107350366,accessed August 2014

In point of fact, from Côte d'Ivoire's independence (1960) to the establishment of a formal relationship between the country and the PRC (1983) the late President Houphouet-Boigny, mostly known as a pro-capitalist unfriendly to communist China, has led the country in a close and almost exclusive relationship with France of General Charles Degaulle, Georges Pompidou, Valery Giscard d'Estaing and Francois Mitterrand.[40] In those days, the country motto was "La Côte d'Ivoire, amie d'un seul, enemy de personne" (Côte d'Ivoire friend of one, enemy of none).[41]

---

40 General Charles Degaulle (January 1959-April 1969), Georges Pompidou (June 1969-April 1974), Valery Giscard d'Estaing (May 1974-May 1981), and Francois Mitterand (May 1981-May 1995) were French 5th republic Presidents who led France during the long reign of President Felix Houphouet-Boigny (1960-1993).

41 Guillaume Moumouni, "China's relations with African Sub-Regions: the Case of West

This clear-cut political choice in a context of a formal ending to French colonialism in West Africa was highly valued by France under General Degaulle. Côte d'Ivoire became French neocolonialism's pivot in the region, with French aid and skills flowing within the country to sustain a non-protectionist economic policy and an export-oriented agricultural policy, which contributed altogether to create what is known as the "Ivorian miracle" of the mid-1970s.[42] Houphouet-Boigny was not a common leader of his time. The Ambassador Donald R. Norland, the U.S. Consul to the country from 1958-1960 made the following observations about him:

> *"it didn't take me long to realize that Houphouet-Boigny was not only a person of considerable stature in his own right, he had been, remember, the number-three man in a post-war French government... A minister of state and minister of health; he was an African doctor. A person of considerable stature within the RDA (Rassemblement Démocratique Africain), which was his political party in all of French West Africa. But his Ivory Coast section of it, which was called the PDCI (Parti Démocratique de la Côte d'Ivoire), was his instrument."[43]*

Beyond this international and regional political stature, Houphouet-Boigny was an enigmatic and charismatic figure at home. He was not only a rich farmer, but also heir to the throne of the Baoule ethnic group in Yamoussoukro. In Côte d'Ivoire he was highly respected and loved but also feared.

Africa," *African Union Fridays Bulletin 3*, no.1, January 2010, p. 40,< http://www.africaunion.org/root/ua/Newsletter/EA/Fridays_of_the_Commission/2010/AUC%20Vol1%20FF%20Low%20Res.pdf>, accessed November 2012. The author explains how France and Côte d'Ivoire work together during Nigerian's Biafra crisis. Côte d'Ivoire even recognized the "Biafran Republic" and was associated with many French neocolonialist tactics within the region.

42 "Ivorian Miracle" is the name given to the spectacular economic growth that happened in the country during the 1960s and 1970s. Confer Denis Cogneau, and Sandrine Mesplé-Somps, "Emerging Africa Program: Could la Côte d'Ivoire become an emerging country", *OCDE Development Center*, June 1999, p. 12, <www.oecd.org/fr/dev/emoa/2674837.pdf>, accessed September 2014.

43 Country Reader, "Ivory Coast", p. 5.

However, from 1983 to 1999, in a context leaning toward the end of Cold War, the "Ivorian miracle" was waning and political and economical support from the "one friend" (France) entered a weak phase. Supporting a policy of multilateralism, Edouard Balladur, French Prime Minister from 1993 to 1995 voiced France's inability to bear the whole world's misery ("la France ne peut pas accueillir toute la misère du monde"), Côte d'Ivoire had no choice but to align with the Breton Woods institutions' regulations.[44] At that time, the country's motto shifted to: "La Côte d'Ivoire amie de tous, enemy de personne" (Côte d'Ivoire, friend of all, enemy of none) to accommodate new "friends" and opportunities while mitigating the effects of a downgraded socioeconomic performance.[45]

In 1983, Houphouet-Boigny was hitting his 23rd year in power. However, the once charismatic leader and architect of the "Ivorian miracle", was facing social discontent instigated by the emerging socialist party of President Laurent Gbagbo within an economically fragile environment.[46] Toward the end of the 1990s, sickness and age further undermined his leadership capabilities. Then, for the first time in the history of the country, in 1989, the constitution was revised to authorize multiparty democracy and the nomination of a prime minister; which dispositions allowed, Allassane Dramane Ouattara, an economist from the West African Central Bank and the IMF, to become the first Ivorian Prime Minister.[47]

---

44 "Edouard Balladur en couverture (Edouard Balladur in Focus)," *Survie.org*, November 17, 1997, <http://survie.org/publications/les-dossiers-noirs/les-candidats-a-la-presidentielle/article/edouard-balladur-en-couverture>, accessed December 2014.

45 Xavier Auregan, "le double-jeu de la Chine en Côte d'Ivoire (Chinese double-game in Côte d'Ivoire)" *La revue géopolitique*, (April 3, 2011), 1-7, <http://www.diploweb.com/La-Chine-en-Côte-d-Ivoire-le.html>, accessed July 2013.

46 Les Echos, "Le père du miracle ivoirien (the Father of Ivorian Miracle)," *Echos*, December 8 1993, <http://www.lesechos.fr/08/12/1993/LesEchos/16534-024-ECH_le-pere-du-miracle-ivoirien.htm>, accessed September 2014.

47 Confer "Le leader politique Allassane Dramane Ouattara (Allassane Dramane Ouattara the political leader)," 2007-2008,< http://www.ado.ci/leader.php?np=1> , accessed September 2014.

The Sino-Ivorian relationship emerged in this context, which explained a shyer Ivorian approach under Houphouet-Boigny and his immediate successor Konan Bedie.[48] The latter became president in 1993, after Ouattara's three years office. Ouattara drove the country closer to the Breton Woods institutions, starting the process of economic stabilization and initiating a significant opening to the PRC with Yang's visit in 1992. Bedie was ousted by a military coup On December 1999 two years after his Beijing tour in 1997, following Prime Minister Kablan Duncan's 1996 voyage.[49]

In conclusion, the early developments in the Sino-Ivorian relations were slow because of France's Cold War neocolonialism impact in Côte d'Ivoire, and former President Felix Houphouet Boigny compliance to this policy. However, in the Post Cold War, especially from 2000, the political landscape in Côte d'Ivoire shifted in favor of the PRC.

1.2 Political Breakthrough (since 2000)

Although the PRC leaders were discreet in diplomatic visits from 2000 to 2011, the Ivorian leadership's rush to Beijing revealed an unexpected political breakthrough for the PRC. During this period, China welcomed three successive political leaders: President Jiang Zemin (1990-2002), Presidents Hu Jintao (2003-2012), Xi Jinping (Since 2012),[50] and under each administration, the PRC interest vis-à-vis Côte d'Ivoire advanced.

For example, the Table 2 (next page) compiles a total of twenty-seven Sino-Ivorian leaders and officials bilateral visits: the double of the previous

---

48 Etienne Kunde, "France-Côte d'Ivoire: histoire d'un couple aux relations ambigües," *Slate Afrique*, February 9, 2012, <http://www.slateafrique.com/82237/france-Côte-divoire-histoire-colonisation-relation-ambigue>, accessed September 2014.

49 Richard Konan, "Les années de Bedie au pouvoir, un vrai cauchemar (Bedie leadership, a nightmare)," *presse ivoirienne*, October 10, 2008, <http://ivoirediaspo.net/anciens/politique/les-annes-de-bdi-au-pouvoir-un-vrai-cauchemar>, accessed September 2014.

50 They, respectively, figure as the third, fourth and fifth generation of Chinese political leadership. See Jeffrey Hays, "China under Jiang Zemin," *FACTORS AND DETAILS*, 2013, <http://factsanddetails.com/china/cat2/sub7/item76.html>, accessed August 2014.

period discussed above. On China's side, only six dignitaries have landed in Abidjan including Chi Haotian; Member of the State Council and Minister of National Defense (September 2001), Wei Jianxing; Standing member of the CPC Central Committee and Secretary of the Secretariat (June 2002), Siao Zhonghuai, Vice-Minister of Foreign Affairs (September 2003), Fu Ziying Vice-Minister of Cooperation and Trade (September 2008), Zhai Jun, Vice-Minister of Foreign Affairs (June 2011), Yang Jiechi, Minister of Foreign Affairs (January 2012).

Beside the aforementioned, no Chinese presidential visit in Côte d'Ivoire was registered during this period. Until now, Minister of Foreign Affairs Yang Jiechi remains the highest-ranking Chinese leader to have visited the country, having made the trip to Abidjan in 2012, some months after Allassane Dramane Ouattara's election when a relative stability was established within the country.[51]

Conversely, this period witnessed a rise in Ivorian visits to Beijing. At least 21 Ivorian leaders and officials visited China from 2000 to 2012. These included Presidents Laurent Gbagbo (February 2002) and Allasane Dramane Ouattara (July 2002) themselves. Most of these visits happened under Gbagbo's governance, beginning with Defense Minister Lida Kouassi and extended to officials visitors from different ministerial department such as economy, national assembly, African integration, mines, transport, solidarity etc.

A possible reason for Chinese cautiousness and Ivorian eagerness was the prevalent Ivorian 2002-2011 sociopolitical crisis. A climate of distrust emerged under Jacques Chirac leadership and reached its climax with Nicholas Sarkozy and Gbagbo's. France, then, disliked Gbagbo because of the rise of the concept of "Ivoirité" and ethnical exclusion under his

---

51 National News Online, "President Hu Jintao welcomed Allassane Dramane Ouattara in Beijing," *Koaci.com*, July 20, 2012, <http://koaci.com/cote-divoire-chine-jintao-recoit-alassane-ouattara-76377.html>, accessed July 2014.

Table 2: Sino-Ivorian Leaders and High Officials Visits 2000-2012

	Chinese Leaders and Officials		
	Names	Titles	Dates
1	Chi Haotian	Member of State Council and Minister of National Defense	Sep .2001
2	Wei Jianxing	Standing member of the CPC Central Committee	Jun. 2002
3	Siao Zhonghuai	Vice-Minister of Foreign Affairs	Sep. 2003
4	Fu Ziying	Vice-Minister of Cooperation and Trade	Sep. 2008
5	Zhai Jun	Vice-Minister of Foreign Affairs	Jn. 2011
6	Yang Jiechi	Minister of Foreign Affairs	Ja. 2012
	Ivorian Leaders and Officials		
7	Lida Kouassi	Minister of Defense	2001
8	Laurent Gbagbo	President	Feb. 2002
9	Mel Eg Theodore	Minister of African Integration	2004
10	Amon Tanoh	Minister of Tourism	2004
11	ClothildeOchouchi	Minister of Solidarity and War Victims	2005
12		Minister of Energy and Mines	2005
13	Anaky Kobenan	Minister of Transport	2005
14		Minister of Economy and Finance	2006
15	Laurent Dona Fologo	President of the National Socioeconomic Council	Nov. 2006
16	Hamed Bakayoko	Minister of New Technologies of Information	Dec. 2006
17	Amadou Kone	Minister of African Integration	Ma. 2007
18	Youssouf Bakayoko	Minister of Foreign Affairs	Ma. 2007
19	Amani Nguessan	Minister of Defense	No. 2007
20	Dagobert Banzio	Minister of Youth Sport and Leisure	Au. 2008
21	Gilbert Bleu Laine	Minister of Education	Oc. 2008
22	Emmanuel Monnet	Minister of Mines and Energy	Oc. 2008
23	Dagobert Banzio	Minister of Economy and Infrastructure	Au. 2008
24	Augustin Kouadio	Minister of Culture and Francophony	Jl. 2009
25	Guillaume Soro	Prime-Minister	Oc. 2009

| 26 | Kaba Niale | Minister of Economy and Finances | Apr. 2012 |
| 27 | AllassaneOuattara | President | Jl. 2012-07 |

Source: "Côte d'Ivoire,"http://www.china.org.cn/english/features/focac/183548.htm. Sino-Ivoirian Relations, *French people daily*, http://french.peopledaily.com.cn/french/200204/24/fra20020424_53994.htmlaccessed August 2014. "Côte d'Ivoire China Relations Report", Ministry of Foreign Affairs (Abidjan), accessed on December 2013. Illustration: Viviane Bayala, August 2014.

leadership, and the latter denounced France for its alleged betrayal and support of the rebel groups.[52]

During an ostentatious ceremony for the transfer of Yamoussokro's Parliament House Gbagbo did not hesitate to express his gratitude to Chinese authorities in the following words: "Thank you for your gratefulness and friendship. Contrary to many other friends, you did not abandon us despite the military and political crisis. Not only did you remain but you support us through tangible actions."[53]

This situation not only damaged Franco-Ivorian relations but also compelled China to adopt a tactical position of discretion in order to advance and secure its position while avoiding any political frictions with France.[54]

---

52 Joseph Sani, "Education and Conflict in Côte d'Ivoire," *United State Institute of Peace*, special report 235, April 2010, p. 1-2, <http://www.protectingeducation.org/sites/default/files/documents/special_report_235.pdf>, accessed September 2014.Winson Saintelmy "la Crise ivoirienne à travers la géopolitique identitaire de Gbagbo (Ivorian Crisis through Geopolitical Identity)," *Le Monde*, April 15, 2011, <http://www.lemonde.fr/idees/article/2011/04/15/une-lecture-geopolitique-de-la-crise-ivoirienne_1507537_3232.html>, accessed September 2014.

53 Antoine Sadia, *Democratic Governance and Foreign Aid in Sub Saharan Africa: Assessing the Cooperation between China and Côted'Ivoire* (French: L'Harmattan,2013), p.152, <http://books.google.com.tw/books?id=NcMwAAAAQBAJ&pg=PA147&lpg=PA147&dq=li+peng+en+Côte+d'ivoire&source=bl&ots=16cZgZnQeS&sig=AxPQvIKxOPNXnbZ7CB7I9iZiULY&hl=fr&sa=X&ei=kezqU- K6KtO68gWsjIL4DQ&ved=0CC8Q6AEwAw#v=onepage&q=li%20peng%20en%20Côte%20d'ivoire&f =false>, Accessed September 2014.

54 The concept of "ivoirité" expressing Ivorian nationalism emerges under Henry Konan

Thus it put a relative freeze on diplomatic visits and acted constructively in the resolution of Ivorian crisis by the UNSC.

Looking at the situation from another angle, President Gbagbo had no other choice than to get a political hook on China. He had definitively lost French financial support but remained assured that China possessed the financial capacity to support the implementation of his internal economic development plan and the political military might to defend his regime internationally, especially at the UNSC. Consequently, he multiplied the number of diplomatic visits to China.

Another important factor was Gbabgo's political background.[55] Unlike Houphouet-Boigny, he is an Ivorian of a modest origin and has, relatively, few ties to French political leaders. He served several stints in jail under the Houphouet-Boigny regime and was the first opposition leader to face him, albeit unsuccessfully, in 1990.[56]

The trend of high diplomatic visits provides a synoptic view of the progress of Sino-Ivorian relations, beginning with restraint in the 80s and culminating in a breakthrough during the 2000s. Côte d'Ivoire, twenty years after independence, finally accepted the PRC's "One China Policy" and severed ties with Taiwan, opening the door to China. In contrast to the confrontational attitude expected of a rising great power, China has been discreet, active and reasonably cooperative with a special focus on Economy.

Bedie to expand during President Laurent Gbagbo's regime. Winson Saintelmy, op-cit, <http://www.lemonde.fr/idees/article/2011/04/15/une-lecture-geopolitique-de-la-crise-ivoirienne_1507537_3232.html>, accessed July 2014.

55 Stephen W. Smith, "The Story of Laurent Gbagbo," *London Review of Books* 33, no. 10 May 19, 2011, p. 10, <http://www.lrb.co.uk/v33/n10/stephen-w-smith/the-story-of-laurent-gbagbo>, accessed December 2014.

56 Pascal Bianchini, "Un Africain à Paris: Retour sur l'exil politique de Laurent Gbagbo dans les années 80 (An African in Paris: Back to Laurent Gbagbo's Political Exile of the 1980s," *Codersia*, p. 184, <http://www.codesria.org/IMG/pdf/9-cotedivoire.pdf>, accessed December 2014.

III. China in Côte d'Ivoire: The Economic Expansion

Starting from 2000, China-Côte d'Ivoire economic relations have expanded with more dynamic trade trend and an increasing Chinese aid provision. In an international context of economic globalization, both countries are exploiting their comparative advantages: with China as a financial investor and Côte d'Ivoire as a raw material producer.

Beginning with the oil-gas sector; Côte d'Ivoire is third only to Nigeria and Ghana in West Africa.[57] According to Carolyn Avery; "Côte d'Ivoire is a regional energy hub centered on Abidjan, which Ivoirians have long envisioned as a "Rotterdam of Africa"."[58] Like fellow West African coastal oil producers, Côte d'Ivoire has an offshore deep water oil potential that requires weighty extraction investments. The country is an established oil refining and emerging oil producing country with estimated oil reserves of 100 million barrels of crude oil located in the Gulf of Guinea and 1.1 Trillion Cubic Feet of recoverable gas reserves.[59]

Besides oil, the country is a haven of barely exploited minerals such as gold, diamonds and ore.[60] However, as highlighted by Omayra Bermúdez-Lugo this sector needs serious public and private investments to fund the research on geologic data, improve the development of mineral's deposit

57 Cindy Hurst, "Oil Rush in Africa", *IAGS:Energy Security*, July 2006, p. 10, <http://www.iags.org/chinainafrica.pdf>, accessed April 2014. She states that the country produced 2.5 million barrels per day (bpd) in 2005, 3.90 million bpd in 2011 and 4.40 bpd expected by 2015.

58 Carolyn Avery, "Côte d'Ivoire's Oil Industry" *IAS Group* ,April 2010, p. 9, <http://iasworldtrade.com/pdf/Côte%20dIvoire%20Oil%20Industry%20Memo.pdf> , accessed November 2014.

59 Mbendi Information, "Oil and Gas in Côte d'Ivoire," *Mbendi Information Services*, 1995-2014, <http://www.mbendi.com/indy/oilg/af/ci/p0005.htm>, accessed March 2014.

60 Extractives Industries Transparence Initiative, "Côte d'Ivoire," *Eiti.org*, May 22, 2013, <https://eiti.org/CôtedIvoire>, accessed March 2014.

exploitation, and the renewal of mineral institutional framework.[61]

Agriculture is, also, another important and under exploited sector waiting for investments. Côte d'Ivoire's economy depends mostly on agriculture with cocoa, coffee and timber, producing more than 40 percent of the Gross Domestic Product (GDP). The is, respectively, the world largest cocoa and fifth largest coffee producer, in addition of the development of products such as cashew nuts, cotton, rubber, and palm oil. All these resources are in demand from China and if well planned the trade trend between the two countries will blossom bringing benefits to both sides.

Moreover, with the end of the civil crisis in 2011, Côte d'Ivoire has returned to a positive GDP growth cycle, with 8.6 in 2012, 8.9 in 2013 and a projected 9.4 in 2014. These optimistic data indicate that the country is reemerging from the economic backdrop of the last two decades where it performed as low as 0.5 from 1991 to 2001 and a negative growth rate of − 0.6 during the period 2001-2011 as described in Figure 5 below.[62]

This recent macroeconomic improvement has, so far, barely impacted social development variables indicating that there is still much to be done with regards to the population's characteristics. With nearly 23 million (July 2014 est.), Côte d'Ivoire is the most populated and potentially multicultural country of the (WAEMU).[63] At the global level, the country is ranked fifty-

---

61 Omayra Bermudez-Leo, "the Mineral Industry of Côte d'Ivoire," *USGS 2012 Mineral Year Book, US Department of Interior*, 2014, p. 1, <http://minerals.usgs.gov/minerals/pubs/country/2012/myb3-2012-iv.pdf, accessed November 2014>.

62 Pascal Yembiline, Bakary Traoré, Luis Padilla, "Perspective Economiques en Afrique: Côte d'Ivoire, (Economic Perspective in Africa: Côte d'Ivoire)," *Africaneconomicoutlook. org*, p. 2, <http://www.africaneconomicoutlook.org/fileadmin/uploads/aeo/2014/PDF/CN_Long_FR/Côte_divoire_FR.pdf>, accessed March 2014.

63 The West African Economic Monetary Union is constituted by former French West African colonies. In terms of population, Côte d'Ivoire comes at the 3rd place after Nigeria (166,629,000 people) and Ghana (25,546,000 people). See "Stratégie de Coopération: Côte d'Ivoire (Côte d'Ivoire's Cooperation Strategy)," World Health Organization, *Who Country Focus*, <http://www.who.int/countryfocus/cooperation_strategy/ccsbrief_civ_09_fr.pdf>, accessed April 2013.

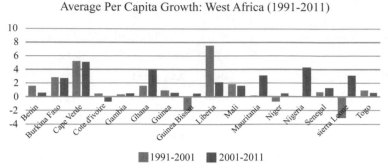

Figure 5: Average Per Capita Growth: West Africa from 1991 to 2011

Source: World Bank http://devdata.worldbank.org, accessed June 2013
Illustration: Viviane Bayala, June 2014.

fifth: 6.5 percent of the population has fifty-five years and over while the remaining, which constitutes the bulk of the population, is young. The median age is 20.3 (male) and 20.2 (female) for a fertility growth rate of 1.96.[64]

Following this brief presentation of Côte d'Ivoire potentials, the remaining of this third section described two important characteristics of China-Côte economic expansions: the rise of Chinese aid, and the changing trade ties.

1. Rising Chinese Aid

Côte d'Ivoire, does not figure among the top-ten Chinese investment destinations in Africa, being only the ninth largest recipient of Chinese aid in Africa and the fourth in West Africa.[65] Almost three years after the political agreement to cooperate, it started to receive a set of grants, and loans from the Chinese government and China Exim Bank. Côte d'Ivoire's Ministry

---

64 U.S. Central Intelligence Agency, "Côte d'Ivoire", *CIA World Fact book*, p. 3, <https://www.cia.gov/library/publications/the-world-factbook/geos/print/country/countrypdf_iv.pdf>, accessed July 2014.

65 "Chinese Finance", *China Aid Data*, 2000-2011,< http://china.aiddata.org/map>, accessed September 2014.

of Economy and Finance reports that between1986 and 2013 the country collected a total sum of US$977.4 million delivered under the form of forty-seven loans (called projects in the original document),[66] and distributed as it follows:US$97.4million (government grants), US$96.6 million (government loans), andUS$783.4 (China Exim Bank loans).[67]

The bar graph (next page) shows a significant increase in the total amount of China Exim Bank loans, shifting from less than US$100 million (1986-1999) to US$760.43million (2000-2013).[68] These inflows were spent on six major projects involving minerals, energy/water, new technologies, road construction, and real estate sectors: the Zéregbo Gold Exploitation (March 14, 2000),[69] the Government Electronic Network (July 2008),[70] the SICOGI Budget Accommodation (February 11, 2010), the Abidjan-Grand Bassam Highway (October 3, 2011),[71] and Soubre Hydro-Electronic Project (January 04, 2013).[72]

---

66 This sum wasconverted from the grand total of CFA 505 billion 510.5 million reported by the original file into US dollar at September 18 2014 conversion rate, <http://www.oanda. com/lang/fr/currency/converter/>, accessed September 2014.

67 These funds are respectively equivalent to about CFA 50.38billion, CFA 49. 934 billion and CFA 405.2 billion, following September 18 2004 dollar to CFA rate, at <http://www. oanda.com/lang/fr/currency/converter/> , accessed September 2014.

68 This initial amount was allocated to four projects including the Hua-KeVehicule, LicPharma, Ywto-CI, and Qinke Chocolate project.

69 Zérégbo is a village located in the western mountainous region of Côte d'Ivoire, and one of the 19th regions of the country. The capital of the region is Man and the total area covers 16km square for about 1.2 million inhabitants. See, "Base de données des noms géographiques (geographic names data base)," <http://civ.geonamebase.com/fr/node/219>, accessed October 2014.

70 "Huawei Going Strong in Africa," *Oafrica*, April 6, 2013, <http://www.oafrica.com/ mobile/huawei-going-strong-in-africa>, accessed October 2014.

71 This project employs 360 workers: 120 Chinese and the remaining are local. Confer "Zoom on Côte d'Ivoire Infrastructure Projects," *Abidjan News*, September 22, 2014,< http://abidjan911.com/projets-dinfrastructures-zoom-les-grands-chantiers-letat>, accessed October 2014.

72 "Amenagement du barrage de Soubre: L'accord de financement avec Eximbank Chine signé (Soubre Hydro-electric Dam: Financing agreement was reached with Exim Bank China," *Côte d'Ivoire Ministry of Energy Website*, 2010, < http://www.energie.

China Aid to la Cote d'Ivoire from 1986 to 2013

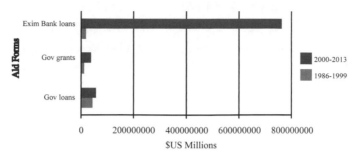

Figure 6: Sequences and Composition of Chinese Aid to la Côte d'Ivoire (1986-2013)

Source: Information from Côte d'Ivoire Ministry of Economy and Finances, accessed January 28 2013.
llustration: Viviane Bayala, October 2014

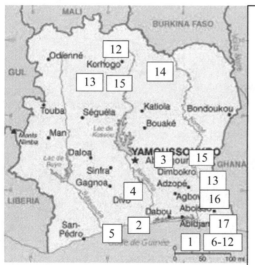

Figure 7: National Distribution of Chinese Aid Projects in Côte d'Ivoire

1986-1999 Projects
1. Culture Palace
2. Guiguidou Rice Farmland
2000-2011 Projects
3. National Assembly
4. Gagnoa Hospital
5. SoubreHydro-Electric Dam
6. Abidjan-Grand Bassam Highway
7. Abidjan Clean Water
8. E-Government
9. Budget Accommodation
Since 2012
10. Bernard Dadie CultureCenter
11. Government Administrative Blocs
12. Malaria research Center Equipment
13. Anyama High School Extension
14. Solar Energy Research
15. Agriculture Training Centers
16. Bassam Excellence High Schoool
17. Olympic Stadium

Source: map, http://www.les7duquebec.com/tag/Côte-divoire/page/2/, accessed October 2014. Projects: "le point de la cooperation Côted Ivoire-Chine, (The State of Côte d'Ivoire-China Relations)" Côte d'Ivoire Ministry of Foreign Affairs, accessed 12 December 2013. Illustration: Viviane Bayala, October 2014.

Albeit the fact that PRC loans delivered at a zero-interest rate reimbursable within 20 years, are much lower in scale than the China Exim Bank loans, they also underwent an increase between 2000 and 2013, rising to US$53.6 million compared to US$38.7 million received between 1986 and 1999. The main project realized with this category of loan was the National Assembly House in Yamoussokro.[73]

The remaining loans were, probably, spent on unspecific projects: "diverse projects" or "economic cooperation projects." Under Gbagbo's governance, some of these funds were spent on social infrastructures building such as Gagnoa Hospital, students and professional training scholarships. Similarly, under Ouattara's leadership (2011-2013), the undefined cooperation projects funds are, probably, allocated to the renovation of the Bernard Dadie Cultural Center, administrative buildings in Abidjan, Anyama's Modern High School, the Center for Research on Solar Energy, as well as the construction of two Agricultural Research Centers in Yamoussoukro (Central of Côte d'Ivoire) and Korogho (Northern Côte d'Ivoire).[74]

Chinese government grants, or "financial gifts" to diplomatic allies, have equally increased from US$8.3million before 2000 to US$35.3 million during the second period. This other type of Chinese aid is as vague as the previously described PRC loans. Under Gbagbo (2000-2010), these funds took the form of "military equipment" (September 10 2001), and then,

---

gouv.ci/index.php/fr/informations-generales/actualites/271-amenagement-du-barrage-hydroelectrique-de-soubre--laccord-de-financement-avec-eximbank-chine-signe.html>, accessed October 2014.

73 The dates of July 20, 2001, April 24, 2002 (loans signature dates), were confirmed by Franck A. Zagbayou's article; "Côte d'Ivoire: Maison des deputes de Yamoussokro: les premiers coups de piochesen fin janvier (Côte d'Ivoire National Assembly House: the beginning of the construction)," *All Africa*, December 6 2013, http://fr.allafrica.com/stories/200312070083.html, accessed October 2014.

74 "Point de la cooperation Côte d'Ivoire-Chine (Brief report of Côte-d'Ivoire – China cooperation)", *Côte d'Ivoire Ministry of Foreign Affairs*, 6, accessed December 2013 in Abidjan.

"undefined projects of economic cooperation." Following a similar pattern, the current government has received several grants with unclear project definition.[75]

Although there is no clear account concerning the use of these funds, one can assume that they were used to finance the numeral socio-cultural projects initiated during the recent decade by both governments. Gbagbo's regime emerged and developed within chaos. Chinese aid packages helped to fill the gaps left by embargos by France and the international community and save the president from falling short in the realization of his domestic governance. For his part, Allassane Ouattara is attempting to reach equilibrium between old and new friends while cooperating closely with the international community to advance his ambitious development plan, which aims to transform Côte d'Ivoire into an emerging county by the year 2020.

2. Changing Trade Trends

Besides financial aid, bilateral trade underwent noticeable changes as described below by Auregan. The graph shows an unprecedented increase in imports with a rise from less than 50 million euros in 2000 to about 400 million euros in 2008 before falling slightly to 350 million in 2009.[76] However, the export trend remains low, culminating in around 50 million euros between the years 2005 to 2006 and decreasing to around 25 million euros from 2007 to 2009.

Cote d'Ivoire's trade data between2010 and 2013 displayed general progress regarding both imports and exports. Exports lead the way with a rise from US$1.05 million in 2009 to US$13.74 million in 2013, after a smooth transition of US$11.56 million in 2010, US$12.54 million in 2011,

---

75 Côte d'Ivoire Ministry of Economy reported that China has also erased about US$ 34.3 million (May 11, 2007 - June 2011) as partial debt forgiveness.

76 Xavier Auregan, "La Chine en Côte d'Ivoire: le double-jeu (China in Côte d'Ivoire: the Double Game)," *Diploweb.com*, April 11, 2011, 5, <http://www.diploweb.com/La-Chine-en-Côte-d-Ivoire-le.html>, accessed August 2014.

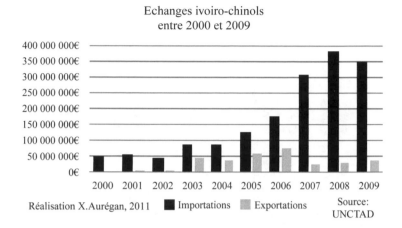

Figure 8: Cote d'Ivoire China Trade Pattern from 2000 to 2009

Source: Xavier Auregan, op-cit,http://www.diploweb.com/La-Chine-en-Cote-d-Ivoire-le.html, accessed July 2014.

and US$12.35 million in 2012. Similarly, although much lower, imports increased from US$6.96 million in 2009, to US$12.89 million in 2013 as described by the figure (next page).

Despite the civil crisis, Cote d'Ivoire remained the largest economy of the WAEMU. In 2013, the country imported 58 percent of manufactured goods, 15 percent of agricultural products, 26 percent of oil and mine products, and exported 49 percent of agricultural products, 28 percent of manufactured products and 23 percent of oil and mineral products.[77] This shows a predominance of agricultural goods in the country's exports to partner countries while manufacture remains the major import category.

Since 2009, China became the third consumption goods provider to Côte d'Ivoire; in 2013 it exported 7.3 percent of these goods, making it the third highest exporter to the country after France (12.4 percent) and Nigeria

---

77 Jean-Herman Guay Dir., "Cote d'Ivoire: commerce des marchandises (Cote d'Ivoire: Trade Goods," *World Perspective*, 2013, <http://perspective.usherbrooke.ca/bilan/servlet/ BMImportExportPays?codePays=CIV>, accessed December 2014.

Cote d'lovire Foreign Trade in USS million (2009-2013)

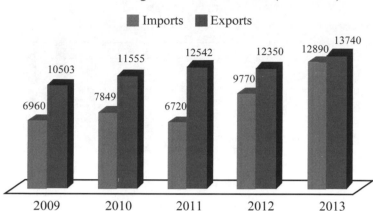

Figure 9: Cote d'Ivoire Trade Trends from 2009 to 2013

Source: Planet Expert, "Cote d'Ivoire: Context Politico-Economique (Côte d'Ivoire: Political and Economic Contexts)," Planet-expert.com, 2012, http://www.planet-expert.com/fr/pays/cote-d-ivoire/chiffres-du-commerce-exterieur, November 2014.

(25.7percent). This trend clearly supports the observation that "China has recently become the continent's largest bilateral trading partner."[78] However, although China has shown interest in Côte d'Ivoire's oil, agricultural products such as cocoa, coffee, cashew nuts and wood constitute most of the country's exports to China. At the same time, Côte d'Ivoire's imports of manufactured goods from China are on the rise.

This exchange of agricultural goods against manufactured commodities presents similar patterns to those of earlier western traditional trade partners such as France and the U.S. but in the current context, it indicates both countries' exploitation of comparative advantages to advance their respective economic development. This pattern is also similar to the general Sino-WestAfrican trade characteristics described below:

78 Johan Lagerkvist, and Jonsson Gabriel, "Foreign aid, trade and development: The strategic presence of china, japan and korea in sub-saharan africa," *Swedish Institute of International Affairs Occasional Papers* 5, 2011.

West Africa's share in China's trade is still quite low, 0.6 percent in 2012, but it is rising rapidly. Exports to China – oil, iron, phosphates, gold, cotton, cocoa and cashew nuts – have grown fast. However, they have not grown as rapidly as imports, resulting in a large trade deficit with China (13 percent of West Africa's GDP over 2009-2012).

Reasons include a strong consumption demand for inexpensive Chinese products as well as the import-content requirements in development assistance agreements. Chinese to their part have the financial power and the less expensive skills for fundamental economic infrastructures building of the moment.

Looking at the impact of China on West Africa, it appears that West African producers do not compete with China on third markets – by and large their products are complementary. However, West African producers are finding difficult to compete with China in their own domestic as well as in regional markets.[79] Most SSA and West African countries are both financially and technically weak and so unable to finance or build key economic infrastructures to launch their respective economies.

As an economic partner, the Chinese currently combine financial power with cheaper know-how for the creation of fundamental economic infrastructures. This combination is what countries such as Côte d'Ivoire, which just emerged from a political crisis and is in a phase of economic reconstruction, need the most.

In the shadow of political and economic relations progress, non-traditional security issues, and new socio-cultural connection are equally growing.

---

79 Miria Pigato and Julien Gourdon, "The Impact of Rising Chinese Trade and Development Assistance in West Africa," *Africa Trade Practice, Working series 4*, May 2014, p 4, <https://openknowledge.worldbank.org/bitstream/handle/10986/18961/883490NWP0Box 30a0Report0May2302014.pdf?sequence=1>, accessed December 2014.

IV. China in Côte d'Ivoire: The Surging Security and Social Ties

The recent spread of terrorism and piracy in the GoG is a threat not only to the U.S. interests but also to those of other European powers and more recently to the PRC. Consequently, as the U.S. and European countries are engaged in a cooperative maritime security mechanism through AFRICOM and Africa Partnership Station as a solution to the security of the GoG,[80] China is also on the process to multiply its security and social connections with most of the countries of this region, Côte d'Ivoire included.

First of all, Côte d'Ivoire owns the most important deep water port infrastructure in the Gulf of Guinea (GoG), and is located on Chinese Oil shipping road departing from Nigeria.[81] Marguerite Egbula and Qi Zheng explain that "for many years trade between China and Africa was dominated by South Africa, ensuring a prominent role for the Cape of Good Hope transit. Now the burgeoning China-West Africa trade is redrawing the map at sea, boosting the significance of Mediterranean shipping lanes."[82]

The map (next page) indicates that the shortest and securest route at the moment for Chinese-Nigerian oil is the sea road transiting through the global oil chokepoints of the Suez channel/SUMED pipelines, Bab el-Mandeb

---

80 The Gulf of Guinea is constituted by 16 countries that share about 6000 km continual coastline including Senegal, Sierra Leone, Liberia, Côte d'Ivoire, Ghana, Togo, Benin, Nigeria, Cameroon, Equatorial Guinea, Gabon, the Island of Sao Tome and Principe, Central African Republic, the Republic of the Congo, the Democratic Republic of Congo and Angola.

81 JeanDebrie, "The West African port system: global insertion and regional particularities," *EchoGéo* ,July 13, 2012 ,p. 11, <http://echogeo.revues.org/13070>. For distances, confer "Sea Routes and Distances," *Ports.Com*, 2010-2014, <http://ports.com/sea-route/port-of-lagos-apapa,nigeria/port-of-abidjan,ivory-coast>.

82 Margaret Egbula and Qi Zheng, "China and Nigeria: A Powerful South-South Partnership," *West Africa Challenges*, no.5 ,Nov., 2011, p. 7, <http://www.oecd.org/swac/publications/49814032.pdf>.

via Hormuz and the Malacca straits to China.[83] This new development has increased Côte d'Ivoire's importance.Besides, the GoG strategic interest with the U.S. and NATO has increased tremendously during the recent decade. Data shows that the proven oil deposits of the region are 50.4 million with a current production of 5.4 barrel per day.[84]

According to Rozoff, the U.S. is a traditional importer of Nigerian oil. Its imports have increased from 30 thousand barrels in 1995 to about 40 thousand between 2005 and 2006. Although the trend is decreasing since 2013, in 2012, Nigeria was still among the top five countries exporting oil to the U.S. The latter has a comparative advantage in offshore oil production in the GoG, with oil quality, ease of transition and safety of location vis-à-vis the U.S. all important factors.[85]

Côte d'Ivoire location in the GoG, its proximity to Nigeria, and advanced maritime infrastructures called for its involvement in the rising maritime security issues within the region. The following sub-sections elaborated the manifestations of this new development.

---

83 Energy Information Administration, "World Oil Transit Chokepoints", *eia.gov*, November 10, 2014, p. 1, <http://www.eia.gov/countries/analysisbriefs/World_Oil_Transit_Chokepoints/wotc.pdf>. According to the U.S. Energy Information Administration, World Oil Chokepoints are narrow channels along widely-used global sea routes and they are a critical part of global energy security because of the high volume of petroleum and other liquids transported through heir narrow straits.

84 Charles Okuje and WullsonMvomo Ela, "African Approaches to Maritime Security: The Gulf of Guinea," *Friedrich Ebert Stiftung: Peace and Security Series*, December 2013 , p. 9.

85 Rick Rozoff, "Militarization of Energy Policy: US Africa Command and the Gulf of Guinea," *Global Research*, January 08, 2011, <http://www.globalresearch.ca/militarization-of-energy-policy-u-s-africa-command-and-the-gulf-of-guinea/22699>.

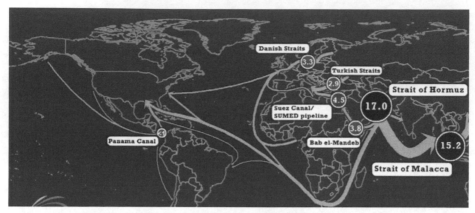

Figure 10: Map of Global Oil Routes Chokepoints Traffic.

Source: U.S. Energy Information Administration analysis based on Lloyd's List Intelligence,Panama
Canal Authority, Eastern Bloc Research, Suez Canal Authority, and UNCTAD, November 10,
2014, <http://www.eia.gov/countries/analysisbriefs/World_Oil_Transit_Chokepoints/wotc.pdf>

1. Surging Security Ties

China-Côte d'Ivoire security is expanding its scope. Traditionally, China-Côte d'Ivoire security related cooperation was symbolized by high military official visits. For example, Abidjan received the successive visits of General Liu Jingsong, Commander of Lanzhou Military Zone in July, 1995, and Lieutenant General Liang Guanglie, Commander of Shenyang Military Zone in November, 1998. While from Abidjan, two military officials visited Beijing, namely, Minister of National Defense Leon Konan Koffi in 1991 and Captain Yacouba Diomande, Commander of the Navy in July 1996.[86]

This trend went forward with two other Chinese tours to Abidjan: Major General Jiang Pumin on April 2001 and General Chi Haotian on September 2001, and one Ivorian visit: the Minister of National Defense Lida Kouassi on February 2002. Recently, following Chinese Foreign Minister Yang Jiechi's formulated will for the development of cooperation in security

---

86 Chinese Foreign Ministry "Cote d'Ivoire," *China.org*, October 10, 2006, <http://www.
china.org.cn/english/features/focac/183548.htm>.

matters between the two countries, the Ivoirians made a proposal for defense and security technical assistance to Beijing authorities in July 2012.

Moreover, in 2014 an unprecedented event shows that beside this traditional military ties, non-traditional relations are negotiating their niche. On May 2014, the fleet led by Admiral Li Pengcheng docked for three days in Abidjan harbor. This first visit, according to the fleet admiral, is a proof of the rising cooperation between the navies of the two countries and contributes to the reinforcement of existing links.[87]

2. The Surging Social Ties

Sino-Ivorian social cooperation has also witnessed some changes: the image of China is improving while educational and cultural cooperation is equally increasing. At the beginning of the year 2000 Chinese perception by Ivorian was restricted to stereotypes. In terms of business, Chinese were generally referred to as corner shops vendors or acupuncture practitioners.[88] These are jobs of low value to most Ivorian who value more privileged white collar jobs instead. There was also the negative perception of the Chinese as stingy dishonest traders of bad qualities products. Although this image still prevails, there has been a noticeable improvement in recent years.

Initial projects, such as the Guiguidou Rice Farmland or the Culture Palace, contributed to build Chinese image in Côte d'Ivoire. They are usually associated with rice production, and rice is a major food staple in Côte

---

87 See "La 16eme flotte de la marine chinoise fait escale à Abidjan (Chinese marine sixteen-escort fleet stopped in Abidjan)," *Xinhua*, May 21, 2014, <http://french.china.org.cn/foreign/txt/2014-05/21/content_32443856.htm>. The fleet of 660 marines comes from the Gold of Alden after a five months mission in Somalia's waters and the escort of Syrian chemical weapons in the Mediterranean. In five recent years, Chinese marines sent seventeen missions to the Gulf of Alden, and Somalia and the frigates have escorted more than 5000 Chinese and foreign Chips and participate to maintain peace and security in the world.

88 Selay Marius Kouassi, "le desamour entre Chinois etIvoiriens (The end of the Love Story between Chinese and Ivorian)," February 17, 2011, <http://www.rnw.nl/afrique/article/le-desamour-entre-chinois-et-ivoiriens>.

d'Ivoire. It is reported that during the 1970s "Taiwanese technical experts were on hand to assist initiate/sic/ viable small scale irrigation schemes and extension programs."[89] When the PRC took over, such intensive rice projects were maintained for the upmost contentment of the population.

Similarly, as a people who are impressed by cultural displays, the promise of the construction of a flamboyant palace to host cultural and country-wide musical events also helped cast the Chinese in a positive light. Moreover, the emergence of civic associations and an increase in two-way diplomatic visits during the recent decade is gradually redrawing the perception of China and Chinese in a more favorable way.[90]

Finally, the changing political reality within the country that came with a younger generation of leaders educated in western universities, mostly as economists, has also contributed to establish the basis for changing social perceptions of Chinese in Côte d'Ivoire. For example, as economists, Allasane Dramane Ouattara, Henry Konan Bedie, and Prime Minister Kablan Duncan, all understood the timely importance of an economic opening toward a rising China.[91]

---

89 Tunji Akande and al, "Streamlining Policies for Enhancing Rice Production in Africa: Past Experiences, Lesson Learnt and the Way Forward," *African Crop Science Journal* 15, no.4, December, 2007, p. 223, <http://www.bioline.org.br/request?cs07023>.

90 The "China Côte d'Ivoire Friendship Association Improves Friendly Cooperation between the two countries," *China World Peace Foundation*, May 28, 2012, <http://www.cwpf.org. cn/index.php/en/a/41/1144.html>. And, "Li Ruohong Leads a Delegation to Côte d'Ivoire Discussing Social Responsibilities," *China World Peace Foundation*, August 14, 2012, <http://www.cwpf.org.cn/index.php/en/a/41/1152.html.>.

91 AllassaneOuattara received a Baccalaureate in Elementary Mathematics from Drexel Institute of Technology, followed by a Master's and Ph.D in Economics at the University of Pennsylvania by 1972. See "AllassaneOuattara Biography," *Ado.ci*, 2007-2008, <http://www.ado.ci/rubrique.php?np=7&ns=21>. Henry Konan Bedie studied economics in France where he obtained a BA in law, MA in political economy and a PHD in economics from the university of Poitiers, August 22, 2012, <http://henri-konan-bedie.org/site/biographie.php>. Kablan Duncan studied trade engineering from High School in Bordeaux and Nancy (France), November 22, 2012, <http://www.primaturecotedivoire.net/site/suite-p.php?newsid=1521>.

In the sector of education, the story started with a 1992 bilateral agreement on cultural cooperation when President Ouattara was Prime Minister of Cote d'Ivoire, followed by protocols for higher education cooperation in 1994, 1998 and 2002 under President Bedie and Gbagbo. However, records from the Ivorian Ministry of Foreign Affair show that even before these formalities, China granted two scholarships to Ivorian student in1985.[92]

Since 1986, China granted more than 400 training scholarships to Ivorian civil servants, diplomats and the military.[93] The Chinese Ambassador to Côte d'Ivoire, Zhang Guoqing, confirmed that from 1985 to 2013, a total of 168 Ivorian students have received scholarships to study in China, and this number does not include those who are still in the process of obtaining their degree.

He explains that, on an annual basis, China provides sixty scholarships to Ivorian students. He also mentioned the existence of self-sustained students receiving grants from universities, private enterprises foreign aid, which brings the total number to about 200 students.[94] The Ivorian ministry of Foreign Affairs confirmed the reception of 160 scholarships attributed to civil servants, thirty training scholarships to students in the hospitality sector, twenty in military academies and twenty general university scholarships in 2012.

---

92 "Chinese leaders who visited la Côte d'Ivoire," *Chinese Foreign Ministry*, October 10, 2006, <http://www.china.org.cn/english/features/focac/183548.htm>.

93 Confer Ministry of Foreign Affairs, op-cit, December, 2013.

94 Chinese Embassy in Côte d'Ivoire, "Allocution de S.E.M Zhang Guoqing, Ambassadeur de la Chine en Côte d'Ivoire, lors de la cérémonie de remise des attestations d'admission des étudiantsIvoiriens (Chinese Ambassador to Cote d'Ivoire, Zhang Guoqing, message during a ceremony of attestation delivery to Ivorian student recipients of Chinese 2014 study scholarship," August 5, 2014, <http://ci.chineseembassy.org/fra/lggx/t1180827.htm>.

Meanwhile, the Chinese language importance is gradually increasing in Côte d'Ivoire. Since 2008 Chinese teachers were sent to the University Felix Houphouet Boigny on request. In May 2015, the country became one of the African countries with a Confucius Center.[95] China has already about twenty-eight Confucius Research Institutes and Centers in twenty-one African countries, and Côte d'Ivoire's request has just been fulfilled.[96]

Also, the increase of socio-economic exchanges prompted the Ivorian government to introduce a request for more cooperation on judiciary and consular matters between the two countries, following the latest FOCAC resolutions. Both parties are aware of the numerous difficulties related to the visa application process additional attention is needed to solve these issues.[97]

Last but not least, further negotiations are underway to extend cooperation related to customs and taxation management, to assure not only the quality of trading products but also widening the scope of opportunities for both sides with the expansion of tourism, transportation and banking cooperation.[98]

---

95 Centre de presse (Press Center) " Inauguration du premier institute Confucius de Côte d'Ivoire ", June 2015, <http://french.hanban.org/article/2015-06/11/content_603906.htm>, accessed July 2015.

96 Confer Ministry of Foreign Affairs, op-cit, December 2013. Another article mentions a total of 25 of these institutes. See MunyaradzyAkoni, "Africa: Chinese institutes Grow Chinese," *University World News*, September 5, 2010, <http://www.universityworldnews.com/article.php?story=20100905072629973>.

97 China has already such kind of agreement with five African countries following the Beijing Action Plan, "Fifth Ministerial Conference of the Forum on China Africa Cooperation," *FOCAC*, July 23, 2012, <http://www.focac.org/eng/zxxx/t954620.htm>. There have been complaints from Chinese citizens living far from Beijing who have experienced delays in visas delivered by the Ivorian authorities. Meanwhile, Ivorian businessmen have had numerous grievances relating to visa requirements from Beijing's consular authorities.

98 Cote d'Ivoire Ministry of Foreign Affairs, op-cit, pp. 7-9.

V. Conclusions: China-Côte d'Ivoire Intimacy Implications

Standing on the past and present development of China-Côte d'Ivoire relationship, the paper observed that taking advantage of the new context of growing economic globalization and interdependence, the two countries have, recently, grown closer than they have ever been, and this new development bears more blessing and less blaming.

1. More Blessing Less Blaming

In perceiving more hope with regard to China-Côte d'Ivoire relations, this paper espouses IR neoliberal's observations on Sino-African relations to state that, China and Côte d'Ivoire deserve more blessings and less blaming for the recent improvements in their relationship.[99] The neoliberal literature argued that China's growing presence in Africa is positively backed by a win-win cooperation framework or a win-win partnership as claimed by Chinese foreign policy discourse. This IR theory perceived States as major actors in international relations (which they share with neorealist) but hierarchy still prevails in international politics and Globalization increases interconnectedness and mutual interdependence between states and positively changes the way states cooperate.[100]

China-Côte d'Ivoire relationship evolvement demonstrated the persistence of both states centrality and the mutual support in preserving it when facing risk of sovereignty annihilation. For example, Côte d'Ivoire recognized China's sovereignty by first complying with the "one China" policy. The establishment of the political relations opened the door to more cooperation. Vis-versa, during the Ivorian crisis, the support of China was

---

99 The neorealist literature is much more pessimistic on China's growing presence within the continent. The country is described as a hungry dragon raping the African continent from its oil and raw material, while encouraging rogues countries to stand up against the traditional western powers, and eroding earlier achievements on democracy and human rights.

100 Keohane and Nye, 2001.

detrimental for Gbagbo's regime willingness to affirm its sovereignty in facing France. In this regard, On January 06, 2011, Hong Lei, representing the Chinese Minister of Foreign Affairs, launched a call for a peaceful resolution of the Ivorian crisis with the implication of all regional actors.[101]

Moreover, authors such as Brautigam,[102] Moyo,[103] or Ronan[104] saw an emerging pattern in Sino-African relations, where each actor is taking advantage of its comparative advantage to maximize its gains from the relationship. Sino-Côte d'Ivoire relationship improvement happened in a context of growing globalization and interdependence where countries tend to complement each other by using their comparative economic advantage. Thus, the trade items are raw material (especially agriculture and forestry) from Côte d'Ivoire, whereas China provides manufactured goods instead. Although realist's critics noticed the North-South nature of this pattern, it's remained that more than earlier times, Côte d'Ivoire had more opportunities to diversify its imports and exports markets. Finally, this relationship is on the right track to impulse both countries national and International Interests through win-win cooperation. China is undeniably the World first growing great power and second largest economy, while Côte d'Ivoire is an ambitious post-crisis African country is search of a lost prosperity. Both countries engorged of underexploited opportunities and drawing well-thought-

101 Xinhua, "La Chine appelle à résoudre la crise en Côte d'Ivoire par le dialogue (China called for a peaceful resolution of the crisis in Côte d'Ivoire)", *Peopledaily*, January 7, 2011, <http://french.peopledaily.com.cn/Chine/7253550.html>.

102 Her researches includes China's Role in Financing African Infrastructure (2007; China's African Aid: Transatlantic Challenges (2008) "China's Challenge to the International Aid Architecture (2009a)"; The Dragon's Gift: The Real Story of China in Africa (2009 b) China, Africa and the International Aid Architecture(2010a); La Chine à l'étranger: "Exporter des hordes d'experts" ou "Apprendre à pêcher"?, (2010 b), Aid with Chinese Characteristics.

103 DambisaMoyo, Interview with CNN, *CNN*, <http://edition.cnn.com/2013/02/28/business/ dambisa-moyo-afric, accessed October 2013>.

104 Morin-Allory Ronan, "Pekin au Congo," *in outré terre*, February 11, 2005, pp. 115-131, <http://www.cairn.info/revue-outre-terre-2005-2-page-115.htm>, accessed August 2014.

out strategies should bring much more earnings and more prosperous cooperation for both parts. And undoubtedly, such a step could help to reverse perceived risks.

2. Reversible Risks

At the image of China recent evolvement in Africa,[105] its growing presence in Côte d'Ivoire instigated the emergence of some risks: such as bureaucratic mismanagement, poor quality of executed projects, and social complaints on Chinese businessmen behavior. These risks are not irreversible.

Regarding bureaucratic mismanagement, the report from Côte d'Ivoire's Ministry of Foreign Affairs informed that more and more businessmen delegations, both Chinese and Ivorian are visiting without a previous notification to their respective authorities.[106] Besides a problem of coordination mentioned by the report, such disorder shows that the bureaucratic units involved are not efficiently accomplishing their respective duties. This required more commitment to monitoring, managing and evaluating the out-in flowing of both countries, but it is definitively reversible.

Another flaw of this relationship is the recurrent mention of the poor quality off projects executed by China within the country. For example, Yvelin Dévérin, denouncing the inopportunity of the building of a legislator's hotel in Yamoussokro, informed that the building is already witnessing some deteriorations regarding the air conditioning system. She explained that the Chinese did not consider the country climate while building the establishment.[107] Many other suffered these criticisms and a much more

---

105 Gill Bates and James Reilly, "The Tenuous Hold of China Inc. in Africa," in *Washington Quarterly*, 30:3 (Summer 2007), pp.37-52, <http://www.ou.edu/uschina/SASD/SASD2007readings/GillReilly2007WQChinaAfrica.pdf>, accessed January 2012.

106 Ministry of Foreign Affairs, op-cit, pp. 9-10.

107 Yvelin Dévérin, "projet inopportun et Inconséquent: 'Chinoiseries' à Yamoussokro (Inopportune and thoughless project in Yamoussokro)" *Le nouveau réveil*, October

diligent coordination and quality control need to be thought-out by the two countries. And this, also, is not a mountain but an ill that could be flattened by a conjoint bureaucratic unit.

Finally, seldom social complaints about Chinese businessmen were mentioned in Abidjan with reference to market dumping by Chinese cheapest products. This is a real problem but also an opportunity to bring local Ivorian traders to more competitive exposition and the maturation of new strategies. Before Chinese communities, French, Lebanese, Syrians, other African communities are sharing the market without any major problem until now. With the increasing number of Chinese, there is a need for an improved of communication, coordination and monitoring in order to create a better climate of open trade.

In conclusion, China-Côte d'Ivoire relationship falls into the bigger framework of China's Africa foreign policy. Belonging to the foundation as other African countries, the countries affairs are dealt with at the bureaucratic level as it comes. However, this does not mean that the country is not important in China policy. The current state of this relationship prefigures better trends in years to come. The rising risks, as elaborated above, are reversible and required more commitment from both countries political leadership: new managerial and social policies, and long term strategic approach.

5, 2007, <http://www.geophile.net/IMG/pdf/projet_inopportun_et_inconsequent_chinoiseries_a_yamoussoukro.pdf>, accessed June 2014.

Economic Integration in East Asia: Implications for Regional Security

Taeho Kim[*]

Three decades into the post-Cold War period and especially since the global financial crisis in 2008, East Asia has been witnessing a creeping yet extraordinary change in its power dynamics—especially among major countries. At least three major trends stand out: One is doubtless China's economic and military rise, whose essence is a double-edged sword to the East Asian states; another is U.S. rebalancing to Asia, which reflects the region's huge and growing stakes to its national interests amid its federal and trade deficits; and still another is the ongoing power transition between China and Japan—the two regional heavyweights.

On the economic front, at the same time, there has been a steady yet sure change that warrants a serious attention from both academic and policy communities. In particular, East Asia now occupies over 20 percent of the world's GDP, and its share is increasing.[1] The region also houses No. 2 (China) and No. 3 (Japan) economies in terms of size as well as other economic powerhouses such as South Korea (ROK), Taiwan (ROC), and ASEAN. Its economic strides would certainly make higher the stake of

---

* Professor, Director, Hallym Institute for Taiwan Studies (HITS), Director, Center for Contemporary China Studies, HallymUniversity of Graduate Studies.

1 For the past 40 years (1969-2009) East Asia's share of the world's GDP has almost doubled, whereas the EU's and U.S. share have declined to less than 30 percent each. See International Macroeconomic Data Set. U.S. Department of Agriculture, Economic Research Service, 2010; as cited in Avery Goldstein and Edward D. Mansfield, "Peace and Prosperity in East Asia: When Fighting Ends," *Global Asia*, Vol. 6, No. 2 (Summer 2011), p. 11, Figure 2. In the author's estimate East Asia's GDP share now amounts to 25 percent of the world's total.

regional stability and vibrancy, as aspired by many in the region and beyond. It is this context of an economically prosperous yet politically uncertain East Asia, against which a new spate of efforts for regional economic integration should be understood.

This brief essay first shed light on several major monetary and financial trends as well as trade and economic blocs to better understand the ongoing movements to economic integration in East Asia. The next section addresses what is called "capabilities competition" or "influence competition" between the U.S. and China as well as the "structural and mutual rivalry" between China and Japan,[2] as they involve complex and interconnected agendas that are yet to unfold. Finally, this essay offers a few policy considerations in a new and more complex phase for a prosperous and safe East Asia.

To telegraph the main arguments of this essay, the current "new normal" in world economy is caused mainly by a faulty monetary policy of the U.S. and other advanced countries, which only generates new bubble in debt, stocks, and currency. It is natural to see the emergence of new initiatives against the U.S. dollar and monetary hegemony. China-led AIIB (Asia Infrastructure Investment Bank) is a case in point. Other alternatives are likely to follow; yet their viability as well as their capability to handle the resistance from the established economic institutions remain a moot question. The impact of economic integration on regional security— interesting and important it might be—is conjectural at most. Not only is regional security based on the continuity, not change, of the established order but the U.S.-China competition is likely to continue. For small and middle-sized countries, at the same time, this means a complication of their economic and security calculus. In brief, an equation of higher degree is likely to unfold in the future of this vital region.

---

2   The term "capabilities competition" was coined by Admiral Mike McDevitt and "influence competition" by former U.S. Secretary of State Hillary R. Clinton. "Structural and mutual rivalry" between Japan and China is the author's.

The Faltering Financial Pillar

It is widelyacknowledged that since the collapse of the U.S. subprime mortgagemarketand the ensuing global financial crisis, the global economy has suffered from "low growth, low interests, and the expansion of governmental intervention"—the so-called "new normal" and has faced a multitude of serious challenges. The fact is that even if the U.S. and other advanced economies have issued an astronomical amount of money ("quantitative easing") and maintained zero-to-minus interest rates—which were unconventional monetary policy unheard of before, the overall situation turned from bad to worse.

In particular, it is galling to note that there have been almost no serious efforts to tackle with the nature of the financial crisis or to rectify the distortedprinciples of the market economy. It is those Keynesian disciples that keep pouring more money into the market in an ad hoc attempt to deal with the economic downturn as well as to create employment by investing in infrastructure by the government. This only leads to new bubble in debt, stocks, and currency,[3] which is often disguised as an economic boom—a flat illusion—and, together with a whopping increase in debts, boils down to a wrong monetary policy in the end.

U.S. dollars have served as key currency in the post-war global economy; for this reason, the U.S. has long enjoyed many privileges. A series of recent U.S. monetary policy in the global financial crisis, on the other hand, has adopted a number of unconventional policy measures, thus raising questions about its role as the "central bank of the world"—a matter of responsibility and trust. Its impacts on most individual states are devastating: its costs are borne by smaller economies; the latter remain on

---

3   For a fuller account of the global financial risks see Brendan Brown, *The Global Curse of the Federal Reserve: Manifesto for a Second Monetarist Revolution* (New York: Palgrave/ Macmillan, 2011); Steve Keen, *Debunking Economics: The Naked Emperor Dethroned* (Zed Books, 2011).

alert about changes in foreign currency markets; and they are susceptible to fluctuations in oil price.

Against this background of U.S. monetary hegemony—that is, unilateral and unfair, there has been a host of policy initiatives and alternatives. The BRICS (Brazil, Russian, India, China, and South Africa) is a case in point. For one thing, China's efforts to internationalize its renminbi(RMB) are gaining momentum and could emerge as a challenge against the U.S.-led dollar system. For another, Russia's declaration on "non-dollar" payment is an effort to shift from the "dollar monopoly."[4] For still another, the NDB (New Development Bank) as well as the AIIB will only accelerate the integration process. All in all, they represent a systemic alternative to the World Bank and the IMF as well as an effort to create a new financial order and a fairer trading system.

According to Korean economist Mihnsoo Kim,[5] three propositions undergird the current rising China's RMB: China—whose economy is now the second-largest in the world—no longer passively responds to the monetary policies of the U.S. and other advanced countries; China also has taken those countries' debt bubble seriously and has prepared for its side-effects and the dawning financial crisis; and China has also decided to build the confidence basis with other countries—e.g., the May 2014 CICA (Conference on Interaction and Confidence-Building) Shanghai—probably in an attempt to hedge against the looming global financial risks.

---

4   Vladimir Kolychev, "Russia's Shift Away from US Dollar Is Welcome," *Financial Times*, October 22, 2014.

5   Mihnsoo Kim, "The U.S.-originated Global Financial Crisis and China's Responses: From the Austrian School of Economics," *Study on Northeast Asian Economy*, Vol. 26, No. 1 (2014), Available at http//neak.or.kr (in Korean).

Trade and Economic Blocs

Regional economic integration in East Asia is not a new issue. For decades it has been discussed in a multitude of forums and at different parts of the region. The issue has been raised in comparison with post-war Europe, between Northeast Asia and Southeast Asia (especially ASEAN), and among Northeast Asian states (China, Japan, and South Korea). While previous efforts at economic integration or cooperation largely fall short of building consensus, recentinitiatives have taken on a new relevance in light of the global financial crisis.

As illustrated above, under the "new normal" condition no matter how much the developed economies keep issuing money ("seignorage") and maintaining quantitative easing, this will not lead to economic recovery. Rather, money is circulated in the financial sector only; the bubble economy is expanded; and debt bomb becomes larger than before. In other words, any policies for economic boost would not bring about improvedproductivity or increased income, thereby hampering the normal operation of a sound market economy. This explains a continued and deepening economic depression in developed and developing countries alike.

China-led AIIB, on the other hand, offers a new and specific message to the current doldrums. New investment on infrastructure—based on a new bank—as well as the "one belt, one road" (*yidai, yilu*) policy linking Asia, the Middle East, Eurasia, and Europe raises the possibility of creating a new economic bloc and improving real productivity. The new initiatives, it is hoped, constitute a solution to the "new normal," which the Bretton Woods-based World Bank or IMF cannot offer.

The AIIB will be launched in early 2016 with great fanfare—with its 57 charter members. Whether or not it functions as a challenge or a supplement to the extant institutions is hard to judge at the moment, as it contains both elements. In the first place, China decided to create the AIIB only after it had failed to raise its share in the U.S.- and Japan-led ADB (Asian Development Bank). Yet, the AIIB's proposed capital of U.S. $100 billion does not overshadow the ADB's 163-billion dollars or the World Bank's 223-billion dollars.[6] In particular, there is no way of telling that China's new investment in so wide an area as cross-Eurasia can generate revenues, let alone profits. In this strictlyeconomic sense, the AIIB is likely to prolong the continuing rivalry among the major powers.

This scheme of things, moreover, is buttressed by rising China's RMB. President Xi Jinping, for instance, announced at the recent Boao Forum that China would increase its import up to ten trillion dollars for the next five years, meaning that ten trillion dollars in RMB would be supplied to the global economy. In light of the 16-trillion dollars being circulated in the global financial system, what would be the basis for international payment in the future? As the growing number of countries—especially United Kingdom and Germany—tried to establish the RMB-based hubs, the RMB-based payment system is likely to grow in the future. As the "new normal" continues, the demand for a new breakthrough and real investment on infrastructure will only increase. A growth in new economic blocs, in brief, raised the real possibility for new economic integration—at least in East Asia.

What then would be impact of economic integration in East Asia—if it is ever successful—on regional security? This is arguably an important yet unanswerable question. There are many hurdles to overcome, such as resistance by the established institutions, transparency and governance issues of the new initiatives, and the future evolution of political and other atmospherics. While used in a different context, to wit, the well-known slogan—"Past, if not forgotten, will be a guide to the future"—applies here as well.

---

6   As cited in Kisoo Kim, "Is China-led AIIB a Challenge to the U.S. Global Economic Hegemony?" *Jungseh wa Jungchaek (Trends and Policy)*, May 2015, p. 9. (in Korean)

The other side of the equation is the causality. The economic factor, in brief, can be a cause, an outcome or an intervening variable at the same time. Thus, it is practically impossible to isolate the economic factor from others and to observe its directeffects on security—at the current state of social science theorizing. Besides, it has been popular in the media in Korea and elsewhere to argue "an Mei jing Zhong" (security with the U.S., economy with China). This simple bifurcation, however, grossly distorts the reality. In brief, there will be no linear equation in the intermix of economy and security. If there is any emerging, it will be an equation of higher degree. The discussions below thus should be seen as tentative and conjectural.

China's Rivalry Relations with the U.S. and Japan

It is trite yet true to note that the future of East Asian prosperity and security will be largely shaped by the economic and security trajectories of China and Japan as well as by U.S. relations with both countries. A continued healthy U.S.-Japan security relationship is vital to American interests and to Asian security, and for the moment the U.S. has a felt need to support a "normal Japan," but without jeopardizing its neutral stance on historical and territorial issues. In particular, a series of recent statements by top Japanese leaders that provoke its neighbors is causing annoyance in U.S. East Asia strategy and its alliance management. At the same time, it is very important to maintain the position that the alliance should not appear aiming at China.

The relationship between the U.S. and China is widely believed today as the most important bilateral ties in the world, whose impact reverberates throughout global and regional issues.[7] It should also be acknowledged that

---

7   For a brief discussion on Sino-U.S. relations as seen by the realist, liberalist, and constructivist perspectives see David Shambaugh, "Tangled Titans: Conceptualizing the U.S.-China Relationship," in David Shambaugh, ed., *Tangled Titans: The United States and China* (Lanham, MD: Rowman & Littlefield), pp. 3-26; For their long-term rivalry see Michael Pillsbury, *The Hundred-Year Marathon: China's Secret Strategy to Replace*

despite their global pretensions and their self-acclaimed role for peace and stability the world over, the U.S. and China are countries with different attitude, diverging perspectives, and conflicting world-views. These differences are often brought to bear in their handling of regional issues in East Asia.

In light of their vast differences in strategic visions, political systems, social values, and regional objectives, the U.S. and China will likely remain divergent over regional issues as well. Beneath the façade of their official camaraderie and formal ties, the U.S. and China more often than not find that their interests are significantly in conflict with each other when confronted with some concrete issues and longer-term agendas. Prominent examples include the missile defense (MD/THAAD) system, Proliferation Security Initiative (PSI), and maritime issues—to name but a few. A host of future developments on the Korean Peninsula, for another example, such as a North Korean contingency, future status of the USFK, and the strategic posture of a unified Korea is an issue of same nature but of greater unknown consequences. They will again affect not only the ROK's relations with the U.S. and China but also the bilateral relationship between the U.S. and China.

In post-Cold War East Asia, China's rise has been a "strategic reality" to the U.S. and regional countries in their economic and diplomatic activities. Moreover, China's ascendancy in the region could incur a change in the regional structure of power in which the U.S. maintains the leading and stabilizing role, a host of bilateral alliance and defense ties, and a set of economic and security objectives. It is in this context, as noted above, against which what Michael McDevitt called "capabilities competition" between the U.S. and China should be seen. Given the recent series of

---

America as the Global Superpower (New York: Henry Holt and Company, 2015). See also Jeffrey A. Bader, *Obama and Chinas Rise: An Insider's Account of America's Asia Strategy* (Washington, DC: The Brookings Institution, 2012).

China's more assertive foreign policy behavior—at a time when its more reassuring attitude is called for—such as its more confrontational behavior in the South China Sea, and its diplomatic row with Japan over a fishing boat collision, it stands to reason that its neighboring countries are concerned about how China might use its new power and influence.[8]

The present-day "strategic distrust" between the U.S. and China is a case in point. The Chinese leadership perceives that, as seen in the recent upgrading of the U.S.-Japan alliance, the thrust of U.S. strategy toward the Asia-Pacific region and China is to contain China, so it needs to hold off America's encroachment as much as possible, whereas the Obama administration relies heavily—and increasingly so at the time of its federal and defense austerity—on the linkage of alliance networks and friendly ties in the region.[9] The net effect is none other than "strategic access vs. strategic anti-access competition" at the regional level. Moreover, it needs only one side to make this vicious cycle tick. To wit, it does not always take two to tango. On this point the realists on both sides of the Pacific can only concur.[10]

On the other hand, China and Japan embody the world's second and third largest economies, respectively, and wield substantial political clout in regional affairs. Militarily, albeit different in nature and size, both countries are major factors to be reckoned with in any East Asian strategic equation. Thus, the current spate of antagonistic ties between Beijing and Tokyo—

8   On this issue of China's "responsible behavior," see for example Joseph S. Nye, "China Is Seriously Miscalculating," *Taipei Times*, March 16, 2010, p. 6; David Shambaugh, "Is China Ready to Be a Global Power?", *BrookINGS* November 10, 2009 ,<www.brookings.edu/opinion/2009/1110>.

9   For the impact of U.S. fiscal austerity on its rebalancing force readiness and defense institutions, see U.S. Office of the Secretary of Defense, *Quadrennial Defense Review 2014* (Washington, DC: DOD, 2014).

10 In the U.S. the writings of Henry Kissinger, John Measheimer, and Aaron Friedberg speak for themselves. In China hard-line views are aired by such scholars as Yan Xuetong at Qinghua, Shen Dingli at Fudan, and Shi Yinhong at Renmin.

as well as those between Tokyo and Seoul, allies of the U.S.—remains problematic. On these two sets of bilateral ties, the U.S. has so far been unable to resurrect normal ties, while continuing to emphasize that the most pressing agenda should be security, not history.

While the future of China-Japan relations will have a substantial impact on post-Cold War East Asia's economic and security order, their traditional rivalry and current and likely future power potentials will continue to be a source for concern in their neighbors' strategic planning. For both historical and contemporary reasons, each country has also pursued its foreign policy goals with an eye on the other.

In terms of future regional stability, what is perhaps more significant in the beginning of the new century is whether the two major regional powers will develop a relationship that is either strong and cooperative or weak and confrontational in the years ahead. Of equal importance is the diverse yet uncertain impact of this evolving relationship on the future of East Asian security, particularly in light of their changing domestic and international contexts.

As China's continued economic growth depends more on securing maritime resources and interests, it stands to reason that the PLA Navy will acquire a wider range of mission capabilities. This type of naval modernization is bound to enhance the level of apprehension by other regional powers and even create an action-reaction cycle at sea. While the current discussion on this subject tends to focus on the U.S.-China rivalry, an important yet under-researched aspect is the creeping regional power transition between China and Japan. Included in this evolving relationship is a combination of "resistant nationalism," a sense of crisis, political immobility—especially by the post-war generation of political leaders—that is sweeping over Japanese society.[11]

---

11 "Resistant nationalism" is this author's understanding of Waseda University Professor Lee Jong Won's discussion on Japanese tendency on nationalism and statism. See an interview

As perhaps best illustrated by the abrupt yet enduring controversy between Beijing and Tokyo over the Senkaku/Diaoyu/Diaoyutai Islands since the late summer of 2012,[12] neither side wants to appear meek on such sensitive and nationalistic issues, due in part to domestic imperatives. New leadership line-ups—President Xi Jinping and Prime Minister Shinzo Abe—have their own agenda to sustain the tense atmospherics in their bilateral ties. China's announcement of its Air Defense Identification Zone (ADIZ) in November 2013 is only the latest manifestation of this deeper and difficult relationship between the two major regional powers.

It is thus argued that despite their huge and growing stakes in maintaining an amicable relationship, China-Japan relations will remain a difficult and often tense process. The persistence of their traditional rivalry and historical distrust over time suggests that they may have more to do with deeply ingrained cultural, historical, and perceptual factors than with the dictates of economic cooperation or shared interest in regional stability that are mutually beneficial. Also underlying their complex but competitive ties is the rise of new-generation leaders in both countries who are tasked with coping with a complex set of challenges from below as well as from outside. How well and in what manner they handle the challenges could significantly affect not only the wealth and health of their respective nation but also the future of the regional order. The future stability in East Asia will hang in the balance as China and Japan continue to seek a new balance between their interdependence and rivalry.

---

with Professor Lee, *Dong-A Ilbo*, September 24, 2012.

12 For a detailed analysis of the island dispute, see Michael D. Swaine, "Chinese Views Regarding the Senkaku/Diaoyu Islands Dispute," *China Leadership Monitor*, No. 41 (June 6, 2013); Paul J. Smith, "The Senkaku/Diaoyu Island Controversy: A Crisis Postponed," *Naval War College Review*, Vol. 66, No. 2 (Spring 2013), pp. 27-44; Noboru Yamaguchi, "A Japanese Perspective on the Senkaku/Diaoyu Islands Crisis," in The East Asia Program, ed., *Tensions in the East China Sea* (Sydney: The Lowy Institute for International Policy, December 2013), pp. 7-17; and Barthelemy Courmont, "Territorial Disputes and Taiwan's Regional Diplomacy: The Case of the Senkaku/Diaoyu/Diaoyutai Islands," *Journal of Territorial and Maritime Studies* (Seoul), Vol. 1, No. 1 (Winter/Spring 2014), pp. 113-134.

Some Implications for Economic and Military Security in East Asia

For decades multilateral cooperation has advanced more in Southeast Asia (SEA) than in Northeast Asia (NEA). A few examples illustrate this point: a) the level of tensions is much higher in NEA than in SEA; b) the nature of conflict in NEA is mostly bilateral and/or land-based, whereas that of SEA is multilateral and maritime; c) the U.S. bilateral alliance networks are thicker in NEA than in SEA; and d) all states seek for "absolute gains" in economic issues; this is not the case for security affairs, in which "relative gains" are pervasive.

Having said that, it is commendable to note that such region-based mechanisms as ASEAN Plus Three, EAS, ASEM, Boao Forum, and CMI have spread throughout the region. At least until the end of 2012 the three NEA countries—China, the ROK, and Japan—agreed to hold a three-way summit meeting regularly on top of their close consultations at the Six-Party Talks. Various forms of FTA including KORUS FTA, CAFTA, and the proposed China-ROK-Japan FTA would consolidate the economic and strategic relationships among the regional powers. In a sense, they are still incomplete (i.e., not fully institutionalized) and at an early stage, but these burgeoning regional mechanisms help understand others' positions and promote the habits of political dialogue.

In particular, the ongoing global economic downturn in tandem with the inexorable globalization trend call for a coordinated effort in the region to develop a common agenda and a concerted step to resolving the economic crisis. A scheme of things has been that the G20, not the extant international institutions, will be a key for global economic governance. Recent regional and sub-regional arrangements in Latin America, Russia and CIS, and East Asia are a case in point, even if the abrupt discontinuation of the ASEAN Plus Three in Thailand and the London G20 Summit a few years ago attests the fragility of the political situation there as well as the anti-globalization forces found elsewhere.

The U.S. may be seen as both a target for and a solution of the global economic crisis, against which the incapacity of several major European economies and of the international institutions should be understood. America's leading role and its strategic presence in East Asia will be inexorably intertwined with its demonstrated capability to resolve the current economic crisis. For its part, China—a key member of the regional community with growing global economic clout—have taken the initiative in regional economic rearrangements so as to help facilitate the global economic recovery. China's responsible behavior in the midst of Asia's financial crisis in the late 1990s is a shining example.In practical terms, they mean a renewed emphasis on institutions, multilateralism, and political dialogue so as not to overburden the economy already in crisis. Whether such efforts would lead to a paradigmatic shift in America's foreign and security policy toward East Asia is not certain, but it remains a possibility.[13]

China and other regional economies have a huge and growing stake in maintaining free trade and market system—for economic and security reasons.[14] They, as a collective entity, should be ableto find the ways to live with and learn from the economic difficulties and to work for greater interdependence and regional integration to ensure stable and sustained growth. As suggested by some economists, East Asian countries' current efforts to rearrange their own economic governance may not be adequate, as the problems run deep and cover the global community.

The growth of new economic blocs in East Asia via real investment on infrastructure could pave the way for economic integration. On the condition that the global economic crisis will not raise its hideous heads and if the

---

13 For a recent call for a change of U.S. policy from assisting China's ascendance to balancing it, see Robert D. Blackwill and Ashley J. Tellis, *Revising U.S. Grand Strategy Toward China* (New York: Council on Foreign Relations, March 2015).

14 The ASEAN, for instance, is to set up at the end of 2015 the ASEAN Economic Community (AEC) among its ten member-states, which is widely dubbed as the "Asian version of EU."

so-called separation of economics from politics—or vice versa—can be sustained, these efforts can contribute to regional stability and prosperity. Thus one may say that the region's future as "cautiously optimistic."

On the other hand, the RCEP (Regional Comprehensive Economic Partnership) whose membership is based on ten ASEAN member-states and six other regional countries is mostly views as a challenge to the TPP (Trans-Pacific Partnership), Washington's preferred trade pact. In the former pact Washington is not included.[15] But the TPP—a giant multilateral arrangement—carries more strategic than economic values, as many have noted.[16] In particular, not only does the TPP showcase the essential element of its rebalancing to the region but it also proves U.S. commitment to engage and maintain the leading role in East Asia.

All in all, given the possibility of prolonged U.S.-China competition, their actual and likely diverging interests on a host of regional issues and China's ascendancy in regional affairs, regional states need to continuously prioritize its strategic relationship with the U.S. over that with China, even if it should also build cooperation and confidence with China. As a corollary, they should be able to reap the benefits of its alliance and friendly ties with the U.S. in addressing the growing importance of the "China factor" to themselves. In the long and often tortuous path to regional stability and prosperity, China will be no substitute for the United States for the foreseeable future. In other words, the quintessence of regional states' strategy is to maintain exchanges and cooperation with China in select yet wider areas, while anticipating and preparing for a reversal of its present course toward East Asia. A hedging strategy will remain the most reasonable approach for the foreseeable future.

---

15 See Evan A. Feigenbaum, "The New Asian Order and How the United States Fits in," *Foreign Affairs, February* 2, 2015,<http://carnegieendowment.org/2015/02/02/new-asian-order/i137>.

16 See, for example, Brad Glosserman, "America's TPP Dilemma," *PacNet*, Number 20 (April 2, 2015).

Regional Economic Integration in Asia: Assessing the Danger of Bubbles and Contagion

David Kleykamp[*]

Abstract

This paper considers the empirical identification and measurement of stock market bubbles for both regional groupings such as the Eurozone, U.S., and East Asia, as well as for five countries in East Asia—Japan, Korea, Hong Kong, Taiwan, and China. In addition, a theory is proposed to explain why that asset bubbles exist despite the low growth—low inflation environment most countries are now experiencing. This theory relies on the existence of a strong wealth effect in money demand and a weak wealth effect in consumption. Such asymmetric wealth effects create a risk of a vicious cycle of money creation and falling income velocity of money, which in turn gives rise to asset bubbles in the midst of weak economic activity. Regional integration is considered in light of possible financial contagion as stock bubbles burst in the major economies. It is suggested that, at the very least, regional integration of financial markets may need to wait for a more hospitable time when the risk of renewed financial crisis is lower.

I. Introduction

Lenin is believed to have said that the best way to destroy capitalism is to ruin the currency through inflation.[1] Most people would interpret this type of hyperinflation as an uncontrolled rise in the general level of prices for

---

*   Associate Professor, Institute of the Americas, Tamkang University.
1   See John Maynard Keynes (1920, pp. 235-248).

current goods and services. Lenin's observation is not generally associated with a dramatic and unsustainable rise in the value of financial assets. But, looked at from another vantage point, a quickly rising nominal value of financial assets represents a corresponding quickly rising perceived stock or pool of future spending and therefore at the very least points to a potential for higher future inflation. Nominal financial wealth is what makes people feel wealthy; this despite the fact that it represents mere paper claims on a tenuous and otherwise quixotic future production. This perceived stock of accumulated future spending will either be realized through a surge in the production of real goods and services (i.e. a strong wealth effect directed at the demand for goods with a highly elastic supply); or it will be manifested in significant future inflation as individuals try to spend their nominal wealth on an inadequate and relatively inelastic supply of goods and services, even as government prints more money; or instead it will end in a catastrophic bursting of the financial bubble that may or may not have consequences for the real economy.[2] In truth, the economy will experience some combination of these three possibilities whenever there is a significant departure of nominal financial markets from the underlying real economy.

There exist other parallels between the cases of goods inflation and asset inflation. Just as households find it difficult to purchase goods during an inflation characterized by the nominal incomes of some groups failing to increase parri passu with inflation, so it is that some savers will find it difficult to purchase new assets at such inflated asset prices and will accordingly suffer extremely low rates of return on whatever conventional lending (i.e. bond purchases) they do undertake. Beyond this similarity,

---

2   There remains the possibility that the distribution of income in the future is generally believed to be skewed in favor of asset holders. In this case, a relatively fixed amount of future nominal output could still be sufficient if divided up with increasing proportions given to the holders of capital. This would manifest itself in a prolonged divergence in market capitalization and nominal GDP, at least until the distributional proportions were once again stable. We exclude this case, while recognizing that such a major social process may in fact be occurring for some countries.

bubbles in financial markets, as with goods inflation, are quite often the direct result of deliberate government and central banking policies aimed at utilizing financial markets as levers to force open spending in the economy. The current fashion in central bank thinking is that if inflation occurs, so be it; such inflation merely represents the justifiable cost of rescuing an economy where households, banks, and firms are aggressively saving income and hoarding money. Higher goods inflation becomes a virtue to central bankers who must inconveniently work with an income velocity of money that is relentlessly collapsing.

But, what if the collapse of velocity (i.e. increase in money demand) is due to surging financial transactions and higher nominal wealth arising because of rampant speculation in financial markets? What if the rise in the propensity to save by households and business is not due to an increased precautionary saving motive, but owes itself instead to enormous and highly disconnected nominal capital gains in financial markets, brought on by excessively loose, but determined, monetary policy, accompanied by oddly low rates of inflation in goods and services. The conventional central bank solution to this will be to maintain rock bottom short term interest rates, provide ever more liquidity to banks, purchase long term bonds to stimulate investment, and seek higher inflation to stop the hoarding of money and the collapse of _measured_ velocity.[3] Unfortunately, if people are entangled in an asset bubble, none of these policies will prevent _measured_ velocity from

---

3   Here is one example of contemporary news accounts trying to explain the ongoing postponements of an interest rate hike by the Fed. Note the emphasis on the apparent lack of inflation as an important reason to continue loose monetary policy.

"Currently, the consensus expectation is that the Fed will raise rates in September at the earliest, which is slightly later than the original prediction of a June rate hike. March's subpar empl1.939oyment data, for one, was one main reason why many economists began predicting a September rate hike. But a lack of substantial inflation pressure may be the leading variable preventing the Fed and other central banks from acting quickly on eventual rate hikes." (our emphasis)

See: <http://www.modernreaders.com/fed-other-central-banks-still-unlikely-to-raise-interest-rates-yet/25618/lorenzo-tanos>.

falling. None of these policies will prevent the hoarding of money. None of the policies will prevent people from saving more to buy financial products with sharply rising values. And what is more, inflation in goods and services will not likely be substantially increased, since such huge sums of money raise the nominal value of asset pools so high that people at last become satisfied with holding more money, whatever the change. In other words, the enormous increase in the supply of money is powering a wealth effect that is causing people to hold more money rather than more goods. The wealth effect, so surprisingly weak in the goods market, is nevertheless surprisingly strong in the money market.[4] In such a case, greater sums of money injected into the economy will only raise financial wealth and will fail to generate a greater desire to produce and purchase real goods and services. The cure has indeed become the sickness with people arguing that things will surely turn around soon, provided we only offer a little more monetary stimulus.[5]

4   Some people would call this a liquidity trap, but the original view of a liquidity trap espoused by Keynes was that people would hold money because they expected that the rate of return on alternative assets was going to rise in the imminent future (i.e. there was a pure speculative motive to holding more money). We are claiming that people hold the additional money because their constantly inflated wealth requires a natural diversification and hence money demand will expand along with the money supply due to a strong wealth effect in the demand for money. There is a significant difference in substitution and wealth effects for the demand for money and in the interpretation of the liquidity trap, in this case. See also the following footnote.

5   D. Patinkin (1984, p. 173) has perhaps made the distinction we are emphasizing here better than anyone before him. He speaks to the subtle and confusing dual natures of the single demand for money, one nature constrained by wealth and the other nature influenced by income. He writes
"...that tangible wealth is the variable that constitutes the budget restraint on the holding of assets, including money — so that an increase in wealth generally results in increased holding of all assets; whereas income is one of the relevant variables explaining the (transactions) demand for money in a portfolio of a given size, so that an increase in income increases the demand for money, at the expense of other assets."
Even here we would disagree with Patinkin since the total transactions demand for money must also be affected by transactions in asset markets, in addition to the goods market. But, the gist of the distinction is clear. Rising wealth drives up the demand for money and this is a separate effect from movements in income. Increased wealth due to speculation could drive up the demand for money, lower the income velocity of money, and produce a moderating effect on prices and growth. This is exactly what we see in the U.S. and other

Unfortunately, the narrative comes within shouting distance of the facts for many of the major economies of the world and presents us with a conundrum. How do we in all good faith promote regional integration and a closer linking together of the goods and asset markets of economies that are quite likely to suffer substantial revaluations in such asset markets in the next few years. Is it enough to look past these near term turbulent times to a longer run where growth returns and opportunities again present themselves? Or, alternatively will the impending short run costs of bringing together these economies and markets outweigh the long run benefits of scale economies and technology sharing? Though there are not likely to be clear and straightforward answers to these questions, it must surely be true that such answers will depend on the following considerations. First, are the major economies indeed enmeshed in a perilous state of financial bubbles and are we at risk of such financial bubbles collapsing? Second, would such a collapse in financial markets produce a significant downturn in real economic activity and if so, how large would that be? Third, does regional integration represent a mechanism for spreading the economic downturn via contagion? And finally, what steps might be taken to proactively safeguard households and businesses from the potential fallout of a major correction in world financial markets. We will address each of these concerns in turn in the following sections of the paper.

II. The Identification and Ultimate Resolution of Bubbles

There are numerous definitions for bubbles and quite technical explanations for how they arise and how they propagate. A great deal of attention has recently been drawn towards the subject of bubbles[6] Gurkaynak

---

countries today with rising stock markets, slow growth, and very weak inflation.

6   Using Google Trends it is possible to count the hits to "stock bubbles" online over the past 10 years. This shows a significant rise in the last 3 years of Google searches for the phrase. This is indirect evidence that more and more people are beginning to realize the markets are deviating from fundamentals and bubbles are occurring.

(2008) has expressed doubts about our ability to detect bubbles. This view is reinforced by other studies that also find it difficult to discern bubbles from fundamentals that are quick to change, see Ahmed (2006), Balke and Wohar (2009), Dezhbakhsh and Demirguc-Kunt (1990). Many of these studies are still focused on the time series properties of stock prices and dividends and seek to demonstrate bubbles in past episodes of U.S. financial history, Phillips and Yu (2011), Hays et.al (2010), Herwatz and Kholidilin (2004),Rapparport and White (1993), Liu et. al (1995), Scheinkman et. al (2014), Homm and Breitung (2012). A common theme is to check for cointegration of the two series. If they fail to be cointegrated, bubbles are suspected, see Diba and Grossman (1988), The Federal Reserve has been targeted as creating bubbles in asset markets and the role of monetary policy has been studied closely Lansing (2015), Gali and Gambetti (2015), Also, much of the discussion has centered on how bubbles get started and why they do not simply burst immediately; since if people are rational, then they should see the risk of holding such an overvalued asset.[7] Scherbina (2013) has recently produced an informative survey of academic studies on asset price bubbles. The usual way of identifying bubbles is done through a comparison of actual market prices with present value outcomes. Bubbles

---

7 In an interview with J. Cassidy (2010), Eugene Fama cast doubt on whether or not the term "bubble" even has any meaning. He says that most people talking about bubbles do not have a clear definition of the phenomenon and moreover, from an empirical point of view, he claims that if bubbles do exist, why doesn't this give rise to consistent predictions of negative returns on stocks? He contends that if bubbles eventually burst, then we should be seeing negative returns in the typical predictions of the market. Our contention is that traders not only use standard structural relationships involving fundamentals in making decisions on the appropriateness of prices, but also simultaneously assess whether the structural relationship, between fundamentals and prices they are currently using, has changed. Bubbles involve the belief that the world has changed substantially. Thus, traders use a statistical model and, at the same time, they doubt the relevance of that very same statistical model. Bubbles burst when the belief in the fundamentalist model returns (i.e. fundamentals matter) and the doubts about the relevance of the fundamentalist model are sufficiently dispelled (i.e. the structural relations really haven't changed). Bubbles occur when there is departure from underlying economic fundamentals and this departure occurs because of sincere and significant doubts about the existence of basics change in the structure of the world.

seen in this fashion are merely deviations in what present value fundamentals imply is the "true" value of the asset. Positive bubbles are more common because of the asymmetric cost of shorting an overvalued asset versus going long an undervalued asset. Positive bubbles persist over time due to a prevalence of traders basing their trading strategies on past price movements, already overvalued for some exogenous reason, most likely perceived structural change. Scherbina points out that the traditional view of positive bubbles is tied to the present value model as follows

$$P_t > E\left[\sum_{k=t+1}^{\infty} \frac{CF_k}{(1+r)^{k-t}}\right] \tag{1}$$

where P_t = current nominal price of the asset, CF_k = cash flows at time $k = t + 1, t + 2, ...,$ and r = an appropriate discount rate. Treating the right hand side of (1) as a single unit called F_t, or fundamentals, the bubble, B_t, can then be written in implicit form as

$$P_t = F_t + B_t \tag{2}$$

This is a particularly succinct and informative way of decomposing the asset price into its natural components. The bubble B_t is highly autocorrelated and remains the subject of much research and conjecture. However, in a rational model, F_t is thought to be quite close to the actual fundamentals being projected out over the future by households. Households are thought to be clear on the potential future outcomes of profits and interest rates. This of course is a difficult assumption to accept and indeed it has been rejected by many followers of behavioral finance after scores of empirical studies apparently failed to confirm it, even indirectly. Rational theorists are nonetheless loath to reject the premise of rationality since learning mechanisms and competition make rationality a powerful and useful tool for analyzing markets. Rationality is something that must prevail in the end since households that are not rational will not succeed financially and will eventually disappear from the market.

Our approach assumes that bubbles are (often significant) deviations from fundamentals, but that such bubbles may nevertheless grow and continue to exist over considerable periods of time. The deviation is due to the preponderance of doubt over whether or not essential economic structural changes have occurred. These bubbles are not entirely independent of policy and other exogenous variables. What is important is that, whenever a bubble forms, a plausible reason must arise that convinces investors to suspend their usual arbitrage activities. Naturally, unless trading in the market is thin, there are millions of investors currently holding the asset who are available to lend strong support to whatever reason is put forward for denying a bubble exists. Since determining whether or not a bubble exists involves comparison of objective current fundamentals to past fundamentals, the obvious reason is that past fundamentals no longer apply and that "this time is different". Note that this cannot be confirmed or denied since structural change is a constant and enduring feature of economies and is difficult to determine immediately by studying the past history of the economy. It is evolutionary and even revolutionary in nature. Structural change is the natural result of competition and invention, and hence, investor appeals to this force can be quite persuasive. Another powerful force affecting investor psychology derives from the substantial perceived capital gains, "received" so-to-speak as the asset's price rises over considerable time, lulling holders of the asset into a false belief that they can always sell their asset before unacceptably large depreciations occurs. Probably not more than one in a hundred people know intuitively that a 100% gain in an asset's value can be completely erased with a 50% fall. Even less realize that declines in asset prices after the bursting of bubbles are often much more rapid than the slow buildup of the bubble. Indeed, the fact that the decline is more rapid down than up indicates that investors become alarmed at the fall and rush to sell rather than calmly follow their original plans to unload their holdings. This asymmetry is prima facie evidence that rational investment plans are not being followed. One can hardly maintain that rational plans are being met when everyone is piling up at the doors and rushing to the exits. How does one reconcile such fear and regret with rationality?

If fundamentals are a long run (weak) attractor for prices, even under conditions of a bubble, then cointegration methods would seem to be the natural analysis to study this. Unfortunately, the very existence of bubbles that drive prices to slowly rise above and quickly fall below the attractor are precisely the things that stand in the way of a clean cointegrating regression. The residuals from the standard cointegrating regression will often be slowly changing and will be judged nonstationary by standard tests and critical values on that account. That is, it is not that the fundamentals attractor does not work, but rather that than the oscillations above and below the fundamentals attractor change too slowly to be statistically classified as strictly stationary. The statistical method of cointegration proves too sensitive by excluding slow moving adjustment in asset values to deviations from fundamentals, whenever there are bubbles.

Our basic methodological assumption is that we should not allow our statistical methodology to straightjacket our theoretical modeling. Rather, our theory should retain its preeminent position and our statistical method should follow along in a supportive role only. We will therefore approach the empirical question by estimating a cointegrating regression without requiring a fast response to deviations from the least squares attractor.[8] Even though the residuals from the cointegrating regression often "appear" non-stationary, this is only due to the fact that bubbles occasionally appear. That is, if we could eliminate such bubbles from a sufficiently long price series, the deviations about the fundamentals variable(s) would once again appear stationary. But, this is precisely the problem we are seeking to solve — how to extract bubbles from the price series.

We have taken the position that bubbles are significant departures from fundamental values. Identification of bubbles is thus dependent on how we

8   The time series Pt is a combination of the fundamentals and the bubble. But, Phillips, Shi and Yu (2012) have stated that bubbles occur whenever there are explosive roots in the time series (say Pt). It follows that no typical cointegration analysis can be undertaken if there are bubbles, since Ft has no explosive root and yet Pt does have one.

define these fundamentals. To better understand this idea, we bring together the ideas of both John Maynard Keynes and Milton Friedman. Keynes has written

"Consumption — to repeat the obvious — is the sole end and object of all economic activity." (Keynes, Chapter 8, The General Theory)

This implies that transactions in asset markets (including those markets experiencing a bubble) are likewise ultimately directed to consumption now and in the future. However, there is clearly no guarantee that the purchasing power of asset values and their related consumption demands (especially during periods of bubbles) are consonant with the output and prices in the goods market now and in the future. Indeed, it is the rise of such assets that supposedly powers the demand to produce the necessary output, and, if such output is yet inadequate, then output prices will rise or asset values will fall. Under stable conditions of the distribution of income, there seems to be little other possibilities left for markets to adjust.

The short observation above by Keynes, which he claims is obvious, is nevertheless helpful in clarifying a much more controversial statement made by Milton Friedman in 1968 and which is particularly relevant to the conduct of monetary policy in recent years by central banks in the U.S., Japan, and now the EU. Friedman remarks came as part of his 1968 Presidential Address to the American Economics Association. The title of his address was "The Role of Monetary Policy". In this important and highly influential paper, Friedman stated that monetary policy could not peg interest rates at an artificially low level without causing a runaway inflationary process. Friedman states

"From the infinite world of negation, I have selected two limitations of monetary policy to discuss: (1) It cannot peg interest rates for more than very limited periods; (2) It cannot peg the rate of unemployment for more than very limited periods...

...The initial impact of increasing the quantity of money at a faster rate than it has been increasing is to make interest rates lower for a time than they would otherwise have been. But this is only the beginning of the process not the end. The more rapid rate of monetary growth will stimulate spending, both through the impact on investment of lower market interest rates and through the impact on other spending and thereby relative prices of higher cash balances than are desired. But one man's spending is another man's income. Rising income will raise the liquidity preference schedule and the demand for loans; it may also raise prices, which would reduce the real quantity of money. These three effects will reverse the initial downward pressure on interest rates fairly promptly, say, in something less than a year...

A fourth effect, when and if it becomes operative, will go even farther, and definitely mean that a higher rate of monetary expansion will correspond to a higher, not lower, level of interest rates than would otherwise have prevailed." (Friedman, 1968, pp. 5-6.)

This process became part of the so-called accelerationist narrative. Friedman claimed that pegging interest rates low (below a natural level) would generate accelerating inflation since faster growing money will not be able to hold down *nominal* interest rates except by continually increasing the growth rate of money. It is interesting that the recent conduct of monetary policy (e.g. forward guidance, quantitative easing, operation twist, etc.) have kept interest rates pegged at near zero levels for more than six years in the U.S. and have kept them at extraordinarily low levels in Japan for up to 15 years. As a result, it is difficult if not impossible to find any economist today quoting Friedman's cautions, despite the fact that his paper is one of the most famous and celebrated papers in all of macroeconomics.

It is tantalizing to guess how that Friedman would explain the odd lack of inflation with short term interest rates pegged at such low levels, but one possibility is that he would surely point to the collapse of the income velocity of money, which has helped to stabilize the price level while at the same time holding back growth in output. This collapse of velocity is in large part due to the enormous rise in asset values. For the U.S. we have seen the stock market (e.g. S&P 500 index) rise over 220% since 2009 while nominal GDP has risen only about 1/10 that much. The burgeoning transactions and rise in value of the stock market, have driven the *measured* income velocity of money much lower.[9] Thus, Friedman's admonition remains true, if we interpret the bubble in the asset market as representing a type of "potential" inflation that will either be realized later, or will be eliminated through enormous growth in output (i.e. a real wealth effect in goods) or through an enormous bursting of the bubble.

Our methodology requires that we have observable series for both asset value and fundamentals. Our dependent variable is taken to be the level of wealth invested in the stock market, which is just the nominal capitalization of the market. As we have previously noted, nominal wealth should be closely related to future spending, while future output and price changes should be closely related to current nominal GDP. The ratio of stock market capitalization to nominal GDP is an indicator preferred by Warren Buffett.

---

9   The CBO in the U.S. has estimated that stock transactions averaged about $240 billion each day and $800 billion was the daily average in the bond market. Thus, every four weeks the U.S. stock and bond markets collectively trade more dollars than an entire year's nominal GDP. See <http://www.cbo.gov/budget-options/2013/44855>. In addition, this is not the first time this type of phenomenon has occurred. Taiwan had a very similar experience during the 1980s. In 1986-1988 average growth of narrow money was about 40% per year and yet the CPI inflation rate remained stable at 3%. Most economists immediately saw that the transactions motive for the demand for money was at the base of the oddity. Transactions in the stock market and housing markets were enormous and supporting a strong demand for money that effectively neutralized the fast growth in money. This is why inflation remained tame in the face of a fantastically growing money supply. But, the social cost of this price stability was asset inflation and bubbles in the stock and housing markets. Output growth by contrast was exceptionally high—in the double digit range. Post-recession U.S. M1 growth has averaged above 10% per year, which is above usual, and has surged at times to 30%. U.S. M2 growth of money has not been particularly high averaging recently around 6-7% per year, surging at times to 20% growth.

He is well known for using this indicator to judge whether or not the stock market is in a speculative bubble. Our view is that bubbles in the ratio of market capitalization to GDP (i.e. substantial increases in the Buffett Ratio and deviations from fundamentals) must generate three possible responses corresponding to higher growth, higher inflation, or a fall in stock prices. Figure 1 shows these three possibilities. As we have said, actual adjustment will be some combination of these three. Naturally, central bankers are hoping that their policies will generate higher growth. Critics of the central bankers are expecting higher inflation. Yet we have already mentioned how that the first two of these are not likely to happen, which leaves only the third channel of adjustment. This then is how bubbles are resolved whenever they occur. Resolution involves a mixture of all three possibilities.

III. Empirical Evidence for Bubbles in Stock Markets

Having postulated that bubbles are identified by values deviating from their fundamental levels, and having explained how such bubbles proceed towards a resolution of the disequilibrium, we now turn to estimating such deviations and thus measuring the extent of bubbles using data from the stock markets of various countries and regional groupings. We seek to empirically investigate the behavior of stock markets and nominal GDP for

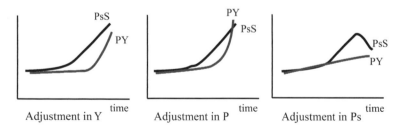

Figure 1: Possible Adjustments to a Bubble in Market Capitalization

Note: PSS is the nominal stock market capitalization (or Price times shares outstanding) while PY is the nominal GDP, or price times real output.

the World, the Eurozone, the U.S., and East Asia, while finally analyzing separately Japan, Korea, Hong Kong, Taiwan, and China.[10]

The data are taken from the World Bank and UN databases. The World Bank collects and disseminates a coherent set of annual data on nominal total capitalization of stock markets in a country as a percentage of nominal GDP beginning in many cases 1989 and ending in 2013. The UN similarly collects and disseminates a coherent set of annual data on nominal GDP (in U.S. dollars) up to 2013.[11] Naturally, all this means that the most important data relating to current market capitalization and nominal GDP is lacking. We have therefore augmented our data set on both market capitalization and nominal GDP (both measured in USD) to include data taken from the major stock markets and government publications, respectively, for 2014.[12] Even so we have no coherent data on the current market capitalization and nominal GDP for 2015. Despite this we argue that bubbles are usually slow in forming, although the recent early—2015 experience in China indicates that bubbles in stocks can at times form in only 3-6 months. China's stock market presents a difficult case since it is not particularly well suited for analysis using the Buffett ratio or nominal GDP, as can be seen by looking at data over the past three or four years. Stocks were essentially flat, even though nominal GDP was growing at well over 10%.

The basic empirical model is represented by a long run equilibrium relation between stock market capitalization and nominal GDP, with nominal

10 All Tables, graphs, and references are available at the following webpage and are not published here for reasons of saving space *http://www.kleykampintaiwan.com/files/Tables_etc_paper2015.pdf.*

11 Of course, data on market capitalization for stock markets in USD is derived from World Bank and UN data by multiplying the World Bank data on percentage market cap to GDP by UN data on nominal GDP in USD.

12 For stock market capitalization in USD in 2014 we have used the following website that provides annual data, <http://www.world-exchanges.org/statistics/monthly-reports>. Because this paper was written in March of 2015, we have not been able to add GDP and Stock Market Capitalization to the model and this has led to a significant omission in terms of China, whose stock market has increased greatly during the first part of 2015.

GDP acting as what we have termed a long run weak attractor for market cap.[13] For any particular regional grouping or country, this can be written as

$$\ln (Mkt\_Cap_t) = \beta_o + \beta_1 \ln (NGDP_{t+1-i}) + \varepsilon_t \quad (3)$$

where Mkt_Cap_t represents stock market capitalization and $NGDP_t$ represents nominal GDP. As we have said, these two variables should be closely related since any deviation between them should generate a movement in real output, goods price inflation, or falling stock prices. This movement may be delayed and may extend over many months or even years, due to the fall in the income velocity of money that occurs with the rise of transactions and nominal capitalization (i.e. wealth) in the stock market. The natural means of analyzing this is with a vector error correction model since this allows us to better see the channel through which the actual adjustment process occurs. We will nevertheless employ several empirical estimation methods to judge whether or not bubbles exist.

Unit root tests were conducted on each grouping, including the world, regional groupings, and countries. The results of these tests are shown below in Table 1.[14] This table shows that nearly in nearly all cases (except for the cases of World and Taiwan market capitalizations using a constant and trend) all variables appear to be I(1) and have unit roots.[15] This is certainly not surprising, since these variables are widely believed to be nonstationary, and casual inspection of their graphs appear to lend support to this. Note that in most cases, a single lag was sufficient to test the variables. This is because

---

13 If β_1 is close to unity, then we have the Buffett Ratio exactly.

14 Note that the sample size is small and the data are annual in frequency. The span of time is generally thought to affect the power of unit root tests, but not the frequency. Thus, in order for our data to be coherent, we use World Bank data that goes back only as far as 1988. If we were able to use monthly data instead, but kept the sample period the same, the power of our unit root tests should not be affected very much. See Shiller and Perron (1985) and the review paper by Campbell and Perron (1991).

15 The power of these tests are known to be low in the presence of structural change, which some might call bubbles.

Table 1: Augmented Dickey Fuller-Generalized Least Squares Unit Root Tests

Region/Country	Lags	Log (Mkt_Cap) ADF-GLS Statistic	Lags	Log (NGDP) ADF-GLS Statistic
World	1	- 0.08	3	0.00
Eurozone	1	- 0.47	2	- 0.65
U.S.	1	- 0.23	1	0.26
East Asia	1	- 0.62	1	- 0.16
Japan	4	- 1.44	2	- 1.46
Korea	2	0.09	1	- 0.08
Hong Kong	1	- 0.41	3	0.10
China	1	0.68	1	- 0.07
Taiwan	1	0.19	3	0.66

Unit Root Tests (with constant and trend)   Sample size = 23

Region/Country	Lags	Log (Mkt_Cap) ADF-GLS Statistic	Lags	Log (NGDP) ADF-GLS Statistic
World	1	- 2.89 *	2	- 1.60
Eurozone	1	- 2.02	1	- 2.42
U.S.	1	- 1.67	1	- 1.26
East Asia	2	- 2.02	1	- 1.88
Japan	4	- 1.66	2	- 2.56
Korea	4	- 1.43	2	- 2.31
Hong Kong	1	- 2.69	1	- 2.00
China	2	- 1.44	2	- 1.82
Taiwan	2	- 3.50 **	1	- 1.65

we are using annual data and therefore most adjustments of the variables are being done over a relatively short time frame. This need not be true of any cointegrating relations, but for the series themselves it is not a peculiar result.

It is important to recognize that a whole literature on unit roots in stock prices was produced in the late 1980s and all throughout the 1990s, beginning with a seminal paper by Summers and Poterba (1987) that asserted stock prices display mean reversion. These writers concluded that mean reversion occurs due to "slowly-decaying 'price fads' that cause stock prices to deviate from fundamental values for periods of several years". In effect, they are saying that bubbles occur and these bubbles delay the return to fundamentals thus masking, to an extent, the nature of this mean reversion. For these writers, stock prices are stationary, but have long memory and therefore have the appearance of being random walks. Summers and Poterba (1987) did not use unit root analysis, which was just becoming popular at the time. Subsequent analyses of stock prices using more and more complicated forms of unit root analysis have not been able to create a clear consensus on mean reversion. Recent work by Balcilar et al. (2015), using a procedure by Gil-Alana (2008), and supplemented by the work of Robinson (1994) and Bai and Perron (1998), assess whether stock prices are nonstationary, or perhaps instead fractionally integrated with multiple periods of structural change. They conclude that nearly all the stock price series they consider are non-stationary, unit root processes and therefore conform to the notion of stock prices being random walks.

In short, we find that there is evidence on both sides of the argument and that stock market capitalization (or value) is not obviously mean reverting and appears to be nonstationary over reasonable horizons, with this non-stationarity possibly being large departures from fundamentals that last over long periods. Nevertheless, our view would seem to be closer to that of Summers and Poterba, but we caution that mean reversion is being masked by periodic bubbles that may last over very long stretches of time, and we do not necessarily endorse the view that these departures are due to "price fads". The fact that enormously complicated time series models have been deployed to try to assess the non-stationarity of stock prices indicates that it is rather moot whether or not stock prices are random walks. Instead, we assert that the difference between stock prices and fundamentals is due to the relatively strong wealth effect in money demand and relatively weak wealth effect in consumption.[16] Given this asymmetry, periodic spans of irrational exuberance or exceptionally low interest rates, that serve to drive wealth higher, will also drive money demand higher, as well. This will reduce the income velocity of money and cool inflation and growth, giving the appearance of a divergence in prices from fundamentals. The divergence can last years, but in the end resolution must involve movements in output growth, inflation, or falling asset prices.

Table 2 contains separate cointegrating regressions for all regions and countries. The regressions are estimated individually and not as a system. We will also estimate the regressions as a system to account for possible correlation between error terms. As we have earlier stated, we do not believe that testing for strict cointegration is necessary since we believe that market capitalization and nominal GDP must be related by a priori reasoning.

---

16 Case, Quigley, and Shiller (2011) investigated the effect of wealth (housing and financial assets) on consumption and concluded —

> "We find at best weak evidence of a link between stock market wealth and consumption. In contrast, we do find strong evidence that variations in housing market wealth have important effects upon consumption. This evidence arises consistently using thirty-one year panels of U.S. states, and this finding is robust to differences in model specification." (p. 31)

We do not find this surprising. If the stock market is rising quickly, we would expect that its rate of return would be dominant and the level of saving could very well rise not fall. In fact, the personal saving rate in the U.S. rose from 2009 to 2013 reaching a high of 10.5% in December 2012. It has since fallen back substantially, but remains double its level during 2005. We suspect this increased saving rate is closely related to the tremendous perceived gains to be made in the U.S. stock market, along with the effort by many Americans to repair their balance sheets.

The intercept β_0 in all cointegrating regressions in Table 2, except for East Asia, are significant at the 1% level, meaning that the traditional Buffett Ratio (i.e. market cap to nominal GDP) is probably inadequate as a measure of bubbles. Except for Japan, the slope coefficient, β_1 , is positive, statistically significant at the 1% level and generally larger than unity. The R^2 statistic is high for the regressions, again except for Japan. We should not be surprised that Japan lacks a strong clear cointegrating relationship since nominal GDP growth as been extremely erratic and low, yet the stock market has experienced several significant ups and downs. Bubbles in Japan have therefore masked any close relation between GDP and market capitalization. A much better cointegrating relation occurs if we limit the sample period to 1992-2014. In this case the slope coefficient is near unity and is significant at the 5% level. Cointegration is found in the Japanese market, regardless of whether we begin the sample in 1992 or 1988. The behavior of the Japanese residuals over the two sample periods is essentially the same, but the shorter sample produces residuals (i.e. bubbles) that are slightly smaller. For the period 1992 - 2014, the adjusted R2 improves considerably to become 0.19. The intercept is found to be insignificant and the slope is unity, meaning that the Buffet ratio is precisely the correct measure to use to assess and measure the size of bubbles in the Japanese stock market, although this is not true for other countries or regions.

Overall, Table 2 shows that strict cointegration is not always achieved between the two variables. Some would argue that this may be due to a rapidly changing distribution of income away from labor and towards the owners of capital. We do not feel that this type of broad social change can explain short and episodic bubbles that form and generate deviations. In addition, if such a change in distribution was in place, we should not see a strong error correction process, which is what we turn to now.

Table 3 includes all single equation error correction regressions, having error correction terms based on the Table 2 cointegrating regressions. We choose to employ the Engle-Granger two step method in deriving these error

Table 2: Cointegrating (Weak) Attractor — Level Regressions

Region/Country	β_0	β_1	R^2	Adj-R^2	D-W	ADF - 1 lag	ADF - 2 lags	ADF - 3 lags	
World	-9.966 ***	1.309 ***	0.86	0.86	0.90	-2.121	-0.993	-1.010	no
US	-20.159 ***	1.674 ***	0.88	0.86	0.59	-1.856	-1.898	-1.921	no
Euro Area	-21.731 ***	1.702 ***	0.69	0.68	0.51	-1.814	-1.925	-2.069	no
East Asia	0.325	0.980 ***	0.75	0.74	1.01	-3.280 *	-2.327	-2.060	yes
Japan	21.410 ***	0.256	0.04	-.01	1.05	-4.067 ***	-2.829	-2.100	yes
Korea	-17.360 ***	1.614 ***	0.76	0.75	1.18	-3.527 ***	-2.386	-1.887	yes
China	-26.280 ***	1.885 ***	0.88	0.87	0.60	-2.217	-1.100	-1.192	no
Hong Kong	-40.048 ***	2.608 ***	0.86	0.86	0.67	-1.954	-1.532	-1.582	no
Taiwan	-7.442 ***	1.600 ***	0.81	0.80	1.50	-4.181	-2.710	-2.040	yes

$\ln(Mkt\_Cap_t) = \beta_0 + \beta_1 \ln(NGDP_{t\text{-}1,t}) + \varepsilon_t$

Annual Data   1989-2014   ··   Number Observations = 26

correction mechanisms.

In general, the results of Table 3 show that the error correction terms all have the expected (negative) sign, and except for Korea, they are all statistically significant. Under typical cointegration analysis, if the cointegrating regression is not significant, there is apparently no long term relation to which these variables correct. We have postulated that our least squares attractor is a good measure of this long run relation regardless of whether or not cointegration is statistically confirmed. The error correction is therefore a confirmation of the adaption of the market capitalization to deviations from fundamentals proxied by nominal GDP. The speed of this adaptation is governed by the size of the coefficient φ_1.

Table 3 assumes that the error correction is accomplished via changes in market capitalization. However, we have pointed out earlier that nominal GDP may instead adapt to the disequilibrium between the two variables. This is possible if inflation is driven up or if there is a steep increase in output due to a strong wealth effect in the demand for goods. To discern whether market cap, nominal GDP, or both adapts or corrects to long run equilibrium, we turn to Table 4 that gives the results of a vector error correction between market cap and nominal GDP. This table confirms that error correction is occurring, but one cannot say that market cap is the sole variable through which resolution of the deviation from fundamentals occurs.

The results of the vector error correction are quite mixed. Only in the Eurozone do we find that there is a complete absence of error correction. All other regions and countries experience some form of error correction. However, in three of the cases (i.e. the World, Japan, and China) we find that market cap is the adjustment variable. In three other cases (i.e. the U.S., Korea, and Hong Kong), nominal GDP adjusts to deviations from fundamentals. Finally, a further two cases (i.e. East Asia and Taiwan) see adjustments in both variables. The variety of adjustment channels makes it difficult to say what may happen in terms of adjustment, if for example the

Table 3: Single Equation — Error Correction Estimations

Region/Country	Constant	φ_1	φ_2	α_1	α_2	R^2	Adj-R^2	Ljung-Box Test Autocorrelation p-value
World	0.1216 *	- 0.3847 **	- 0.0141	- 0.2083	- 0.7108	0.22	0.06	0.983
US	- 0.1354	- 0.3514 *	- 0.3011	6.4356 *	- 0.9227	0.26	0.11	0.937
Euro Area	0.0841 **	- 0.1900 *	0.0594	- 0.0857	- 0.2566	0.11	- 0.07	0.871
East Asia	- 0.0588	- 0.6981 ***	- 0.0340	1.9256 **	- 0.4794	0.43	0.32	0.856
Japan	- 0.0175	- 0.7569 ***	0.3503 *	0.6686	- 0.4894	0.48	0.37	0.929
Korea	0.1348	- 0.2824	- 0.3752	1.9726 *	- 2.0437 ***	0.51	0.42	0.962
China	0.3819 **	- 0.2950 **	0.1905	- 1.6343	0.7010	0.23	0.04	0.707
Hong Kong	0.0737	- 0.2710	- 0.2194	4.2018 **	- 2.3688	0.31	0.18	0.948
Taiwan	0.0787	- 0.8338 ***	- 0.0641	0.5523	- 1.1540	0.61	0.53	0.971

$$\Delta\ln(Mkt\_Cap_t) = \varphi_0 + \varphi_1 EC_t + \sum_{i=2}^{p+1} \varphi_i \Delta\ln(Mkt\_Cap_{t-i}) + \sum_{i=1}^{p+1} \alpha_i \Delta\ln(NGDP_{t-1-i}) + \nu_t$$

$$EC_t = \ln(Mkt\_Cap_{t-1}) - \hat{\beta}_0 - \beta_1 \ln(NGDP_{t-1})$$

Annual Data 1990-2014 -- Number Observations = 25   p = 1

U.S. or Japan were caught in a stock bubble.[17] We might also say that this is the adjustment on average for any deviation of market cap from nominal GDP, however small or large such a deviation may be. There is no saying what may happen for any one particular large bubble that might occur.

Finally, we recognize that Table 4 assumes each vector error correction regression is independent of others. There is no reason to expect that this is true. Indeed, there is every reason to expect that the VECMs are closely connected through correlated error terms due to the possibility of contagion. We approach the problem of correlated errors by estimating the single equation error corrections using seemingly unrelated regressions (SUR). This is accomplished by first estimating Table 2 regressions again using a system of SUR, first for the three regions (Eurozone, U.S., and East Asia) and then for the five countries (Japan, Korea, Hong Kong, Taiwan, and China). After this, the residuals are calculated and two corresponding systems are estimated for the three regions and five countries. Table 5 and Table 6 present the estimation results of this modeling. We suppress the output for the SUR estimation of the attractors and present only the error correction estimations. In the table, these SUR estimates are then compared with the original single equations error corrections.

The outcome of the SUR estimations confirms again that there is an active error correction mechanism operating in nearly every market. Ostensibly, market capitalization adjusts to restore equilibrium whenever there is a sufficient deviation from fundamentals. We now ask which markets appear to have significant bubbles and threaten economic stability.

---

17 Although we have not addressed it in this paper, it is always possible for a bubble to be resolved by government creating another bubble.

Table 4: To Equations — ector Error Correction Estimations

Region/Country	μ_{Cap}	μ_{GDP}	β_2	α_1	α_2	R_1^2	R_2^2	D-W 1	D-W 2	ECM significant for
World	-3.73**	0.58	1.31***	-0.38**	0.05	0.20	0.19	2.04	1.41	Mkt Cap
US	-3.25	1.43	2.18***	-0.09	0.04***	0.02	0.39	1.98	1.21	NGDP
Euro Area	-4.5	1.6	1.90**	-0.16	0.05	0.08	0.07	1.88	1.59	—
East Asia	0.02	0.07***	0.993***	-0.45**	0.11**	0.19	0.17	1.96	1.43	Both
Japan	4.46**	-0.30	0.678	-0.49**	0.04	0.24	0.01	1.76	1.32	Mkt Cap
Korea	-6.38	5.07	1.91***	-0.26	0.20***	0.07	0.18	2.15	1.79	NGDP
China	-5.54***	0.47*	1.48	-0.40***	0.02	0.42	0.08	1.79	1.13	Mkt Cap
Hong Kong	-2.84	4.51***	3.96***	-0.04	0.06***	0.01	0.49	2.29	1.00	NGDP
Taiwan	-6.36**	1.52***	2.07***	-0.48**	0.11***	0.22	0.28	2.31	1.82	Both

$$\begin{pmatrix} \Delta\ln(\text{Mkt\_Cap}_t) \\ \Delta\ln(\text{NGDP}_t) \end{pmatrix} = \begin{pmatrix} \mu_{\text{Cap}} \\ \mu_{\text{GDP}} \end{pmatrix} + \begin{pmatrix} \alpha_1 \\ \alpha_2 \end{pmatrix}\left(1 \quad -\beta_2\right)\begin{pmatrix} \ln(\text{Mkt\_Cap}_{t-1}) \\ \ln(\text{NGDP}_{t-1}) \end{pmatrix} + \sum_{k=1}^{p}\begin{pmatrix} \ln(\text{Mkt\_Cap}_{t\,k}) \\ \ln(\text{NGDP}_{t\,k}) \end{pmatrix} + \begin{pmatrix} \varepsilon_t^1 \\ \varepsilon_t^2 \end{pmatrix}$$

(p = 0 , unrestricted constant)

Annual Data 1989-2014 — Number Observations = 26

Table 5: SUR Regional System — Error Correction Estimations

	μ_{EZ}	μ_{US}	μ_{EA}	φ_{EZ}	φ_{US}	φ_{EA}	R^2_{EZ}	R^2_{US}	R^2_{EA}
SUR Estimations	0.07	0.07	-0.07	-0.16 **	-0.34 ***	-0.39 ***	0.06	0.15	0.28
Single Equation Estimations	0.08	-0.14	-0.06	-0.19 *	-0.35 *	-0.70 ***	0.11	0.26	0.43

$$\begin{pmatrix} \Delta\ln(Mkt\_Cap_t)_{EZ} \\ \Delta\ln(Mkt\_Cap_t)_{US} \\ \ln(Mkt\_Cap_t)_{EA} \end{pmatrix} = \begin{pmatrix} \mu_{EZ} \\ \mu_{US} \\ \mu_{EA} \end{pmatrix} + \begin{pmatrix} \varphi_{EZ} & 0 & 0 \\ 0 & \varphi_{US} & 0 \\ 0 & 0 & \varphi_{EA} \end{pmatrix}\begin{pmatrix} EC_{EZ} \\ EC_{US} \\ EC_{EA} \end{pmatrix} + \begin{pmatrix} \alpha_{EZ}\ \ln(NGDP_t)_{EZ} \\ \alpha_{US}\Delta\ln(NGDP_t)_{US} \\ \alpha_{EA}\Delta\ln(NGDP_t)_{EA} \end{pmatrix} + \begin{pmatrix} \varepsilon_{EZ} \\ \varepsilon_{US} \\ \varepsilon_{EA} \end{pmatrix}$$

Annual Data 1989-2014 -- Number Observations = 26

Note: EZ = Eurozone, US = United States, and EA = East Asia. Single equation estimations are taken from Table 3.

Table 6: SUR Country System — Error Correction Estimations

	μ_J	μ_K	μ_{HK}	μ_T	μ_C	φ_J	φ_K	φ_{HK}	φ_T	φ_C	R^2_J	R^2_K	R^2_{HK}	R^2_T	R^2_C
SUR Estimations	0.00	0.03	0.01	0.05	0.50	-0.51***	-0.72***	-0.32**	-1.19***	-0.43***	0.35	0.23	0.18	0.55	0.36
Single Equation Estimations	-0.02	0.14	0.07	0.08	0.38	-0.76***	-0.28	-0.07	-0.83***	-0.30**	0.48	0.51	0.31	0.61	0.23

$$\begin{pmatrix} \Delta\ln(Mkt\_Cap_t)_J \\ \Delta\ln(Mkt\_Cap_t)_K \\ \Delta\ln(Mkt\_Cap_t)_{HK} \\ \Delta\ln(Mkt\_Cap_t)_T \\ \Delta\ln(Mkt\_Cap_t)_C \end{pmatrix} = \begin{pmatrix} \mu_J \\ \mu_K \\ \mu_{HK} \\ \mu_T \\ \mu_C \end{pmatrix} + \begin{pmatrix} \varphi_J & 0 & 0 & 0 & 0 \\ 0 & \varphi_K & 0 & 0 & 0 \\ 0 & 0 & \varphi_{HK} & 0 & 0 \\ 0 & 0 & 0 & \varphi_T & 0 \\ 0 & 0 & 0 & 0 & \varphi_C \end{pmatrix} \begin{pmatrix} EC_J \\ EC_K \\ EC_{HK} \\ EC_T \\ EC_C \end{pmatrix} + \begin{pmatrix} \alpha_J \ln(NGDP_t)_J \\ \alpha_K \Delta\ln(NGDP_t)_K \\ \alpha_{HK}\Delta\ln(NGDP_t)_{HK} \\ \alpha_T\Delta\ln(NGDP_t)_T \\ \alpha_C\Delta\ln(NGDP_t)_C \end{pmatrix} + \begin{pmatrix} \varepsilon_J \\ \varepsilon_K \\ \varepsilon_{HK} \\ \varepsilon_T \\ \varepsilon_C \end{pmatrix}$$

Annual Data   1989-2014 -- Number Observations = 26

Note: Single equation estimations are taken from Table 3

IV. Evaluating Bubbles and Possible Contagion

Our definition of bubbles involves a deviation between stock market capitalization and nominal GDP. While it is true that this is an absolute indicator, we will find it is more useful for each regional grouping or country to compare the current bubble with a previous reference bubble. This is done because past bubbles (such as the dotcom bubble in the U.S.) are generally agreed to have existed. The bubbles we have computed are equal to the residuals from the SUR systems estimation of the cointegrating attractors. The estimated bubbles for regions and countries are shown in Figures 2 and 3 respectively.

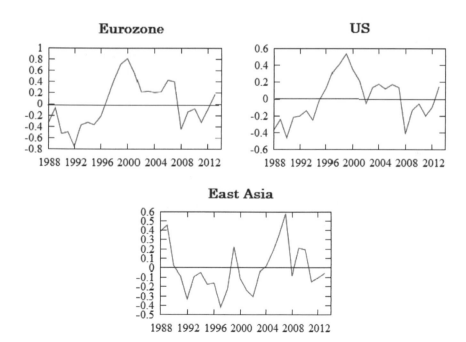

Figure 2: Measurement of Bubbles in Major Regional Economies Deviation of Stock Capitalization from Nominal GDP SUR System Estimates

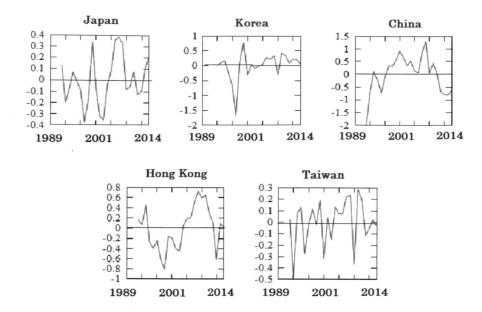

Figure 3: Measurement of Bubbles in East Asian Countries Deviation of Stock Capitalization from Nominal GDP SUR Systems Estimates

With respect to Figure 2, it seems clear that East Asia as a whole is not currently in the midst of a stock bubble. There is simply no evidence for a stock bubble for the entire region. By contrast, both the U.S. and the Eurozone appear to be in the early stages of having bubbles, with the Eurozone bubble about 1/4 the size of its 2000 bubble and the U.S. currently about 1/3 its 1998 stock bubble. It should be remembered that our estimations only extend to 2014 and more recent data may show a slight worsening of these bubbles. Also, it is not clear which of the individual stock markets in the Eurozone are in bubble territory. The recent acceleration of QE policies in the EU are likely to have increased the size of the bubble there.

With respect to Figure 3, Japan is in the midst of a clear bubble that is about 1/2 the size of the large 2006 stock bubble. The importance of Japan to the regional and indeed global economy makes this bubble particularly dangerous. None of the other East Asian stock markets appear to have stock bubble problems, although they may have bubbles present in other assets such as bonds or housing. What is more, there may be financial contagion in the form of heightened correlation between bubbles during this period.

To determine the extent of possible contagion, we use our constructed bubble series estimated by SUR methods and look at the simple correlations between regions and countries. This are shown below in Table 7-A and 7-B. Simple correlations are generally thought to be poor indicators of relations when there are more than two variables under consideration. In addition, there is no lag structure to propagate causality and contagion. However, in our case, we are using annual data. Lag structures in this case, whether we use vector autoregressions or cross correlations, will not be precise. However, such tests show that the U.S. bubbles (or deviations from fundamentals) tend to lag Eurozone bubbles and tend to be positively correlated with such bubbles. Cross correlations with Japanese bubbles and U.S. bubbles tend to show that U.S. deviations drive Japanese below their fundamentals. This may be due to funds being attracted out of Japan to the U.S. bubble. Nevertheless,

Table 7-A: Correlation Matrix between Bubbles - Regional Groupings

EZ	U.S.	EA	
1	0.848***	0.174	EZ
	1	-0.103	U.S.
		1	EA

Table 7-B: Correlation Matrix between Bubbles - Country Groupings

J	K	HK	T	C	
1	0.582**	0.524**	0.435**	0.048	J
	1	0.391	0.285	0.013	K
		1	0.244	0.142	HK
			1	0.333	T
				1	C

attempts to correlate these bubbles across the region are quite tenuous. Japan is the only country that has any large contemporaneous correlation with the other Asian countries (especially Korea, Hong Kong, and Taiwan). A bubble bursting in Japan would be expected to bring down these particular stock markets in the region. Considering that Japan currently has a rather large stock bubble (right now about half the size of its next most recent bubble), it is reasonable to be concerned about extending greater linkages within the region. China on the other hand does not seem to have this problem. The Chinese stock market is relatively small compared to its GDP and it is quite isolated with the regions other stock markets. Bursting of a stock bubble in China would not be expected to bring down the other markets in the region, unless it affected the Chinese economy greatly. China's credit markets and banking sector in particular, remain unknown quantities and financial integration with Chinese banking interests would probably be ill advised. Stock participation is quite another thing. Opening the Chinese stock market to greater foreign participation would not seem to be dangerous.

The Korean, Hong Kong and Japanese stock bubbles have a similar temporal profile in relation to the U.S. bubbles. Typically expansion of U.S. bubbles will drive down the bubbles in these markets, drawing funds from them. This is not true of Taiwan which has a positive contemporaneous correlation with the U.S. market and rises along with the U.S. bubble. Adjustment of the Taiwan market to the U.S. market is quick with no lags or leads present in the cross-correlogram.

V. Conclusions

Naturally there will be some who will claim that it is better to go ahead an try to better integrate the economies of East Asia. For one thing, such integration might in some cases allow decoupling of the economies in East Asia from the major Western economies. Decoupling was the watchword of the 1990s and it proved to be disastrously true as the U.S. spread a global recession due to its excesses in the housing market. For another, the typical recessionary period does not last very long and therefore development plans must be made well in advance and without thought about what may happen in the intervening short run period. However, the 1997-1998 Asian financial crisis showed that financial and economic contagion within Asia, quite unrelated to the major Western economies, can also be disastrous. Malaysia was one of the few economies that sought to place tough capital controls on its markets and reign in the impact of foreigners and fear in financial markets. The problem is assessing whether the economies of the world are under a bubble. Our study here shows that the major economies of the U.S., the Eurozone and Japan do indeed have the appearance of bubbles, at least in the stock market. Bursting of these bubbles in the future, perhaps even simultaneously, could generate a massive global financial crisis. Since many of the usual policies used to fight such crises are already spent, it is not clear how that governments could defend their domestic economies against the global downturn. During times of upheaval, economies simply cannot have rampant and uncontrolled capital outflows occurring which cause bets to be placed on currency depreciations. During more placid times, when growth is normal and there is no talk of outrageous bubbles among the large economies, regional integration might be a policy worth pursuing. Clearly governments must pick and choose among the various sectors they wish to open up and integrate during these uncertain times. Financial integration would surely be at the bottom of that list.

The Changing Landscape of Taiwan-ASEAN Economic Relations: Value Chain Clustering in ASEAN

Kristy Hsu[*]

I. Introduction

The establishment of the ASEAN Economic Community (AEC) by end-2015 will mark a major milestone in the Southeast Asian integration, which will be further acknowledged when negotiations of the Regional Comprehensive Economic Partnership (RCEP) agreement conclude by year end. To respond to the opportunities and challenges in the integrated regional and global economy, Taiwan businesses are re-shaping their regional strategy by expanding value chains in Southeast Asia. As a result, the past years have witnessed a changing landscape of Taiwan-ASEAN economic relations, which may bring Taiwan businesses out of the "FTA anxiety". This paper first examines the latest development of East Asian economic integration by analyzing the AEC 2015 and the RCEP initiative. The paper then presents the changing Taiwan-ASEAN economic and trade relation and analyzes the transformation of Taiwan's investments in Southeast Asia driven by the business community's response to the AEC and RCEP. Finally, the paper concludes and suggests policy recommendations for Taiwan and ASEAN Member States.

---

*   Program Director, Taiwan ASEAN Studies Center, Chung Hua Institution for Economic Research (CIER), Taiwan.

II. The Latest Development of East Asian Economic Integration

1. The AEC 2015 in Shaping

On 7th October 2003, the ASEAN Leaders adopted the Declaration of ASEAN Concord II (Bali Concord II) in Bali, Indonesia, to establish an ASEAN Community by 2020. On January 13, 2007, the ASEAN Leaders at their 12th ASEAN Summit in Cebu, the Philippines, further affirmed their strong commitment to accelerating establishment of the ASEAN Community by 2015. The Leaders believed "the strengthening of ASEAN integration through the accelerated establishment of an ASEAN Community will reinforce ASEAN's centrality and role as the driving force in charting the evolving regional architecture."[1]

The ASEAN Community will comprise three pillars — the ASEAN Political-Security Community (APSC), the ASEAN Economic Community (AEC) and the ASEAN Socio-Cultural Community (ASCC). The three pillars are closely intertwined and mutually reinforcing for the purpose of ensuring durable peace, stability, and shared prosperity in the region.

With respect to the second pillar — the ASEAN Economic Community (AEC), the ASEAN Leaders agreed to transform ASEAN into a region with free movement of goods, services, investment, skilled labour, and freer flow of capital by 2015. The AEC envisages four characteristics — a single market and production base, a highly competitive economic region, a region of equitable economic development, and a region fully integrated into the global economy.[2]

---

1   Cebu Declaration on the Acceleration of the Establishment of an ASEAN Community by 2015, January 13, 2007, <http://www.asean.org/news/item/cebu-declaration-on-the-acceleration-of-the-establishment-of-an-asean-community-by-2015>.

2   Declaration on the ASEAN Economic Community Blueprint, November 20, 2007.

According to the ASEAN Economic Community Blueprint, in order to enable ASEAN businesses to compete internationally, to make ASEAN a more dynamic and stronger segment of the global supply chains and to ensure that the internal market remains attractive to foreign investors, it is crucial for ASEAN to look beyond the borders of the AEC. In order to achieve the goal of integration into the global economy, the Blueprint points out two approaches: coherent approach towards external economic relations and enhanced participation in global supply networks. With respect to the former approach, ASEAN shall work towards maintaining ASEAN Centrality in its external economic relations, including, but not limited to, its negotiations for free trade agreements (FTAs) and comprehensive economic partnership (CEPs) agreements (ASEAN 2007).

To stock-take and assess the latest development of the AEC, at the ASEAN Summit in 2013 in Brunei Darussalam, ASEAN leaders reviewed the work of the three areas of the AEC. According to the ASEAN Secretariat, an average of 82.5 percent of all action lines towards the ASEAN Community 2015 have been completed or are being implemented — representing 78 percent for the political security, 79.7 percent for the economic and 90 percent for the socio-cultural pillars.[3]

As the end of 2015 is approaching, ASEAN's post-2015 vision is also being frequently discussed. In October 2013, ASEAN Leaders adopted the "Bandar Seri Begawan Declaration on the ASEAN Community Post-2015 Vision" during the 23rd ASEAN Summit in Brunei Darussalam. The Leaders tasked the ASEAN Community Councils to expedite their work on developing the ASEAN Community's post-2015 vision, and instructed that realising a politically cohesive, economically integrated, socially responsible, and a truly people-oriented, people-centred and rules-based ASEAN would

---

3 Post ASEAN Summit Highlights- ASEAN Leaders to intensify efforts towards ASEAN Community 2015, *ASEAN Secretariat News*, October 16, 2013, <http://www.asean.org/news/asean-secretariat-news/item/post-asean-summit-highlights-asean-leaders-to-intensify-efforts-towards-asean-community-2015#>.

be the central elements of a Post-2015 Vision of the ASEAN Community.[4]

ASEAN had experienced robust economic growth in the past decades, notably its "golden decade" of the late 1980s and early 1990s before the Asian Financial Crisis in 1997/1998. The high economic growth rate of ASEAN is correlated with high investment rate and a higher share of international trade to national output. And then the outbreak of Asian financial crisis in 1997/1998 hit the fast growing economy of most ASEAN Member States, and changed ASEAN's plans of economic integration – shifting from focusing on internal cooperation towards an outward looking partnership with larger East Asian countries.[5] Since the early 2000s, ASEAN gradually expanded economic cooperation with its six Dialogue Partner countries. On the one hand, ASEAN successfully concluded bilateral ASEAN+1 free trade agreements (FTAs) with its six Dialogue Partner countries, starting from China in 2004, South Korea in 2006, Japan in 2008, and India, Australia and New Zealand in 2009.[6] As of 2009, these six countries have separately or jointly developed ASEAN+1 FTAs with ASEAN.

---

4   The Leaders requested the ASEAN Coordinating Council (ACC) to further develop the central elements of the post-2015 vision for endorsement by the ASEAN Summit in 2014, and for the ACC to establish a Working Group of the ACC at the level of Senior Officials of the three pillars to oversee the overall process of developing this post-2015 vision by the 27th ASEAN Summit, with progress reports submitted to the 24th, 25th and 26th ASEAN Summits. See "Bandar Seri Begawan Declaration on the ASEAN Community Post-2015 Vision," *Asean*, <http://www.asean.org/images/archive/23rdASEANSummit/bsb%20declaration%20on%20the%20asean%20communitys%20post%202015%20vision%20-%20final.pdf>.

5   On 17 December 1997, ASEAN leaders in Kuala Lumpur adopted "ASEAN Vision 2020", emphasizing its aim to build ASEAN as a "...outward looking, living in peace, stability and prosperity, bonded together in partnership in dynamic development and in a community of caring societies".

6   Among the ASEAN+1 FTAs, Australia and New Zealand together negotiated and singed with ASEAN the ASEAN-Australia-New Zealand Free Trade Area (AANZFTA). The AANZFTA Agreement is the first region-to-region FTA for both ASEAN and Australia and New Zealand. Agreement is the first region-to-region FTA for both ASEAN and Australia and New Zealand.

According to a Mid-Term Review of the Implementation of the AEC Blueprint conducted in 2012, the Mid-Term Review highlights a number of significant achievements of ASEAN towards AEC 2015 (Intal, Ponciano et al, 2014). The most significant and visible achievement would be the tariff reduction. Intra-ASEAN tariffs have drastically come down under the decade long integration under the Agreement on the Common Effective Preferential Tariff (CEPT) for the ASEAN Free Trade Area (AFTA). For the ASEAN-6, the percentage of items with zero tariffs in CEPT rose from 40 percent in 2000 to 99.11 percent in 2012, while the percentage of zero tariffs in CEPT for CLMV countries rose from about 10 percent in 2000 to 67.6 percent in 2012. Averagely, the ASEAN-6 tariff rate has been virtually zero (0.05 percent) since 2010, and the rate for CLMV countries is 1.69 percent in 2012 (see Figure 1). The elimination of tariffs is made possible with the political commitments of ASEAN Leaders, widely conceived as the highlight of the success story of the integration of ASEAN.

ASEAN has also progressed significantly in the services liberalization and investment liberalization. According to the results of the ASEAN

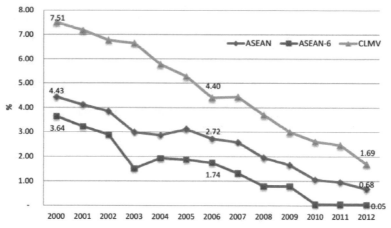

Figure 1: Average CEPT Rates in ASEAN Countries: 2000-2012

Source: ASEAN Tariff Database 2013

Business Outlook Survey 2014 conducted by the American Chambers of Commerce in ASEAN, the report indicates ASEAN has incremental improvements in most factors affecting investors' satisfaction of local environment in many ASEAN Member States (Intal, Ponciano et al, 2014).

According to the Mid-Term Review of the Implementation of the AEC Blueprint, ASEAN is moving towards the goals of the AEC 2015 Vision. However, there are challenges ahead for ASEAN as follows:

(1). There are still large number of poor and marginally non-poor in most of the ASEAN member states. The Review estimated that there were around 100 million people in ASEAN who were still poor (1.25 $ PPP per capita per day) in the late 2000s. Eliminating the number of the poor is the dominant key challenge facing ASEAN now and beyond 2015.

(2). ASEAN's overall competitiveness is still weak and needs to improve. In a study of labour productivity growth and total factor productivity growth during 1996-2011 for ten ASEAN Member States as well as China, India, Korea, Taiwan, Japan, USA and Latin America, the results show robust growth in labour productivity, particularly in Cambodia, Viet Nam, and Indonesia, and the Philippines. However, the growth of total factor productivity has been very modest or even negative for most ASEAN Member States. ASEAN needs to improve its total productivity growth performance relative to its East Asian neighbors in order to improve its competitiveness and move up the global value chains (GVCs).

2. The RCEP Negotiation and competition with the TPP

At the 19th ASEAN Summit in November 2010, the ASEAN Leaders adopted the ASEAN Framework for Regional Comprehensive Economic Partnership (RCEP). In November 2012, at the 21st ASEAN Summit, ASEAN Leaders announced the commencement of RCEP negotiations in early 2013 and aim to complete them by the end of 2015. The RCEP is comprised of 16 participating countries, namely ASEAN Member States, China, Japan, Korea, Australia, New Zealand, and India. The leaders commit to achieve a "comprehensive, high-quality and mutually beneficial economic partnership agreement establishing an open trade and investment environment in the region to facilitate the expansion of regional trade and investment and contribute to global economic growth and development".[7]

Since the announcement of the RCEP negotiations, the world's largest FTA in terms of population has attracted increasing attention from within and around the region. The total of RCEP participating countries' combined output reached USD 21.3 trillion in 2013, accounting for nearly 30 percent of world output. With regards to trade and investment flows of RCEP economies, in 2013 total trade of RCEP participating countries amounted to USD 10.7 trillion, equal to 29.0 percent of global trade, while total FDI inflows to these countries reached USD 339.8 billion, equal to 23.4 percent of global FDI inflows.[8]

ASEAN's decision to promote the RCEP was regarded by many a response to the U.S.-led TPP which was considered as a threat to ASEAN's integrity and its central role in leading the regional economic integration. The RECP is emphasized as an ASEAN-driven or ASEAN-led regional initiative, and as it encompasses a population and international trade volume lager than that of the TPP, it is economically more attractive than the TTP. It is ASEAN's most important initiative so far in stepping up further regional integration in East Asia as well as ASEAN's major expression of a global ASEAN (Intal, Ponciano et al, 2014). Furthermore, the possible expansion of RCEP's membership with its open accession clause to allow "other FTA Partners and external economic partners" to join in the future will contribute further to ASEAN's ambition to have a larger voice in the global economy.[9]

---

7   "Joint Declaration on the Launch of Negotiations for the Regional Comprehensive Economic Partnership," November 20, 2012 in Phnom Penh, Cambodia.

8   Joint Media Statement, "the Second RCEP Ministerial Meeting," *ASEAN*, 27 August 2014, <http://www.asean.org/images/Statement/2014/aug/2nd%20RCEP%20Minsterial%20 Meeting%20JMS%2028FINAL29.pdf>.

9   According to the Guiding Principles and Objectives for Negotiating the Regional

The TPP became strategically important when in November 2009 when the President of the United States Barak Obama announced an intention to participate and to conclude an "ambitious, next-generation, Asia-Pacific trade agreement that reflects U.S. economic priorities and values."[10] There are four ASEAN Member States participating in the TPP negotiations: Singapore, Brunei, Malaysia and Vietnam. Among them, Singapore and Brunei are the original members in the TPSEP, while Malaysia and Vietnam participated in the negotiations since 2009. Several economies have expressed their interests in joining in the agreement, including Thailand, Philippines, Korea and Taiwan. Other ASEAN Member States may also consider participation when they think they are better prepared in the future. If more ASEAN Member States turn their attention to the TPP, it may undermine the RECP.

A few factors clearly demonstrate that the design of the RCEP initiative is affected by the TPP. Firstly, facing TPP's original timeline to complete negotiations by 2013, the RCEP sets a very tight timeline to conclude negotiations by end of 2015. Secondly, the TPP adheres to APEC's open regionalism, and has an open accession clause that allows accession by "any other APEC economies or countries" in the future. The RCEP follows suit and also sets an open accession clause to open for "any other ASEAN FTA partner countries or any other extra economic partners in the region" to participate in the future. In fact, quite contrary to APEC's open regionalism, ASEAN has been a rather closed forum and has never adopted an open accession clause in its existing FTAs. In addition, the open accession clause also reflects ASEAN's consideration of expanding economic integration beyond its current Dialogue partner countries.

Comprehensive Economic Partnership, the RCEP will allow ASEAN's other FTA Partners and external economic partner to participate after it concludes negotiations of the current 16 participating members.

10 The TPP began in 2005 as the Trans-Pacific Strategic Partnership Agreement (TPSEP) with 4 members – Singapore, Brunei, Chile and New Zealand, and then expanded to the current 12 negotiating members (Australia, Brunei Darussalam, Canada, Chile, Japan, Malaysia, Mexico, New Zealand, Peru, Singapore, United States, and Vietnam)

Thirdly, the TPP pursues high standard and comprehensive liberalization, the RCEP also targeted at an ambitious and comprehensive trade agreement when it was launched. However, as the RCEP moved into more detailed negotiations, the liberalization targets for both goods and services were lowered due to difficulty to reach consensus among all participating countries.

In terms of economic incentives or potential gains, it is often argued that RCEP will create larger economic gains to individual ASEAN Member States and its FTA partners. Firstly, with China and India participating in the RCEP, the population and market size of RCEP will provide larger economic gains than the TPP. Secondly, the flexibility and respect for participating members' different nature, instead of the "one size fits all" approach adopted in the TPP, make RCEP negotiations easier than the TPP. Last but not least, RCEP will build on the existing ASEAN+1 FTAs, meaning less adjustment costs for ASEAN Member States.

As of June 2015, the RCEP has conducted eight rounds of negotiations and two ministerial meetings, focusing on the agreed negotiation areas which include trade in goods, trade in services, investment, economic and technical cooperation, intellectual property rights, competition, dispute settlement, and other areas. Under the Trade Negotiation Committee (TNC), working groups are organized on Trade in Goods, Trade in Services, Investment, Economic and Technical Cooperation, Intellectual Property, Competition, and Legal and Institutional Issues.[11] In order to conclude the negotiations by year's end, the RCEP may wrap up its negotiations of major issues while leave other unfinished items in the built-in agenda in its subsequent negotiations. As such, the RCEP is clearly distinct with the TPP as the latter adopts a single undertaking approach and will not conclude until all negotiating issues are agreed upon.

---

11 Japan Ministry of Economy, Trade and Industry, "*Joint Press Release with the Ministry of Foreign Affairs*," Feb. 5, 2015, <http://www.meti.go.jp/english/press/2015/0205_01.html>.

III. The Changing Taiwan-ASEAN Economic and Trade Relation

1. The investment-driven Taiwan-ASEAN Economic Ties

Taiwanese firms began to relocate their manufacturing facilities in Southeast Asia since the 1980s as a response to the scarcity of natural resources and increasing land and labour costs in the home market.

However, in the 1990s the rise of China has changed Taiwanese firms' investment decisions and since then gradually replaced Southeast Asia as the hub for Taiwanese manufacturing operations.[12] Despite the government's "Go South" policy in the 1990s trying to encourage investors to "go South" instead of "go West", Taiwanese investment in China continued to grow. The Asian Financial Crisis in 1997/1998 in Southeast Asia and anti-China riots in 1998 in Indonesia further scared Taiwanese investors away from the region.

In the past decades, Taiwan's FDIs in Southeast Asia have undergone significant changes in different periods of time. According to statistics, prior to the middle to late 1990s, Indonesia, Thailand and Malaysia remained the top three destinations of Taiwan's outbound FDIs in the region, accumulated FDIs in these three countries accounting for up to 85% of the total FDIs in the region. Most of the FDIs focused in manufacturing sectors, aimed at exporting to North America and other international markets. Most of the investors were small and medium sized companies. It was only until around middle of the 1990s that Taiwanese investors, particularly larger companies, began to seriously look into the potentials of the domestic markets of certain host countries and then adjusted their investment decisions accordingly.

---

12 The government of Taiwan had adopted a No-Engagement policy with China since 1949 until Present Lee relaxed the bans and allowed Taiwanese citizens to visit China and indirect trade and investment in 1992.

In addition to investing in the old ASEAN Member States, some Taiwanese investors began to set foot in the new ASEAN Member States, mainly Vietnam and Cambodia. To take advantage of the low labour cost in these emerging economies, Taiwanese investment focused in labour intensive manufacturing industry in Vietnam and then Cambodia. Same as the expansion trend in other ASEAN Member States, FDIs in Vietnam then expanded to more capital- and technology-intensive industry, with locations also moving from South Vietnam to North Vietnam.

According to Taiwan's FDI Statistics, between 2004 and 2014, total Taiwanese investment in mainland China reached USD109.65 billion, accounting for 68.16 percent of the total outbound FDI in this period, while total investment in ASEAN reached USD 17.31 billion, accounting for 10.76 percent of the total outbound FDI. If informal estimation of total FDI stock is considered, Taiwanese FDI stock in mainland China may reach USD250 to USD300 billion, accounting for more than 70 to 75 percent of Taiwan's total overseas FDI stock.

According to data of host countries in ASEAN, the total volume of FDI stock from Taiwan to ASEAN as of end-2014 amounted to around USD 84.12 billion. However, as this amount does not include the Taiwanese investment via third country or by a holding company registered in a third country, it is estimated that the total investment from Taiwan, direct and indirect, may be significantly larger. For example, according to Ministry of Planning and Investment in Vietnam, Taiwanese FDI stock totaled USD 27.87 billion, while Taiwan's informal estimation was around USD 45 billion. Therefore, Taiwanese investment is ASEAN has been under-presented due to the incomplete statistics.

According to ASEAN statistics, as of end-2014, Taiwanese FDI stock ranks as No. 3 in Thailand, No.4 in Malaysia and Vietnam, No. 6 in

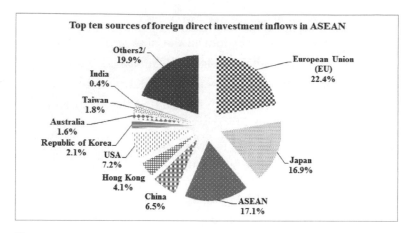

Figure 2: Top 10 Sources of FDI inflows in ASEAN (2011~2013)

Source: ASEAN Secretariat.

Cambodia, No. 9 in the Philippines and No. 10 in Indonesia.[13] Although Taiwan is still a principle investor in Southeast Asia, it lags far behind major competitors such as Japan and Korea, and the new comer Mainland China.

Furthermore, when considering newly registered FDI projects by Taiwanese firms and not including indirect FDI projects from a third country, according to statistics released by ASEAN Secretariat, Taiwan ranked only as the 9th among the 10 largest source of FDI in ASEAN during 2011 and 2013, accounting for only around 1.8 percent of ASEAN's total FDI inflows during the 3-year period. (see Figure 2).

There is a close correlation between Taiwanese FDI in ASEAN and its FDI in China. Since the mid-2000s when investment environment in China began to appear less favorable, some Taiwanese firms began to look outside China in search of both overseas investment destinations and new markets. Wage increase, shortage of labour in Southeast coastal provinces of China

---

13 經濟部投資業務處，《我國在東協各國投資統計表》，<http://www.dois.moea.gov. tw/asp/relation3.asp>。

and enforcement of more stringent labour and environmental legislations all drove an increasing number of Taiwanese firms away from the once "World Factory". Some ASEAN Member States, particularly the most populous Indonesia and the Philippines, as well as the CLMV countries, notably Vietnam, Cambodia and Myanmar, hence began to entice these investors with their abundant labour force and lower wages. The sharp growth in contrast to the consecutive decline of Taiwanese FDI outflows in China since 2009 suggests an emerging trend of Taiwanese firms "returning" to Southeast Asia.

According to Taiwanese Customs, China (including Hong Kong) has become Taiwan's largest trading partner since the mid-2000s, while ASEAN remains the second largest export market for decades. In 2014, trade with China (including Hong Kong) accounted for 39.78 percent of Taiwan's total exports, reaching USD 124.80 billion, and 18.15 percent of its total imports, reaching USD 49.73 billion. Trade with ASEAN accounted for 18.98 percent of Taiwan's total exports, totaling USD 59.53 billion, and 12.45 percent of its total imports, totaling USD 34.12 billion.

It is important to note that a large share of bilateral trade between Taiwan and China and between Taiwan and ASEAN is made with intermediate goods, representing a close links of intra-industry trade between Taiwan and its two major FDI destinations. Among Taiwan's exports to ASEAN, a significant share is made by local manufacturers (including Taiwanese and other foreign and local manufacturers) importing from Taiwan machineries, raw materials, components, spare parts and semi-finished products needed for local assembly for re-exporting to international markets. However, growth of imports from Taiwan has slowed down in recent years resulting from gradual development of local industries and trade diversion from other countries, such as China and South Korea which have signed FTAs with ASEAN and receive preferential treatments than Taiwanese products. Such market access barriers made by differential tariffs are one major factor that has driven Taiwanese firms to relocate manufacturing operations from Taiwan to the region in the past years.

2. Taiwan Businesses' Response to the AEC and RCEP: Clustering Value Chains in Southeast Asia

Some ASEAN Member States show relatively higher trade orientation than others, including Singapore, Malaysia, Thailand, Viet Nam and, to a lesser extent, Cambodia. Among them, Singapore, Malaysia and Thailand are the main ASEAN participants in regional production networks or global value chains (GVCs). Since recent years Vietnam has also participated in the production networks, which contributes further to ASEAN's increasingly important role in the rise of the "Asian Factory".

ASEAN's participation in the global value chains can be attributed to inflows of FDIs in the past four decades which have disseminated capital and technology in the region. The major FDI sources include Japan, the earliest pioneer, followed by Taiwan and then Korea, and China catching up in the recent years. The FTAs ASEAN has signed with China, Japan and Korea further facilitated trade of intermediate goods and encouraged FDIs from these three FTA Partners into the region to establish their manufacturing operations.

Different from other three ASEAN FTA Partners, Taiwan has not yet negotiated an FTA with ASEAN, so Taiwanese FDI into the region mainly resulted from market-driven activities. The production networks established by Taiwan-invested manufacturing operations since the 1980s have made possible development of manufacturing sectors and economic restructuring in the host ASEAN member States. The intra-industry trade and investment links between Taiwan and ASEAN have formed deep economic interdependence and contributed to Taiwan's de facto integration in the region. They have also enhanced ASEAN Member States' participation in the regional or global value chains.

In order to further respond to the accelerated development in the ASEAN-centric integration, including the initiatives of the RCEP and the TPP currently under negotiation, more Taiwanese firms are planning or considering relocation or expansion of their operations into ASEAN. According to a recent informal survey by Chung Hua Institution for Economic Research, Taiwan, three types of relocation activities are now taking place: relocation from Taiwan into ASEAN, relocation from China into ASEAN, and relocation within ASEAN region from more advanced countries to the CLMV countries.[14]

First of all, the trend of relocation from Taiwan into ASEAN reflected Taiwan businesses' more acute concerns towards the proliferation of FTAs in the East Asia, including the ASEAN+1 FTAs and the upcoming mega FTA of the RCEP. The accelerated economic integration among ASEAN and other countries is driving Taiwanese firms to relocate their operations from Taiwan into the region in order to avoid high tariffs of ASEAN Member States. Taiwanese firms can also take advantage of ASEAN's increasing FTA networks to export to other international markets. For example, Vietnam's participation in the TPP and conclusion of FTA negotiation with EU has attracted investment boom from Taiwan to set manufacturing operations in the hub for exporting to the US and the EU markets.

Different from consideration of tariff barriers, the relocation from China into ASEAN and relocation within ASEAN region from ASEAN's six old Member States to CLMV countries reflect consideration of operational costs. For example, an increasing number of Taiwanese firms move to ASEAN from China as the production costs and other indirect costs in China are becoming less affordable. As for relocation within ASEAN region, for example, some Taiwanese firms relocate from Thailand to the Philippines or Myanmar in order to take advantage of the latter's abundant and cheaper labour force.

---

14 Kristy Hsu, "AEC 2015: Taiwan Industry Response," Paper present at the "Toward ASEAN Economic Community: Investment Liberalization, Protection, and Emerging Trends" (Taipei: CIER, Oct. 29, 2004), <http://www.aseancenter.org.tw/upload/files/20141029_1-2.pdf>

It is important to note that, in order to respond to the AEC that aims to make ASEAN a single market and production base, larger Taiwanese firms also consolidate their separate manufacturing operations into one or two ASEAN Member States and thus have made clusters of sector-specific value chains. For example, the textile industry is building value chains in Vietnam that include downstream, middle stream and upper stream production processes. Thanks to the "Yarn Forward" Rules of Origins demand in the TPP, Vietnam has seen increasing investment into the country from manufacturing fabrics, yarns, dying to cloths and garments. Another example is an emerging cluster of electronics industry in the Philippines. Taiwanese electronics firms are relocating from China (mostly from Southeastern coastal provinces), Thailand and even Vietnam to the populous country. It is also reported that Taiwan's electronics industry plans to establish a Taiwan-based industrial zone in Myanmar to facilitate Small and Medium Sized Taiwanese electronics companies to invest in the emerging market.

Following the manufacturers, Taiwan's services sector is also actively setting foot in the region. The financial services, logistics and transportation, ICT-enabled services and e-commerce are among the most active investors. However, decause of the restrictions in services sector in certain ASEAN Member States, most of the service companies choose to invest in joint venture or through merge or acquisition of local firms.

IV. Conclusions and the Way Forward

The AEC 2015 Vision is not yet fully fulfilled, but ASEAN has managed to make significant achievements, particularly in eliminating tariffs and other forms of non-tariff barriers among ASEAN Member States and with its FTA Partner countries. When the RCEP is concluded and implemented in the future, ASEAN's centric role in the regional economic integration will be further enhanced.

Taiwan has played an important role in the economic development of Southeast Asia. However, as Taiwan does not yet have an FTA with ASEAN and may not be part of RECP in the near future, Taiwan businesses cannot afford to be excluded from the ASEAN-centric integration. The changing investment climate in China also drives the investment activities into ASEAN. The emerging trend of Taiwanese companies "returning" to ASEAN after the "Go South" policy in the 1990s explains the importance of ASEAN to Taiwan.

In early 2014, President Ma Ying Jeou of Taiwan announced that Taiwan will try all efforts to join the TPP and the RCEP in order to help Taiwan industry to compete with its Korean and Japanese competitors on a level playing field. The decision is based on the fact that both the TPP and the RCEP have an open accession clause that enables new member economies to accede on a consensus base. However, given the accession clause, the path to the TPP and RCEP is full of political and economic barriers.

There are growing concerns that Taiwan will be excluded and discriminated in the regional integration. While ASEAN moves towards an economic and political community, Taiwan has to work with ASEAN and its Member States to promote a new partnership that would respond to common interests and shared prosperity. ASEAN also needs to work with Taiwan in order to further benefit from Taiwan's outward investment trends and unique role in regional/global value chains.

On ASEAN side, it has been a policy choice for most ASEAN developing Member States to participate in the GVCs with more value addition. All leaders in Indonesia, the Philippines, Vietnam, Cambodia and even Myanmar wish their countries to play a more important role in certain GVCs and continue to upgrade their export structure by capturing larger value-added share in trade. The establishment of more Taiwan-based industrial clusters in ASEAN may create a win-win solution for both Taiwan and the region.

This paper suggests the following policy direction for Taiwan to work with ASEAN Member States to help develop a stronger manufacturing sector and enhance participation in the global value chains.

The first recommendation is to prepare sufficient skilled human capital. In order to promote higher value added activities in supply chains, such as textile, electronics and ICT products, a large supply of skilled and experienced work force is needed to handle a full range of supply chain functions. This involves training and skill enhancement of the workers in resource-based and low-level manufacturing sectors towards more technology and management sophisticated activities. Taiwan has experienced similar transformation when it began to upgrade its industrial structure from labour intensive industry to technology-based industry in the 1980s. Taiwan and ASEAN can share experiences and create joint efforts to promote human resource development in the ASEAN Member States.

The second recommendation is to remove trade barriers that hinder international trade and Taiwan's investment activities. Increasing studies indicate that tariffs and non-tariff barriers, such as rigid product standards and customs practices not in compliance with international standards, may become significant impediments to trade of intermediate goods and functioning of GVCs. For example, due to severe competition in electronics industry leading to very low profit margin for mass-produced electronics parts and components, even very low tariffs may hinder their trade activities. This explains why a lot of GVCs are developed among countries that have FTAs to provide zero tariffs and other facilitating treatments for trade of intermediate goods among the countries. By removing tariffs and non-tariff barriers, ASEAN can encourage more Taiwanese firms to invest in the region.

Last but not least, this paper suggests Taiwan government to create a supportive business climate and provide investment assistance. Taiwan should create a supportive environment and friendly climate to help and guide

Taiwan's outbound FDI activities, while also provide investment assistance to encourage companies to establish main functions in Taiwan, such as logistics hub, R&D and marketing. This will help strengthen business links between Taiwan and ASEAN (and with China).

To sum up, ASEAN and Taiwan can work together in participation in the regional production networks. The past three decades of industrial development and overseas investment in the region have enabled Taiwan to stand at a strategic position in the GVCs. As an increasing number of Taiwanese firms are relocating their manufacturing bases in ASEAN and consider it a potential new "Factory of Asia", ASEAN and Taiwan can work together to improve productivity and quality in the manufacturing sector. They can develop a comprehensive partnership that covers cooperation in high value added manufacturing industries and knowledge based services, R & D collaboration, and joint human resource development, among others. Moreover, Taiwan's investment in China will strengthen the triangular collaboration among Taiwan, ASEAN and China, and hence contribute to ASEAN's efforts to climb up the ladder of the GVCs.

Trend and Determinants of Pan-Asian Economic Integration: Evidence from Regional Trade Statistics

Jeet Bahadur Sapkota[*]
Motoko Shuto[**]

Abstract

This paper examines the trend and determinants of economic integration in Asia in terms of the trade intensity index (TII) and intra-regional trade share. ADB's ARIC database revealed that despite rapid increase in intra-Asian trade volume of all countries from 1990 to 2012, the trends of intra-regional trade share of different countries are different indicating that countries in the region are functioning independently and stronger economic tie is yet to build within the Asian region and its sub-regions. Furthermore, the dynamic panel data analysis resulted that FTAs/RTAs are one of the main determinants of growing intra-Asian trade share. Other determinants are countries' level of economic development, FDI stock, urban population growth and access to ICT. Thus, it is argued that active participation in FTAs/RTAs, open FDI policy, urbanization and technological development of Asian countries create enabling environment for pan-Asian economic integration.

I. Introduction

Recent regional integration efforts are increasing towards Pan-Asian economic integration (Wignaraja 2014). Despite continued efforts on deeper

---

*   Assistant Professor, Humanities and Social Science, University of Tsukuba.
** Professor, Humanities and Social Science, University of Tsukuba.

integration at each sub-regional level, countries from East Asia, Southeast Asia, South Asia, Oceania and Pacific are involving in the negotiations of large integration initiatives, such as Regional Comprehensive Economic Partnership (RCEP) (Chia 2013). However, there is no such a bold effort that can pave the way for realizing Asia-wide regional integration in the near future. In this context, this paper examines the trend and determinants of economic integration in Asia in terms of the trade intensity index (TII) and intra-regional trade share.

Asian trade within the Asia and with the world is increased rapidly over the last two decades. This trend is contributed by continuous unilateral as well as plurilateral liberalization by many Asian countries and sub-regions at various time (Rai 2010). However, unlike Europe and North America where regional integration is driven by policy and institution, Economic integration in Asia is still largely market driven. As Kumar (2009) argued, Asian economic integration followed the "flying geese pattern", which means capital, technology, and know-how moved from more developed to less developed nations. For instance, it first moved from Japan to the Asian economic tigers[1] and then to other Southeast Asian countries, mainly to Thailand, Malaysia, Indonesia, and the Philippines. The economic integration process was further fueled by trade and investments liberalization along with the production fragmentation across countries. Policy driven regional integration is also becoming visible after the Asian financial crisis (1997/98). Different forms of bilateral free trade agreements (FTAs) and regional trade agreements (RTAs) are proliferating within and outside Asia, and currently, every country is engaging in some FTAs or RTAs. However, most of the RTAs are at sub-regional level, and the broader pan-Asian level cooperation is not progressing well. Furthermore, these agreements are very different

---

1   The "Asian economic tigers" is a widely used term in development discourse, which refers to the newly emerged economic powers in Asia namely Hong Kong, Singapore, South Korea, and Taiwan. These countries achieved rapid economic development achieved rapid economic development through outward looking open economic policies for development.

from each other, in terms of its scope, coverage, and commitments, therefore, Kawai and Wignaraja (2009) argued that multiple trade agreements can be detrimental to increasing trade due to the "spaghetti bowl effect".[2] Similarly, various studies revealed that broader and deeper economic cooperation at the pan-Asian level would generate tremendous gains, hence opposed integration among a small group of countries at different sub-regional levels (Urata, 2013). Thus, it is worthwhile to observe the progress toward broader pan-Asian regional integration though it is still largely market driven.

The paper is organized as follows. Section 2 examines the trend of inter sub-regional and intra-regional trade in Asia. Economic Integration database of Asian Development Bank's Asian Regional Integration Center (ARIC) revealed that the trade volume of each country in Asia toward Asia as well as toward the world increased dramatically over the last two decades. However, the trends of intra-regional trade are not similar across countries. Section 3 assesses the determinants of intra-regional trade in the region, which finds the positive and significant impacts from FTAs/RTAs with Asian countries, GNI per capita, foreign direct investment (FDI) and urbanization. However, the economic size of the countries or economies has negative and significant impact on intra-regional trade share. Section 4 concludes the paper.

II. Pan-Asian intra-regional and inter sub-regional trade

In terms of population and geographical sizes, Asia is the largest continent. Asia covers 30% of the global terrestrial surface providing shelter for about 60% of global population. Hence, Asia possesses a high degree of sociocultural, developmental as well as political diversity. Thus, there are many sub-regions within Asia involving in sub-regional integration initiatives, such as Association of South East Asian Nations (ASEAN) of

---

2   A well-known economist Jagdish Bhagwati first used the term "spaghetti bowl effect" in 1995, which refers to the problems likely due to many rules of origin of a product and other complexity cause by involving in many FTAs.

10 countries from Southeast Asia and South Asian Association for Regional Cooperation (SAARC) of 7 countries of South Asia.[3] However, broader regional integration initiatives across the sub-regions are underway with little progress. For instance, Regional Comprehensive Economic Partnership (RCEP) widely known as ASEAN plus six, and ASEAN plus three (APT) groupings of integration are under discussion.[4] Interestingly, Asian regional integration initiatives broaden its scope bringing its neighboring regions, especially from Oceania and Pacific Islands, in the integration process.

Therefore, Asia is defined in a broader perspectives comprising from East to West Asia, North to South Asia, two Oceanian countries, Australia and New Zealand, and the Pacific Island countries.[5] All the countries are included as long as data are sufficiently available for analysis. Based on the ADB's country grouping, Appendix 1 shows the list of countries for each group highlighting the countries, which are covered in this study.

1. Intra-regional trade by country/economy

Figure 1 shows the trend of total trade volume of Asian countries to Asia from 1990 to 2012. It clearly indicates the increasing trend of trade volume towards Asia from its member economies; People's Republic of China (PRC), Japan, and Hong Kong remained at the top 1st, 2nd and 3rd rank in 2012, respectively. We can observe the similar trend of total trade volume from Asian economies to the world in Figure 2. Although Republic of Korea

---

3   Member countries of ASEAN include Brunei Darussalam, Cambodia, Indonesia, Lao PDR, Malaysia, Myanmar, the Philippines, Singapore, Thailand and Vietnam. Similarly, current member states of the SAARC are Afghanistan, Bangladesh, Bhutan, India, Maldives, Nepal, Pakistan and Sri Lanka.

4   CEP or ASEAN plus six consist of 10 ASEAN countries plus China, Japan, Republic of Korea, India, Australia and New Zealand. Similarly, ASEAN plus three (APT) includes 10 ASEAN member states plus China, Japan and Republic of Korea.

5   ARIC regional integration database of ADB covers 48 countries from Asia, Oceania and the Pacific as a group of Asia. This study follows the same groupings as it uses the ARIC database. It is rationale, indeed, to include Australia, New Zealand, and the Pacific countries because some of these countries are already in the broader Asian integration process.

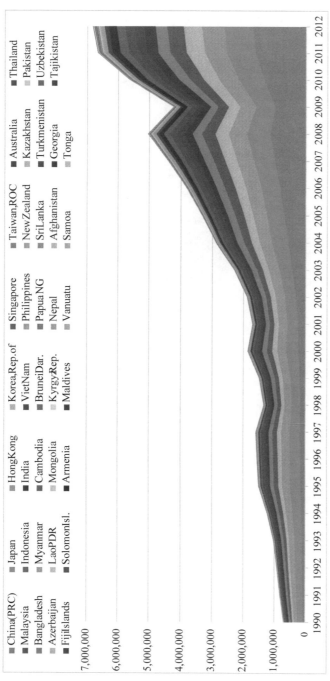

Figure 1: Total trade volume from Asian countries to Asia, 1990-2012 (million US$)

Notes: PRC=People's Republic of China, Rep.=Republic, NG= New Guinea, ROC=Republic of China, Dar.= Darussalam, Isl.=Island

Source: The author using the data from ARIC Regional Integration Indicator database, available at: <http://aric.adb.org/integrationindicators>, accessed: March 7, 2015.

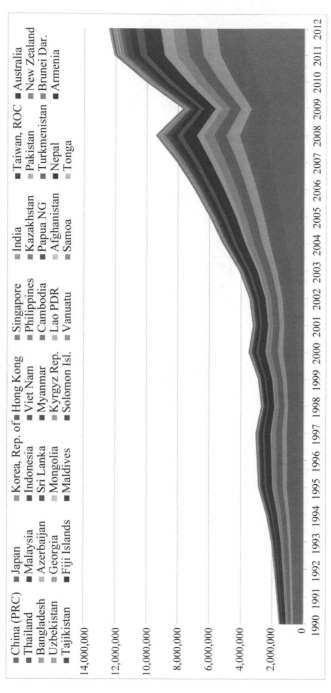

Figure 2: Total trade volume from Asian countries to the world, 1990-2012 (million US$)

Notes: PRC=People's Republic of China, Rep.=Republic, NG= New Guinea, ROC=Republic of China, Dar.= Darussalam, Isl.=Island

Source: The author using the data from ARIC Regional Integration Indicator database, available at: <http://aric.adb.org/integrationindicators>, accessed: March 7, 2015.

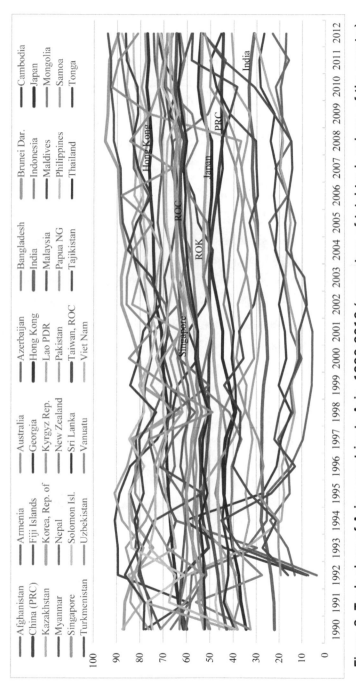

Figure 3: Trade share of Asian countries to Asia, 1990-2012 (percentage of total trade volume of the country)

Notes: PRC=People's Republic of China, Rep.=Republic, NG= New Guinea, ROC=Republic of China, Dar.= Darussalam, Isl.=Island

Source: The author using the data from ARIC Regional Integration Indicator database, available at: <http://aric.adb.org/integrationindicators>, accessed: March 7, 2015.

(ROK) replaced the 3rd place, the overall trend is mostly similar. In general, the trade volume of Asian countries to Asia as well as to the world increased over the time but rapid growth observed from 2002. Despite a sharp drop in 2009 due to the huge global economic crisis, the trade volume rose sharply thereafter for most of the major economies of Asia in general. As the total trade of Asian economies to Asia and the world follow the similar trend, it cannot point out whether the regional economic integration is advancing within the region vis-à-vis with the world.

In order to examine the depth of regional economic integration in Asia, Figure 3 shows the trade share of Asian economies to Asia.[6] Unlike the trend of trade volume, trade share to Asia of its countries and economies are not similar. For example, trade share to Asia is growing slowly for Japan, Hong Kong, Taiwan, ROK, and Singapore; whereas, it is declining for PRC, and some Central Asian and the Pacific countries. Interestingly, the trade share of Hong Kong to Asia remained more than 75%, Taiwan and Singapore remained more than 60%, and Japan and ROK remained more than 50% in 2012. In the same year, trade share to Asia remained at 44.5% and 31.13% for PRC and India, respectively.

These trends indicate that trade integration in Asia is not progressing significantly over the last two decades as some countries' Asian trade share is declining where as it is increasing or remained stable for other countries. Huge diversity, prolonged territorial disputes among major economic powers,[7] and relatively cold bilateral relations among neighboring countries are hindering the regional integration process.

---

6   As defined by ADB, "trade share is the percentage of trade with a partner to the total trade of a country/region. It is computed as the dollar value of total trade of country/region i with country/region j expressed as a percentage share of the dollar value of total trade of country/region i with the world. A higher share indicates a higher degree of integration between partner countries/regions" (Available at: http://aric.adb.org/integrationindicators/ technotes, Accessed: March 18, 2015).

7   In Asia, PRC, Japan, ROK, and India are among the major economic powers having problems in their bilateral relations.

2. Intra-regional trade by sub-region

Figure 4 presents the trend of intra-regional and intra sub-regional trade share in Asia. Sub-regions of Asia and the list of countries for each sub-region are presented in Appendix 1. It shows gradual but slow increasing intra-East Asian and intra-Southeast Asian trade share. Intra-regional trade in East Asian rose from 28.58% in 1990 to about 40.6% in 2004, which declined to 35.87% in 2012. Intra-regional trade in Southeast Asia rose from nearly 17% to 24.56% from 1990 to 2012, respectively.

However, there is rather a stable trend for South Asia, whose intra-regional trade share remained around 2% to 3% over the period of 1990 to 2012. Other sub-regions; the Pacific, Oceania, and Central & West Asia experienced even decreasing trend (especially from around 1995).

Intra-regional trade in Asia, however, increased (slowly though) from 45.2% in 1990 to 55.94% in 2010. Then, the region experienced slowdown

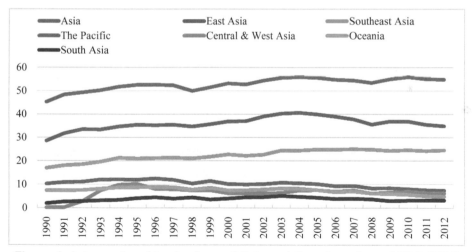

Figure 4: Intra-regional trade share of Asia and its sub-regions, 1990-2012 (% of total trade)

Source: The author using the data from ARIC Regional Integration Indicator database, available at: http:// aric.adb.org/integrationindicators, accessed: March 7, 2015.

marginally reaching 54.85% in 2012. The trend also clearly indicates the adverse effect of regional and global financial crisis on regional economic integration process as the trend are declining around 1997-98 and 2008-09 when the region was suffered severely from the Asian financial crisis and global financial crisis respectively.

In the context of growing efforts on pan-Asian integration, there is increasing interest on inter sub-regional trade flows in Asia. To detect such flows in relation to global trade, trade intensity index (TII) is used. TII shows the relative importance of trade of a region with another region vis-à-vis global trade.[8] Specifically, as defined in the Integration Indicators technical notes of ARIC home page, TII of region A to region B is the ratio of the proportion of trade from region A to region B with region A's total trade with the world and the global trade share to region B. Specifically, TII from region A to region B (TII_{AB}) is calculated as:

$$TII_{AB} = \cfrac{t_{AB}/T_{AW}}{t_{WB}/T_{WW}}$$

where, t_{AB} is the amount of total trade of region A with region B, T_{AW} is the amount of the total trade of region A with the world, t_{WB} is the amount of world trade with region B, and T_{WW} is the total dollar value of world trade.

The TII_{AB} value exceeding one means the trade flow between the region A and region B is more than expected given their importance in the world trade. TII for Asia and some of the sub-regions over the period of 1990 to 2012 are presented as follows.

Figure 5 presents the TII of East Asia with Asia and its other sub-regions from 1990 to 2012. TII with Oceania, the Pacific, Southeast Asia and

---

8   The original definition of TII is available at: <http://aric.adb.org/integrationindicators/technotes, accessed: March 20, 2015.

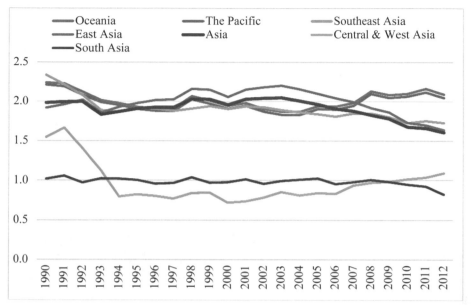

Figure 5: TII of East Asia with other Asian sub-regions, 1990-2012

Source: The author using the data from ARIC Regional Integration Indicator database, available at: http://
aric.adb.org/integrationindicators, accessed: March 7, 2015.

East Asia itself remained around 2 with small fluctuation during the period. Surprisingly, TII for East Asia, and with Southeast Asia is declining since 2003 indicating the reducing relative trading importance with the region. In fact, efforts and discussion of pan-Asian integration are concentrated on Association for South East Asian Nations (ASEAN) plus frameworks that primarily includes China, Japan, ROK and all the economies of Southeast Asia. It is also troublesome that East Asian TII with overall Asia is declining sharply from 2.05 to 1.61 from 2003 to 2012, respectively.

Interestingly, the relative importance of East Asian trade with the Pacific and Oceania is not only remained high with TII more than two since 2007 but also increasing since 2004. Thus, it is worthwhile including these regions in overall Asian integration.

On the other hand, TII value of East Asia remained about one for South Asia until 2008, but declined to 0.82 in 2012. It indicates that East Asia should develop strategies to increase trade with South Asia to increase the gain from pan-Asian integration. It is encouraging for East Asia that the TII with Central and West Asia is climbed over one in 2010 and sharply increasing since then as well.

Figure 6 presents TII of Southeast Asia with Asia and its other sub-regions from 1990 to 2012. TII with the own region, Southeast Asia, remained highest around four, but it fluctuated sharply reaching the lowest of 3.27 in 1996 and reached the highest of 4.33 in 2007. However, it declined sharply since then and reached 3.57 in 2012. TII with East Asia declined from 2.27 to 1.71 during the period. Similarly, TII with South Asia also declined particularly from 2002. Although TII with Oceania increased up

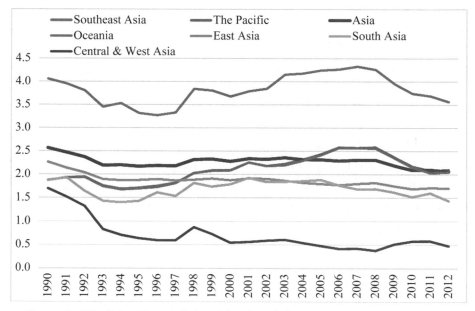

Figure 6: TII of Southeast Asia with other Asian sub-regions, 1990-2012

Source: The author using the data from ARIC Regional Integration Indicator database, available at: http://aric.adb.org/integrationindicators, accessed: March 7, 2015.

to 2006 reaching 2.57, it declined sharply since then. TII with Central and West Asia showed the worst record, which declined from 1.7 to 0.47 during the period. These results indicate that Southeast Asia need to revise its trade policy towards its neighboring regions in Asia if they aspire to be the key player in Asian integration.

Similarly, although TII with overall Asia remained over two during the period, the trend is declining from 2.57 to 2.07 over the period. It indicates Southeast Asia will face more challenges to play the key role in pan-Asian integration. However, as the most integrated sub-region in Asia with stronger institutional setup compared to other sub-regions, ASEAN is expected to play a key role in the pan-Asian integration process (Kurlantzick 2012).

Figure 7 presents the TII of South Asia with Asia and its other sub-

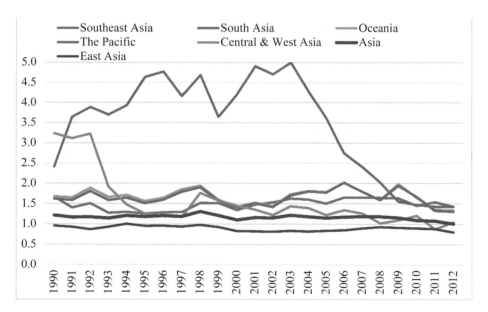

Figure 7: TII of South Asia with other Asian sub-regions, 1990-2012

Source: The author using the data from ARIC Regional Integration Indicator database, available at: http://aric.adb.org/integrationindicators, accessed: March 7, 2015.

regions from 1990 to 2012. TII with the own region, South Asia, remained highest until 2008 reaching the apex to nearly five but it dropped sharply right after that and reached the lowest point at 1.42 in 2012. The relative importance of trade to East Asia remained at the lowest level, which mostly remained below one, and the trend is declining over the period.

However, the TII value for other regions remained more than one but the trends are declining in general. Similarly, TII with overall Asia declined and remained marginally over one, which was declined gradually from 1.21 to 1.0 during the period. These results indicate that South Asia need to improve its trade policy with its neighboring regions in order to play a significant role in pan-Asian integration.

TII of Central and West Asia, Oceania, and the Pacific are presented in Appendix 2a to 2c. In case of Central and West Asia, TII for South Asia has is more than one since 1990; however, it is declining. TII with the own region, Central and West Asia, remained very high at 24.31 in 1995. However, it continuously declined and reached 7.58 in 2012 (Appendix 2a). TII of Oceania with the Pacific remained highest among with other sub-regions over the period, which reached the top at 7.66 in 1995. However, the trend declined sharply since 2003 reaching 3.88 in 2012 (Appendix 2b). Except for Central and West Asia, TII for other sub-regions is around two over the period indicating the key importance of Asia for the region. A similar trend can be observed for the TII of the Pacific with other sub-regions (Appendix 2c).

In overall, despite having the high importance of trade among sub-regions and the Asia as a whole, the importance is decreasing, which arguably reduces the motives for pan-Asian economic integration. The declining importance can also observe through the declining TII of Asian sub-regions with Asia as a whole as shown in Figure 8.

In order to examine the importance of whole Asian trade with its sub-regions, Figure 9 presents the TII of Asia as a whole with Asia and its sub-

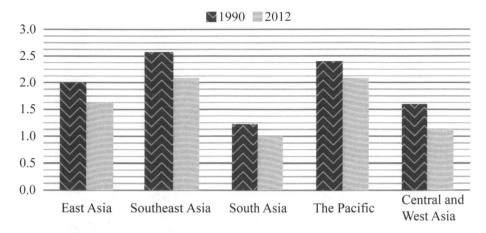

Figure 8: TII of sub-regions with Asia, 1990 and 2012

Notes: There is no data for Oceania
Source: The author using the data from ARIC Regional Integration Indicator database, available at: http://
         aric.adb.org/integrationindicators, accessed: March 7, 2015.

regions from 1990 to 2012. Interestingly, the TII for all the sub-regions are more than one, which indicates the greater importance of trade flows with its sub-regions vis-à-vis with the world. Among the sub-regions, TII with Southeast Asia remained highest around 5, but fluctuating in between 4.4 and 5.8 during the period. The Pacific and Oceania follows the similar trend ranging from 2.4 in 1990 to 2.1 in 2012. The similar trends of TII follow with Asia as whole itself and East Asia, which also declined from about two to about 1.6 respectively during the same period. South Asia and Central & West Asia remained at the bottom with TII about one.

The TII of Asia as a whole to its sub-regions indicates that the relative importance of trade within the region is greater than with the world. A similar conclusion can be drawn from the TII of Asian sub-regions discussed above. These results signify a strong desirability of pan-Asian economic integration, which supports the enormous benefits that showed by many empirical assessments.

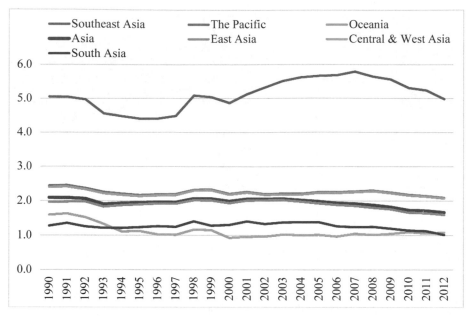

Figure 9: TII of Asia with its sub-regions, 1990-2012

Source: The author using the data from ARIC Regional Integration Indicator database, available at:
<http://aric.adb.org/integrationindicators>, accessed: March 7, 2015.

However, it is not welcoming results that the TII trends are decreasing for most of the sub-regions, and the Asia as a whole as well. It is more worrisome that the declining trend is sharper in recent years for most of the sub-regions. This might be due to the faster pace of growth in global trade integration compared to the regional trade integration.

Thus, what determines the pace of regional economic integration in general and intra-regional trade, in particular, is one of the main concerns for regional integration efforts. Next section explores major determinants of intra-regional trade in Asia.

III. Determinants of intra-regional trade share

1. Model specification

In order to find out the determinants of intra-regional trade share of Asian countries and economies, we employ the dynamic panel data model implemented by Roodman (2005), which is explained in detail by Roodman (2009) in Stata. The intra-Asian trade share of each of the 39 selected countries is the dependent variable.[9] The annual data from 1990 to 2012 is used which is mainly taken from two online databases namely ADB-ARIC Integration Indicators and the World Development Indicators (WDI).[10] As trade share of each country in Asia changes slowly over time and current level of intra-regional trade share also depends on their past level of intra-regional trade share. Thus, the lagged dependent variable is also included in the explanatory variables as one of the major determinants. However, this creates a dynamic structure of the model hence fixed country effects, and the OLS estimator becomes biased and inconsistent in short panels (Nickell, 1981). In order to overcome such problems, Arellano and Bover (1995) and Blundell and Bond (1998) suggested system generalized method of moments (GMM) estimator (Sapkota 2014). The model is specified as follows:

$$Y_{it} = \alpha + \beta_1 Y_{it-1} + \beta_2 X_{it} + \eta_i + \eta_t + \varepsilon_{it}$$

where; Y_{it} represents the dependent variables of country i at year t. Y_{it-1} is one period lag of the dependent variable, X_{it} represents the set of determinants of intra-regional trade share, η_i is the country fixed effect, η_t is the time-varying effect, and ε_{it} is an error term. β_1 and β_2 are the coefficient of each explanatory variable, which are the parameters of interest. α is the constant term. The correlation matrix and the summary statistics of the

---

9   Selected countries are listed in Appendix 1.

10 The ADB-ARIC Integration Indicators is available at: <http://aric.adb.org/ Integrationindicators> and the World Development Indicators (WDI) is available at: <http://data.worldbank.org/data-catalog/world-development-indicators>.

dependent and independent variables are given the appendix 3a and 3b.

GMM is appropriate for our data for several reasons. Firstly, if the independent variables and the error term "ε_{it}" in the model are not independent, unobserved variables can affect both the outcome variable and independent variable, so the estimated coefficients can be biased. Such problem of endogeneity can be partially solved by controlling fixed effects and time trend, but if some unobserved variable changes over time and across the countries, this problem will remain in the error term. GMM deal with this problem (Blundell and Bond 1998). Secondly, GMM is also appropriate for fixed individual effect (in our case, the country-specific effect), and heteroskedasticity and autocorrelation within individuals but not across them (Roodman 2009).

Several trade-related variables are considered as the major determinants of intra-regional trade share. Apart from the lag dependent variable, we consider each country's number of Free Trade Agreements (FTAs) or Regional Trade Agreements (RTAs), which are in effect with the Asian countries or sub-regions. Although the quality of FTAs and RTAs are different, gravity model revealed that FTAs/RTAs brings trade creation effect, and trade diversion effect is far limited in general (Urata and Okabe 2010). Similarly, countries' trade as a percentage of GDP is considered to examine whether the countries with more trade dependence trade more within the region.

Gross Domestic Product (GDP) in purchasing power parity (PPP) term is considered as one of the determinants of intra-regional trade because the traditional gravity model of trade considers size of economy and distance between trade partners as the major determinants of trade between them (Helpman, Melitz and Rubinstein 2008). It is expected that the bigger economy in Asia trade proportionately more within the region as Thornton and Goglio (2002) found the same in the case of Southeast Asia. The distance is ignored as this study uses intra-regional trade as the dependent variable instead of bilateral or inter-regional trade.

Gross National Income (GNP) per capita is considered another determinant of intra-regional trade share. GNP per capita is one of the widely used measures of the level of economic development, and it is expected to make positive impacts on intra-regional trade (Sharma and Chua 2000).

Similarly, foreign direct investment (FDI) stock as a percent of GDP is considered as another determinant. The literature, including Bilas and Franc (2010), suggest that the foreign capital creates dynamic, positive effects on regional economic integration. In addition, mobile cellular subscriptions (per 100 people) is included because mobile technology boost environment for international interaction and networking that helps to increase intra-regional trade (Bankole, Osei-Bryson and Brown 2013).

We also include urban population growth as a prospective determinant of intra-regional trade. Brakman and Marrewijk (2013) suggest that trade patterns may also depend on the level of urbanization between countries. Finally, value added from the service sector to GDP is considered as another determinant. As the service sector contribution to GDP increase along with human resource and other forms of development (Wagner 2012), service sector growth is expected to generate a positive effect on intra-regional trade.

System GMM uses a large matrix of available instruments and weights them properly to overcomes endogeneity problem. We assumed only trade-related variables, such as lag dependent variable, total trade as percentage of GDP, and number of FTAs as endogenous variable, and used as *gmmstyle* instruments in xtabond2 command in Stata as suggested by Roodman (2009). Rests of the variables are used as *ivstyle* instruments. The Sargan/Hansen test supports the joint validity of the instruments.

2. Results and Discussion

Table 1 presents the results. The asterisk (*) indicates the level of significance, where one asterisk (*) means 10% level of significance, two

Table 1: Determinant of intra-regional trade in Asia, 1990-2012
Dynamic panel-data estimation, two-step system GMM
Dependent variable: intra-regional trade with whole Asia (%)

Explanatory variables	
Trade Share (%) with the partner to whole Asia in prev. year	0.402***
	(0.035)
Trade (% of GDP)	0.003
	(0.009)
Number of FTAs/RTAs with Asian countries or sub-regions	0.476***
	(0.133)
Log of GDP, PPP (current in Billions $)	-2.240***
	(0.217)
Log of GNI per capita, Atlas method (current US$)	2.161***
	(0.444)
FDI stock (% of GDP)	0.022***
	(0.005)
Mobile cellular subscriptions (per 100 people)	0.014*
	(0.007)
Urban population growth rate (annual %)	3.213***
	(0.254)
Services (% of GDP)	0.009
	(0.033)
Constant	16.38***
	(4.709)
Observations	858
Number of countries	39

Notes: *** $p<0.01$, ** $p<0.05$, * $p<0.1$; Standard errors in parentheses; all data are annual. GDP and GNI per capita are in natural logarithm, because these two variables are in natural numbers, not in percent form.

Source: Data for dependent variable, FDI stock and number of FTAs/RTAs of all countries are taken from ARIC Regional Integration Indicator database of the Asian Development Bank available at: http://aric.adb.org/. Data for the remaining variables (except for Taiwan) are taken from the World Bank's WDI online database, available at: http://databank.worldbank.org/Data/ Databases.aspx. Data for Taiwan are taken from the ADB's Statistical Database System available online at: https://sdbs.adb.org/sdbs/index.jsp.

asterisks (**) means 5% level of significance, and three asterisks (***) means 1% level of significance. No asterisk means no significant effect. The sign of the coefficients indicates the direction of effect.

Among the trade-related variables, lag dependent variable and number of FTAs/RTAs are found highly significant at one percent level to increase intra-regional trade share of countries in Asia. While it is intuitive that past level affects the current level of intra-regional trade, the positive and significant effect of FTAs is consistent with the existing literature as Baier and Bergstrand (2007) empirically argued that bilateral FTA approximately doubles the trade between the members. Ghosh and Yamarik (2004) also found the trade-creating effect of RTAs as well. However, total trade and service sector value added both as a percent of GDP are found insignificant indicating that the trade dependence and service sector growth do not affect intra-regional trade. The reason behind these results needs further investigation.

The level of development measured by the log of GNI per capita is highly significant to increase intra-regional trade. It indicates that countries level of development boosts their trade capacity. However, the size of the economy measured by the log of GDP has significant negative impact on intra-regional trade in Asia. It captured the fact that bigger economies, such as China, trade more outside Asia than inside the region (Gaulier, Lemoine and Deniz 2007).

FDI, measured as the percent of GDP, is also highly significant to increase intra-regional trade in Asia. It is consistent with the existing literature that FDI has been instrumental for production fragmentation especially in East and Southeast Asia, which contributes increasing trade of parts and components within the region (Fukao, Ishido and Ito 2003).

Similarly, technological advancement also has significant positive impact on intra-regional trade. The results show that mobile cellular subscription per 100 people is significant at 10% level to increase intra-regional trade in Asia. The result is consistent with the recent findings of Bankole, Osei-Bryson and Brown (2015) as they found a significant positive impact of ICT on intra-African trade. Moreover, we found a significant positive impacts of urbanization measured by urban population growth on intra-regional trade in Asia. Urbanization can contribute intra-regional trade through increasing cross-border movement of people (Skeldon 2006) and promoting international networks (Smart and Smart 2003). Thus, results are firmly consistent with the existing literature.

IV. Conclusion

In the context of growing interest and efforts on pan-Asian integration, this paper examines the trends of pan-Asian intra-regional trade by countries/ economies and by sub-regions. ADB's ARIC database revealed that despite the rapid increase in intra-Asian trade volume of all countries from 1990 to 2012, the trends of intra-regional trade share are found different for different countries. For instance, during the same period, intra-Asian trade share increased significantly for Taiwan from 42.79% to 64.41% and for Japan from 34.38% to 53.95%. The intra-Asian trade share is moderately increased for India from 22.03% to 31.13% during the period. However, some countries intra-Asian trade even declined considerably, such as China from 59.9% to 40.5% during the period. These mixed results indicate that countries in the region are functioning independently, and stronger economic tie is yet to build. Furthermore, despite institutionalized regional integration efforts within the Asian sub-regions, the importance of trade within the region is declining for all the sub-regions in Asia (Figure 8). It indicates that as countries trading capacity grows they tend to trade globally rather than regionally. This is also the impact of open regionalism that all the regional integration institutions in Asia are following.

Employing the dynamic panel data approach, this paper also found that FTAs/RTAs are one of the main determinants of growing intra-Asian trade share. Other determinants are countries' level of economic development, FDI stock, urban population growth and access to ICT. Thus, it is argued that active participation in FTAs/RTAs, open FDI policy, urbanization and technological development of Asian countries create enabling environment for pan-Asian economic integration.

Appendices

Appendix 1: List of countries (underlined included in the analysis) with sub-regional grouping as per the ADB

Central Asia sub-region	Armenia, Azerbaijan, Georgia, Kazakhstan, the Kyrgyz Republic, Tajikistan, Turkmenistan, and Uzbekistan
East Asia sub-region	People's Republic of China, Japan, Hong Kong, the Republic of Korea, Mongolia, and Taiwan (Republic of China)
Southeast Asia sub-region	Brunei Darussalam, Cambodia, Indonesia, the Lao People's Democratic Republic (Lao PDR), Malaysia, Myanmar, the Philippines, Singapore, Thailand, and Viet Nam
South Asia sub-region	Afghanistan, Bangladesh, Bhutan, India, the Maldives, Nepal, Pakistan, and Sri Lanka
The Pacific sub-region	Cook Islands, Fiji, Kiribati, the Marshall Islands, the Federated States of Micronesia, Nauru, Palau, Papua New Guinea, Samoa, Solomon Islands, Timor-Leste, Tonga, Tuvalu, and Vanuatu
Oceania sub-region	Australia and New Zealand

Source: Integration Indicators groupings of ADB's ARIC database, available at <http://aric.adb.org/integrationindicators/groupings>, accessed: March 17, 2015.

Appendix 2a: TII of Central and West Asia with other Asian sub-regions, 1990-2012

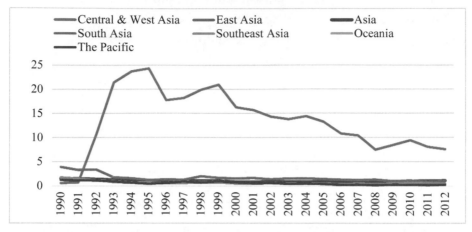

Source: The author using the data from ARIC Regional Integration Indicator database, available at:< http://aric.adb.org/integrationindicators>, accessed: March 7, 2015.

Appendix 2b: TII of Oceania with other Asian sub-regions, 1990-2012

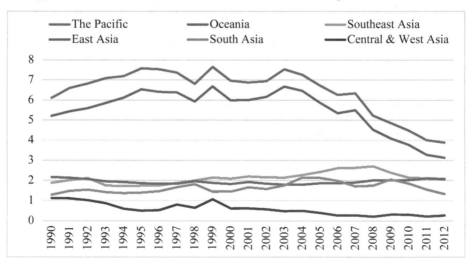

Source: The author using the data from ARIC Regional Integration Indicator database, available at: <http://aric.adb.org/integrationindicators>, accessed: March 7, 2015.

Appendix 2c: TII of the Pacific with other Asian sub-regions, 1990-2012

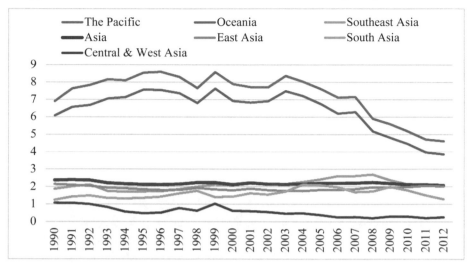

Source: The author using the data from ARIC Regional Integration Indicator database, available at:
      <http://aric.adb.org/integrationindicators>, accessed: March 7, 2015.

Appendix 3a: Correlation Matrix

	tras	trade	ftas	gdp	gnipc	fdi	mob	pop	se
Intra-regional trade in Asia (tras)	1								
Trade (% of GDP)	0.17	1							
No. of FTAs/RTAs within Asia (ftas)	-0.04	0.07	1						
GDP, PPP (current in Billions $) (gdp)	-0.12	-0.17	0.26	1					
GNI per capita, (current US$) (gnipc)	0.15	0.28	0.19	0.20	1				
FDI stock (% of GDP) (fdi)	0.20	0.73	0.14	-0.09	0.47	1			
Mobile subscriptions (per 100 people) (mob)	0.14	0.32	0.47	0.15	0.54	0.49	1		
Urban population growth (annual%) (pop)	0.38	0.03	-0.13	0.03	-0.19	-0.10	-0.13	1	
Services value added (% of GDP) (ser)	0.14	0.13	0.02	0.10	0.45	0.32	0.40	-0.20	1

Source: Data for Intra-regional trade in Asia, FDI stock and number of FTAs/RTAs of all countries are taken from ARIC Regional Integration Indicator database of the Asian Development Bank available at: <http://aric.adb.org/>. Data for the remaining variables (except for Taiwan) are taken from the World Bank's WDI online database, available at: <http://databank.worldbank.org/Data/ Databases.aspx>. Data for Taiwan are taken from the ADB's Statistical Database System available online at: <https://sdbs.adb.org/sdbs/index.jsp>.

Appendix 3b: Summary Statistics

Variables	Obs	Mean	Std. Dev.	Min	Max
Intra-regional trade in Asia	897	54.636	21.161	2	95.171
Trade (% of GDP)	897	93.759	72.416	0.1	449.99
No. of FTAs/RTAs within Asia	897	2.295	2.210	0	13
GDP, PPP (current in Billions $)	897	467.488	1305.829	0.22	14790.12
GNI per capita, (current US$)	897	5981.52	10276.17	110	59770
FDI stock (% of GDP)	897	32.932	57.939	0	579.78
Mobile subscriptions (per 100 people)	897	29.753	42.065	0	229.24
Urban population growth (annual %)	897	2.291	1.861	-3.103	10.92797
Services value added (% of GDP)	897	47.980	15.349	6.7	93.115

Source: Data for Intra-regional trade in Asia, FDI stock and number of FTAs/RTAs of all countries are taken from ARIC Regional Integration Indicator database of the Asian Development Bank available at: <http://aric.adb.org/>. Data for the remaining variables (except for Taiwan) are taken from the World Bank's WDI online database, available at: <http://databank.worldbank.org/Data/ Databases.aspx>. Data for Taiwan are taken from the ADB's Statistical Database System available online at: <https://sdbs.adb.org/sdbs/index.jsp>.

China's Economic Statecraft toward Taiwan[*]

Szu-Yin Ho[**]

Since President Ma Ying-jeou assumed Taiwan's top office on May 20, 2008, relations across the Taiwan Strait have undergone a significant turnaround. Rapprochement has become the predominant policy objective for both sides, while outright confrontational tactics have been put on the back-burner. Both sides have so far signed twenty-one agreements, including a free trade agreement, i.e., the Economic Cooperation Framework Agreement (ECFA) that has China making significant trade concessions to Taiwan without reciprocal gains. In addition, since the warming of relations, Taiwan's economy has also benefited from the influx of Chinese tourists (four million to date) and the numerous purchasing missions led by Chinese delegations. Cross-strait relations are expected to remain peaceful and prosperous as long as both sides are satisfied with the pace of progress they are making. Yet all these progresses have raised concerns for many Taiwanese. One such concern is how China's new economic statecraft will impact Taiwan. Another is the perceived unjust social distribution of the benefits from cross-Strait commercial exchanges. Both of these concerns, among others, were evident in the large-scale student movement that erupted in March, 2014. The student movement ultimately derailed the passing in Taiwan's legislature of a Service Agreement signed between Taiwan and China in mid-2013, thus stalling the further development of cross-Strait relations. The student movement

---

[*] This paper has been presented, in part or in whole, under different titles, in other conferences. All comments are welcome. Citation requires permission by the author.
[**] Professor, Graduate Institute of International Affairs and Strategic Studies, Tamkang University.

also proved instrumental in the resounding defeats of the ruling party KMT in the local elections in the end of 2014, thus paving the way for the pro-Independence opposition party, DPP, to win the presidential election to be held on January 16, 2016. A DPP administration will most certainly dampen the cordial relations built across the Strait since 2008.

This paper intends to assess Taiwan's economic security against this background. First, it will briefly review the literature surrounding this topic. Next it will discuss China's economic statecraft toward Taiwan, presenting it as an iterative bargaining game between the two sides of the Taiwan Strait. Then, the paper examines the variables that may impact China's use of economic statecraft. A conclusion follows.

I. Literature Review

For the purpose of this paper, I found three genres of literature are relevant. The first has to do with the effectiveness of deterrence, compellence and sanctions (both positive and negative) as power levers between states. This area of research, accumulated in security studies during the Cold War, is vast. A complete review of this literature is beyond the scope and purpose of this paper.[1] Briefly, deterrence refers to the use of military threat to prevent an adversary from carrying out an action undesired by the other state. In the words of Schelling, a leading scholar in deterrence theory, to deter is "to turn aside or discourage through fear; hence, to prevent from action by fear of consequences."[2] In contrast, compellence employs the threat of punishment to persuade the target state to do something desired by the other state.[3] Although both deterrence and compellence involve the use

---

1   Morgan, among others, offers an excellent review of the development of deterrence and compellence, both as a theoretical concept and a strategy during the cold war. See Morgan, Patrick M., *Deterrence Now* (New York: Cambridge University Press, 2003).

2   Thomas C. Schelling, *Arms and Influence* (New Haven, CT: Yale University Press, 1966), p. 71.

3   *Ibid.*, p. 71. Schelling uses the term "compellence" to emphasize the offensive nature in the threat employed by the initiating state. In contrast, deterrence emphasizes the

of threat to change the incentive structure of the adversary, they are different in terms of the underlying dynamics, i.e., time horizons, and expectations.[4] Some of these variables will be applied to analyze China's statecraft toward Taiwan in Section 3. Underlying deterrence or compellence is the assurances the initiating state offers in return for compliance by the target state. If the target state chooses to comply, it should expect the initiating state to refrain from carrying out punishments. In actuality, the assurances offered by the initiating state can go beyond merely the retraction of threats should the target state comply. The initiating state can reward, make concessions to, or compensate the compliant state.[5] Deterrence and compellence are about the use of "sticks," while assurance is about the use of "carrots."

The second genre of literature relevant to this research is the effectiveness of economic statecraft. It examines how an initiating state employs its economic strength to change the policies of a target state in its favor. Albert O. Hirschman's 1945 classic *The National Power and the Structure of Foreign Trade* serves as the foundation to this genre of scholarly

---

defensiveness in the threat. George, on the other hand, believes that "coercion" is a better theoretical concept, in the sense that it not only captures the defense/offense distinction in statecraft, but also denotes a wider spectrum of levers that states can employ to change the incentives, hence the behavior, of their opponents. See George, Alexander L., "Coercive Diplomacy: Definition and Characteristics," in Alexander L. George and William Simmons, eds., *The Limits of Coercive Diplomacy* (Boulder, CO: Westview Press, 1994), pp.7-11. Despite the theoretical nuances between compellence and coercion, scholars in general tend to use these two terms interchangeably. For example, Sperandei, Maria, "Bridging Deterrence and Compellence: An Alternative Approach to the Study of Coercive Diplomacy," *International Studies Review* 8:2, June 2006, pp. 253-280. In this paper I also use these two terms interchangeably.

4 Thomas C. Schelling, *Arms and Influence* (New Haven, CT: Yale University Press, 1966), pp. 69-91.

5 David A Baldwin's theoretical treatment of how positive incentives (inducement) work with negative incentives, i.e., threats, provides an incisive review of the exercise of power. Baldwin, David A., "The Power of Positive Sanctions," *World Politics* Vol. 24, No.1 (October 1971), pp. 19-38. For case studies, see Davis, James W., *Threats and Promises: the Pursuit of International Influence* (Baltimore, MD: Johns Hopkins University Press, 2000).

research. Hirschman argues that when trade interdependence between states is asymmetrical, the stronger state can use bilateral trade as an effective lever to extract political concessions from the weaker state. Trade asymmetry exists when one state is less dependent on the bilateral trade relations than the other state. Hirschman uses Germany's inter-war trade relations with Central and Eastern European small states to illustrate his theoretical points.[6] Hirschman's work failed to generate meaningful interest in this area of research during the Cold War years, as international relations scholars were preoccupied with the high-politics statecraft of the two superpowers. However, since the waning years of the Cold War scholarly interest has revived in research of how states use sanctions, embargos, currency manipulations, trade preferences, direct investments, technology transfers, foreign aid programs, and general market power to deter, compel, cajole or induce a target state to change its foreign policy. The main area of research has focused on the effectiveness of these economic levers in achieving the initiating state's foreign policy goals.[7] Since its inception, this area of research has relied largely on American-centric case studies and datasets as the US has been the largest economy for over a century and hence has had the means to exercise economic statecraft. However, lately, case studies have shown that, for example, Russia has also attempted to use its vast energy resources to exact political compliance from its CIS neighbors.[8] Similarly, China's impressive economic growth of the past thirty years has not only transformed it into the second largest economy in the world but also armed

6   Hirschman, Albert O., *National Power and the Structure of Foreign Trade* (Berkeley, CA: University of California Press, 1945). Also, Abdelal, Rawi, and Jonathan Kirshner, "Strategy, Economic Relations, and the Definition of National Interests," in Blanchard, Jean-Marc F., Edward D. Mansfield, and Norrin M. Ripsman, eds., *Power and the Purse: Economic Statecraft, Interdependence and National Security* (Portland, OR: Frank Cass, 2000), pp. 119-156.

7   See Baldwin, David A., *Economic Statecraft* (Princeton University Press, 1985). Baldwin's book is especially good in conceptualizing "economic statecraft," which is inevitably related to the concept of "economic security."

8   Drezner, Daniel W., *The Sanctions Paradox: Economic Statecraft and International Relations* (New York: Cambridge University Press, 1999).

it with significant economic might. According to recent reports, China has employed economic coercive strategies in its foreign policy with the Philippines, Japan, and Norway.[9] And China also uses positive economic incentives to lure small states to have foreign policies in favor of China.[10]

The third genre concerns economic statecraft in the China-Taiwan dyad. Undoubtedly, both sides of the Taiwan Strait have adopted a strategy of economic engagement in hopes of influencing the other side. For China, economic engagement is the mainstay of its "peaceful offense" grand strategy toward Taiwan.[11] The ever-growing mainland market and the host of trade and investment preferences China has offered to Taiwan have attracted Taiwanese investment, trade, and tourism. China has become Taiwan's largest trade partner and recipient of Taiwan's outgoing investments as well as the primary destination for Taiwanese tourists. On the other hand, until 2008 Taiwan was quite leery of the negative effects that the exodus of Taiwanese businesses to China would have on its economy and politics.[12] As a result, Taiwan adopted its own set of strategies to counter China's economic statecraft. President Lee Teng-Hui installed a "Go Slow, Be Patient" policy in the late 90s to slow the outflow of Taiwan businesses

9   Glaser, Bonnie S., "China's Coercive Economic Diplomacy: A New and Worrying Trend," *CSIS*, August 6, 2012, <http://csis.org/publication/chinas-coercive-economic-diplomacy-new-and-worrying-trend>. Also, using aggregate trade data, scholars have shown that the bilateral trade between China and the country that received the Dalai Lama would decrease in the wake of his visit. See Davis, Christina, Andreas Fuchs, and Kristina Johnson, "State Control and the Effects of Foreign Relations on Bilateral Trade," paper presented at the Annual Meeting of the International Political Economy Society, Charlottesville, Virginia (November 10, 2012). For a general description of China's use of economic sanctions, see Reilly, James, "China's Unilateral Sanctions," *The Washington Quarterly*, Vol. 35, Nol. 4 (Fall 2012), pp. 121-133.

10 French, Howard W., *China's Second Continent* (Vintage Books, 2014).

11 Zhao, Suisheng, "Military Coercion and Peaceful Offence: Beijing's Strategy of National Reunification with Taiwan," *Pacific Affairs*, Vol. 72, No. 4 (winter, 1999-2000), pp. 495-512.

12 Tung, Chen-yuan, "Cross-Strait Economic Relations: China's Leverage and Taiwan's Vulnerability," *Issues & Studies*, Vol. 39, No. 3 (September 2003), pp. 137-175.

to China. President Chen Shui-Bian followed suit with "Active Opening, Effective Management" from 2000-2008, which in practice emphasized the latter part of the policy. Both policies were aimed to reduce Taiwan's economic dependence on China.[13] However, China's expanding market proved too much of a lure for Taiwan's businesses, which effectively circumvented government regulations to increase their presence in China.[14] On the domestic front, both the Lee and Chen administrations set up tariff and non-tariff barriers to reduce China's economic presence in Taiwan's economic presence in Taiwan. As a result of these developments, there has been a growing literature that examines the political economy across the Taiwan Strait. Tanner has thoroughly researched on China's economic "weapons" —conduits China can use to exercise its economic influence— and Taiwan's vulnerabilities. But Tanner did not draw any firm conclusion from his study, citing that it is hard to forecast Taiwan's possible response to Chinese coercive attempts.[15] Saunders and Kastner speculate on the bargaining situation between China and Taiwan over a peace agreement, assuming Taiwan is already willing to sit at the negotiation table.[16] However, Taiwan may not be willing to negotiate with China over its future. In addition to the literature written in English, there is a great deal of research in Taiwan written in Chinese (e.g., government reports, think tank analyses, academic papers, op-eds, etc.) with regard to the political implications of Taiwan's dependence on the Chinese mainland market. By and large, two schools of thought emerge from the Chinese-language researches. The first,

---

13 Kahler, Miles, and Scott L. Kastner, "Strategic Uses of Economic Interdependence: Engagement Policies on the Korean Peninsula and Across the Taiwan Strait," *Journal of Peace Research*, Vol. 43, No. 5 (September, 2006), pp. 534-539.

14 Leng, Tze-kang, "State and Business in the Era of Globalization: the Case of Cross-Strait Linkages in the Computer Industry," *China Journal*, No.53 (January 2005), pp. 63-79.

15 Tanner, Murray Scott, *Chinese Economic Coercion against Taiwan: A Tricky Weapon to Use* (Rand Corporation, 2007).

16 Phillip C. Saunders, and Scott L. Kastner, "Bridge over Troubled Water: Envisioning a China-Taiwan Peace Agreement," *International Security*, Vol. 33, No.4 (Spring 2009), pp. 87-114.

based on standard trade theory, argues that trade is mutually beneficial to both sides of the strait, thus it is only natural for both Taiwan and China to consolidate their economic relations. China is unlikely to exploit Taiwan's economic dependence on the mainland market with coercive strategies, because doing so will only boomerang. At least for the foreseeable future, China cannot afford to dismiss the business and employment opportunities generated by Taiwanese businesses. The second school of thought argues that China has both the intention and capability to use its economic strength to force Taiwan into unification (the historical analogy of Zollverein that led to German unification is often a convenient reference point). Assuming that China has both the capability and ill-intent, this school of thought believes that to survive China's economic menace Taiwan has no other choice but to reduce its trade with and investment in China. While both schools of thought recognize the deepening business relations across the strait, one views this as an opportunity for Taiwan to piggyback on China's rapid growth, while the other views this as a crisis for Taiwan's autonomy.

II. China's Economic Statecraft toward Taiwan

Chinese statecraft toward Taiwan is three pronged: military, diplomatic and economic. Before 2008, China emphasized military and diplomatic measures over economic strategies. While Chinese military strength may be the ultimate deterrence against de jure Taiwan independence, it has some shortcomings. First, prevailing international norms no longer view war as a legitimate means to solve sovereignty disputes. If China ever employs force against Taiwan, it will have to bear the brunt of world opinion. Second, America's policy of "constructive ambiguity" deliberately obfuscates the potential course of action the US would take in the event of a China-Taiwan conflict, hence according it a greater degree of freedom in policy decisions. Third, China's saber-rattling toward Taiwan has raised alarms in other East Asian nations regarding its true regional intentions. These incidents work against China's national interest of creating a stable international environment conducive to its goal of "peaceful development." Compared with military deterrence, China's diplomatic statecraft against Taiwan has fewer consequences. Through the years, China has relentlessly strived to limit Taiwan's international space and reduce the number of countries that recognize its sovereignty. Taiwan can participate in only a handful of international organizations with the participation severely conditional. Presently, only 23 countries formally recognize Taiwan, all of which are small players on the international stage. However, Taiwan has been able to navigate around the diplomatic isolation imposed by China. For example, 127 countries offer visa-free entry or landing visas to Taiwanese nationals. Taiwan has 97 representative offices in 65 countries that do not formally recognize Taiwan. These examples demonstrate that Taiwan has been moderately adept at compromising China's diplomatic offensive. The marginal utility of diplomatic isolation of Taiwan has decreased over the years. If anything, it only further alienates the Taiwanese public from China. Since the Ma administration came into office in 2008, China 's use of economic statecraft has become much more apparent than before, with military and diplomatic statecraft serving as a fallback method.

As Hirschman suggests, the precondition for economic statecraft is asymmetrical interdependence in a trade dyad. State A, if it intends to exert economic statecraft, must be economically powerful enough so that it becomes exorbitantly costly for State B to replace country A as a market. Asymmetry indeed exists in cross-strait economic relations. First of all, while in 1995 China's GDP was only 3.66 times that of Taiwan's, at the end of 2015 it will become 20.66 times bigger. IMF projects that through 2019 the figure will remain around 20.67 times. That is, Taiwan's GDP will be about only 5% of China's GDP. Moreover, China is Taiwan's largest trading partner, accounting for 28% of Taiwan's total exports. If including Hong Kong, China accounts for 42% of Taiwan's total exports. In 2011, Taiwan's trade surplus with China was 78.8 billion US dollars, dwarfing its global trade surplus of 26.8 billion US dollars. Taiwan's trade dependence on China was ultimately driven by the outflow of Taiwanese businesses to the Chinese mainland market. By and large, these businesses primarily choose the mainland market as the final destination of their companies' FDI, as oppose to other countries.[17] In contrast, Taiwan is China's 7th largest trading partner, absorbing only 1.85% of China's total exports. Taiwan's economy is also highly dependent on trade, more so than that of China's. According to the most recent WTO statistics, foreign trade is 132% of Taiwan's GDP, but only 55% of China's. Taiwan's democratic system and periodic elections make the government highly accountable to trade-related interest groups (e.g., export-oriented manufacturers, trade-related financial and insurance companies, transportation companies, etc.). On the other hand, China's authoritarian single-party state is comparatively autonomous of special interests groups (other than those within the Communist Party).[18] The Chinese state controls strong administrative leverages that can be instrumental to the exercise of economic statecraft. For example, the number of tourists that are allowed to visit Taiwan is decided by city and provincial governments. Furthermore, the process of obtaining travel permits is highly opaque at the local level. In contrast, the Taiwan government has little control regarding its citizens' decisions to travel, invest, trade, or receive education in China. As a result, the Chinese government is undoubtedly capable of exercising economic statecraft as a lever against Taiwan. If it so chooses, China can exercise economic statecraft in the form of inducements, deterrence, or compellence.

Since May, 2008, as a result of Ma's election to office, China began to increase economic inducements to Taiwan. China was willing to cooperate with the Ma administration's rapprochement policy, because it no longer feared inadvertently rewarding Taiwan's "defecting" behavior, i.e., the pursuit of Taiwan independence. Other than signing ECFA that granted Taiwanese goods preferred access to the Chinese market, Chinese

---

17 Leng, Tze-Kang, unpublished manuscript, July 2012.

18 For a general picture of state-enterprise relations in China, see *China 2030*, The World Bank, 2012.

tourists and purchase missions to Taiwan received a high degree of public attention in Taiwan, as reflected in local media coverage. For many in Taiwan, Taiwan's investments in and exports to China cannot be "seen." In fact, from their perspective, China is to blame for Taiwan's outflow of capital investments, loss of job opportunities and slow-growing economy. However, Chinese tourists and purchase missions are a different matter; the obvious economic benefits from their activities are tangible and highly visible. Tourism infrastructure, i.e., hotels, restaurants, duty-free shops, tour buses, bus drivers, tour guides, night stands, etc., have expanded to meet the demands of Chinese tourists.

While Chinese tourists bring profits to Taiwan's small enterprises, China's purchase missions bring business to Taiwan's large industrial enterprises and agricultural producers. According to the data collected by this author, between May 2009 to July 2011 China sent 55 purchase missions to Taiwan, which averages to slightly over two missions per month. These missions committed over 50 billion US dollars to the purchase of Taiwan's industrial products, and over 500 million US dollars to agricultural products.[19] Tables 1 and 2 show the origins of these purchase missions.

Table 1 shows that a significant number of Chinese purchase missions were from the inland provinces, which presumably would have fewer trade interests with Taiwan. This may indicate China's ability to mobilize provinces, inland or coastal, to provide economic inducements to Taiwan. Table 2 shows the level of purchase missions. Again, it is noteworthy that the purchase missions were not just limited to the central government; they also included those dispatched by provincial and city governments.[20] What

---

19 The dollar amount of actual delivery is difficult to find. There are two reasons for this: first, the contracting parties have no incentives to make public the terms of their contracts; and two, many of the contracts span multiple years, hence there are no specific figures for any one year. To put things in perspective, the committed amount to purchase industrial goods is worth about 20% of Taiwan's exports to China in 2009.

20 The administrative jurisdictions of cities in China, such as Chongqing, can sometimes be more important, both politically and commercially, than the province.

Table 1: Chinese Purchase Missions to Taiwan by Provincial Location

	N	%
Inland Provinces	23	41.8
Coastal Provinces	32	58.2
Total	55	100

Table 2: Chinese Purchase Missions to Taiwan by Government Level

	N	%
Central Government	13	23.6
Provincial Governments	30	54.6
City Governments	12	21.8
Total	55	100

is not shown in Table 2 is that purchase missions formed by provincial and city governments tended to be quite high-profile, as they were frequently led by the top officials from the administrative units, thus attracting considerable press coverage in Taiwan. For example, a purchase mission from Jiangsu Province in November 2009, was led by the provincial party chief and deputy-governor. Clearly, China intends to highlight the economic benefits it can bring to the island.

As Table 3 demonstrates, there were more purchase missions for agricultural products than for industrial goods. Specifically, of the 55 purchase missions, 23 bought agricultural products exclusively, 17 bought industrial products, and 15 bought both. This reflects China's claim that it wants to build a more lasting relationship with Taiwan's agricultural sector, which has been a strong voting bloc for the Independence-leaning DPP. Qualitative evidence also supports this assessment. In July 2011, when Taiwan's banana farmers suffered from a long stretch of bad market prices as a result of overproduction, Shangdong provincial governor, who was leading a purchase mission to Taiwan, announced an emergency plan to purchase

6,800 tons of bananas at above-market price. This announcement quickly raised banana prices in Taiwan.[21] Frequent visits to Taiwan's agricultural areas by Mr. Zheng LiZong, Vice President of China's Association for Relations across the Taiwan Straits and Deputy Director of PRC State Council's Taiwan Affairs Office, also indicate China's efforts in reaching out to "villages, households, minds, and hearts" (入村 , 入戶 , 入腦 , 入心). Figure 1 shows the routes of a visit to Taiwan by a Chinese official that mostly concentrated on agricultural areas.

The significance of Chinese tourists and purchase missions is that they are more visible and directly felt by the general public. These business opportunities have political implications. As Nincic observes, there are two models underlying economic inducements, the exchange model and the catalytic model.[22] In the exchange model, the quid pro quo was specified ex ante. For example, West Germany offered a handsome total to the USSR in exchange for Gorbachev's promise to withdraw the Red Army from East German territory. In the catalytic model, however, there is no specification of quid pro quo. The initiating state that provides economic inducements (as a catalyst) only aims to change the overall policy preferences of the target state so that the latter's policy preferences becomes better aligned with those of the initiator. West Germany's economic aid to Poland in the 1980s and 1990s is a case in point.[23] Although China's economic inducements to Taiwan as described appear to adhere to the catalyst model, i.e., "winning the hearts and minds of Taiwan's people," and China's purchase missions never mention the politics of economic engagement, it should be noted that there may be a tacit understanding of the quid pro quo between the two sides. As Baldwin observes, "Today's reward may lay the groundwork for tomorrow's threat,

---

21 康子仁,〈大陸緊急採購　台蕉價格水漲船高〉,《中國評論新聞網》, 2011 年 7 月 22 日,<http://www.chinareviewnews.com>。

22 Miroslav Nincic, "Getting What You Want: Positive Incentives in International Relations," *International Security*, Vol. 35, No. 1 (Summer 2010), pp. 138-183.

23 Patria A. Davis, *The Art of Economic Persuasion* (Ann Arbor, MI: The University of Michigan Press, 1999).

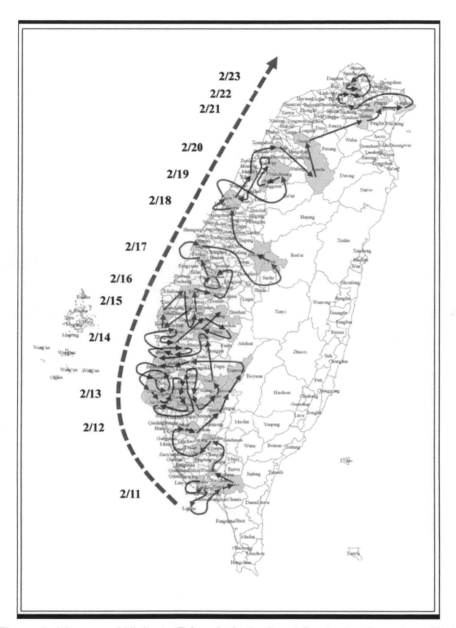

Figure 1: Itinerary of Visits to Taiwan's Agricultural Producing Areas by a High Chinese Official in 2012

Table 3: Chinese Purchase Missions By Purchased Products

	N	%
Agricultural Products	23	41.8
Industrial Products	17	30.9
Both	15	27.3
Total	55	100

and tomorrow's threat may lay the groundwork for a promise of the day after tomorrow."[24] Furthermore, subsidy can be a source of bargaining power for the subsidizing state that can be exploited to gain political concessions from the subsidized state, regardless of asymmetrical dependence.[25] Therefore, if Chinese tourists and purchase missions to Taiwan are considered by China as subsidies to Taiwan, rather than part of a trade relationship that will benefit both sides, then suspension of tourism and purchase missions to Taiwan can be used by China as a threat.

China implicitly used (possible suspension of) economic inducements as basis for deterrent threat in the months leading to Taiwan's presidential election held in January, 2012. The focus was the "92 Consensus," a formula employed by both the KMT and CCP governments as the foundation for cross-strait negotiations since Ma's assuming presidential office in 2008.[26]

---

24 David A. Baldwin, "*The Power of Positive Sanctions,*" p. 24.

25 Wagner, R. Harrison, "Economic Interdependence, Bargaining Power, and Political Influence," *International Organization*, Vol. 42, No3 (Summer 1988), pp. 479-481.

26 Coined by Su Chi, former-Secretary-General of the National Security Council under the Ma administration, the "92 Consensus" means the consensus of "One China, Different Interpretations" agreed by both sides of the Taiwan Strait allegedly in 1992. This is a formula that has helped navigate the differences between the two sides' legal interpretations of the situation across the Taiwan Strait, which has existed since 1949. For China, Taiwan is part of China; therefore, in principle Beijing cannot negotiate with

Since the pro-Taiwan independence DPP denies the very existence of such a consensus, a presidential victory by DPP's candidate Ms. Tsai Ing-wen would mean Taiwan can become a flash point, once again, for China. As a result, China undertook a series of actions to "remind" Taiwan the importance of the "92 Consensus." On August 26, 2011, when Taiwan's presidential campaign season just started, Wang Yi, Director of PRC State Council's Taiwan Affairs Office, had these words to say in an opening speech to a major meeting attended by China's local officials and Taiwan businessmen in Southern China, "Cross-strait relations can be compared to a mansion with the '92 Consensus' as its foundation…if the foundation is emptied out then the progresses people across the Taiwan Straits achieved so far will be reversed." Two months later, when the incumbent President Ma was in a neck-to-neck race with Ms. Tsai, China again drummed up the "92 Consensus." On November 7, 2011, Jia Qinglin, Chairman of the National Committee of the Chinese People's Consultative Conference, addressed a group of Taiwanese businessmen visiting Beijing that, "If the '92 Consensus' is denied, cross-strait negotiations will have to be stopped, the current development will be arrested, and cross-strait relations may be thrown into turmoil." Five days later, Chinese president Hu Jintao met with Lien Chan, Taiwan's former vice president, during the 2011 APEC meeting, reiterated that "identification with the '92 Consensus' is a major precondition to cross-

---

Taipei, the capital of a renegade province. For the KMT, both Taiwan and the Chinese mainland are part of the Republic of China; therefore, the KMT government cannot recognize the government in Beijing. For the DPP, Taiwan is not part of China; Taiwan's national title should be Republic of Taiwan. For Beijing, the DPP's position that Taiwan is an independent state is political anathema. Beijing has long maintained that should Taiwan declare independence, Beijing will use force against Taiwan. On the other hand, from Beijing's perspective, the KMT's position on cross-strait relations is more compatible with that of its own; that is, KMT considers both Taiwan and the mainland as part of China (though not People's Republic of China.) Since the "92 Consensus" equivocates on the contentious issue of sovereignty, it is used by both the KMT government and Beijing as a device for agreeing to disagree. However, for the DPP, the "92 Consensus" will invalidate the sovereignty of the Republic of Taiwan, which explains the DPP's vehement denial of its existence.

strait negotiations, and it is also the foundation for peaceful development in the Strait." And on November 17, Wang Yi warned again that the consequences would be grave if the "1992 Consensus" is to be denied. In a keynote speech at the Taiwan Week exhibition in Chongqing, Wang stated that "China will not tolerate the denial of the '92 Consensus', nor the backpedalling of cross-strait relations, nor the lapse of peace in the Taiwan Strait, and nor the destruction of the welfare of the people on both sides of the strait." Wang Yi's last salvo was immediately followed by an "academic" conference that sounded off the dire consequences from the denial of the "1992 Consensus." It should be noted that occasions used by the Chinese officials to send their warning signals, with the possible exception of Hu's remarks to Lien Chan at the APEC, were all business-related. This sequence of actions demonstrates a classic deterrence strategy whereby Beijing publically drew a line in the sand, and waited to see if Taiwan would cross the line.[27]

China's attempt at deterrence was quickly picked up by Taiwan's businesses.[28] Between mid-November, when China voiced its threats, and Election Day (January 14, 2012), Taiwan businesses gradually came out to support Ma's campaign. This surge in support for KMT's Ma would have been unlikely had it not been for China's deterrence strategy, given that various surveys showed that in terms of candidate likability and personal quality Tsai was equally popular. A case in point is that five of the traditionally pro-DPP conglomerates rallied behind the "1992 Consensus"

27 Theoretically, in Taiwan's two-candidate presidential election, deterring against votes for DPP's Tsai is tantamount to compelling votes for KMT's Ma. But given that China's actions in this period of time were aimed at maintaining the "1992 Consensus"-based status quo, Beijing's actions were more of deterrence in character than of compellence. I want to thank Professor Wu Yu-shan to point this out.

28 It should be noted that measuring the effectiveness of deterrence can be problematic due to context-specific variables. In determining the success or failure of deterrence, researchers are required to prove that a non-event (i.e., the fact that the target country does not cross the red-line) was due to the deterrent threat, and not the target country's own voluntary decision to comply even in the absence of threat.

(hence, by default, Ma's candidacy) for the first time. Furthermore, rarely had Taiwan's businesses come out to support one policy on such a significant scale or number. Historically, businesses tended to remain neutral in presidential elections, at least superficially, lest they wager on the wrong bet. The 21 big businesses that publically pledged their support for the "1992 Consensus,"— the majority of which refrained from mentioning Ma's candidacy —ranged from electronics, retailing, transportation, general manufacturing, to banking.[29] Moreover, according to Taiwan's most respectable business magazine, *The Commonwealth*, Taiwan's top 1,000 businesses were overwhelmingly supportive of Ma's candidacy.[30] This indicated that by and large, Taiwan's business sector preferred the status-quo to possible changes under a DPP administration.

However, in contrast to Taiwan businesses, traditionally DPP electoral districts, mostly agricultural areas, did not respond to China's economic deterrence strategy in any clear way. This is the case for the five townships that were historically DPP strongholds that since 2008 have greatly benefited from China's economic inducements in terms of tourism or large-scale purchases of agricultural produce. Presumably, if there was a fear of China's threat to withdraw its economic favors from these five townships, voter turnout rate should drop accordingly, thus harming the DPP's election prospects. Based on aggregate electoral data (Table 4), this author found that the respective voter turnout rates remained relatively constant compared with the previous two elections. In comparison with all other townships, the voter turnout rates of these five townships were well within ±1 standard deviation. Therefore, the data does not indicate that the townships in question were significantly impacted by China's deterrence strategy. However, anecdotal evidence suggests otherwise. According to an in-depth reportage on Xyue-

29 〈台灣首富王雪紅宣佈挺馬 企業家表態大集合（圖）〉，《美國中文網》，2012 年 1 月 3 日，<http://gate.sinovision.net:82/gate/big5/news.sinovision.net/portal.php?mod=view&aid=201335>。

30 *The Commonwealth*, December 27, 2011.

Table 4: Voter Turnout in Presidential Elections: Measured in Deviation from All-Townships Mean

	2012	2008	2004
Yu-Chih (tourism)	-2.03	-2.65	-2.17
Gu-Keng (citrus)	-1.04	-1.27	-0.60
Alishan (tourism)	-2.45	-2.45	-2.25
Xyue-Jia (milkfish)	-0.73	-0.70	+0.03
Yong-An (grouper)	-0.55	-0.09	+0.40
±1 Standard Deviation	±3.98	±4.01	±3.35

Jia Township by *Business Weekly*, a major business magazine in Taiwan, the township's heavy dependence on milkfish exports to China had a dampening effect on its voter support for the DPP.[31] In addition, the DPP's post-election report that reviewed why DPP lost the presidential election surmises that China's deterrence "card" negatively impacted voter turnout in DPP strongholds, whereby Tsai received significantly fewer votes than DPP's legislative candidates. This author's tentative observation is that China's deterrence did not change the orientation of DPP supporters, but may have changed their intensity of supports. Therefore, it is difficult to forecast the effects on Taiwan voters of China's economic deterrence in the future. This is because the variables that impact Taiwan's presidential elections are multifarious, ranging from international politics (China and the United States, in particular), to party identification, policy issues, and to the popularity of the candidate.

I now conjecture whether China's economic engagement with Taiwan will become an effective means of compellence to force Taiwan into political negotiation. China is yet to show any intention to do so, but should it become impatient with the rate of progress in the Taiwan Strait, economic compellence is clearly in its tool box.

---

31 Yi-ling Kuo, "Communists, Money, and Milkfish," *Business Weekly*, No.1249(October 26, 2011).

To analyze this problem, I use a decision tree, as shown in Figure 2, to layout the possible scenarios in the event China exercises economic coercion against Taiwan. In this simple model, China and Taiwan place different values on each outcome, as indicated by the paired numbers. The first number indicates the value of China's preference, while the latter is that of Taiwan's, with higher numbers representing higher ordinal preference. In the first decision tier, China, as the initiator, has two options: making no move against Taiwan or using economic threats to compel Taiwan to engage in political negotiations. The threats may include suspension of tourism and purchase missions to Taiwan, stalling trade negotiations under the ECFA framework, thwarting Taiwan's efforts to sign FTAs with other countries by pressuring its trading partners, etc. On the other hand, if China makes no move then the status quo is preserved. Under the first scenario whereby China chooses compellence, Taiwan can resist or comply. However, it is important to note that China will never directly demand of

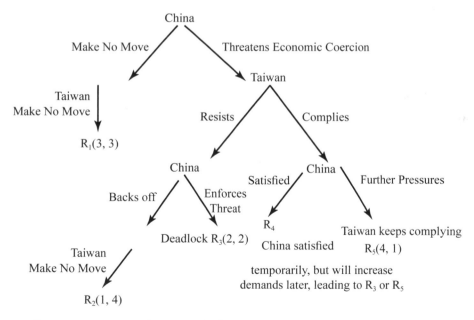

Figure 2: Decision-Tree in a China/ Taiwan Economic Coercion Game

Taiwan to engage in negotiations over reunifications. Rather, the demands will usually be crouched in terms more politically palatable, such as "talks over reasonable arrangement for cross-strait political relations," or "talks over military confidence-building measures," or "talks over peace accord."[32] However, no matter how the demands are worded, Taiwan will essentially have two options: to comply or not to comply. If Taiwan decides to sit at the negotiation table for political talks, its greatest concern would be whether China will be sufficiently satisfied with the move or will it construe this action as a sign of appeasement to be further exploited, i.e., China making further demands on direct negotiations over reunification terms. This author postulates that Taiwan is more likely to view the latter scenario to be true; the reason is what Sechser calls the "Goliath's curse."[33] According to Sechser, coercive threats in a highly asymmetric power relationship tend to make the target state leery of reputation costs. The challenger state then should compensate the target state's reputation cost so that it is more willing to acquiesce. But the overwhelming power of the challenger often leads it to underestimate the reputation cost of the target state, hence resulting in insufficient compensation. For Taiwan, China's relentless pursuit of military power and diplomatic maneuver against its international space means only one thing—reunification. Therefore, should Taiwan comply with China's demands, it would only be appeasing an aggressor that will continue to demand more in the future. Even in the former scenario whereby Taiwan complies and China is satisfied in the short-term (Result4), there is no guarantee that China would not be recidivist given its national goal of reunification. Even if Taiwan continues to comply (R_5), the result is the least desirable for Taiwan, while most desirable for China, i.e., $R_5(4, 1)$.[34]

---

32 These terms appeared in a speech delivered by China's retiring-president Hu Jintao at the 18th Party Congress of the Chinese Communist Party on November 8, 2012.

33 Sechser, Todd S., "Goliath's Curse: Coercive Threats and Asymmetric Power," *International Organization* 64 (Fall 2010), pp. 627-60.

34 Reputational cost is the main reason why economic coercion tends to be unsuccessful. And reputational cost is closely related to conflict expectations. See Drezner, Daniel

However, if Taiwan resists China's threat of economic compellence and China subsequently retreats, the result would be most preferable for Taiwan and least preferable for China, R_2 (1, 4). In this scenario, Taiwan would learn that it is capable of warding off China's economic pressures and maintain the status quo. However, China's reputation would suffer. Should Taiwan resist and China follow through with its economic threats the Taiwan Strait would inevitably be deadlocked. As a consequence, cross-strait relations may revert back to its prior state before the Ma administration came into office in 2008. In this scenario, China will lose its economic leverage over Taiwan, while Taiwan will lose the economic concessions it enjoyed from China, hence slowing down its economic growth. For both China and Taiwan, this scenario R_3(2, 2) is inferior to the current status quo R_1 (3, 3), where China continues its economic engagement with Taiwan while keeping Taiwan Independence at bay, and Taiwan refrains from provoking China while reaping profits from its business relationships with China. It is clear that the status quo is the better option given the other three scenarios. But if China makes an economic compellent threat, a deadlock could easily result, making both sides worse off. The preference structure across the Taiwan Strait is therefore similar to that of a prisoners' dilemma game. But there is one important difference: in the compellence scenario only China has the capability to make the first move. Such may be the reasoning behind an editorial of the generically nationalistic Huanqiu Shibao, an affiliate of the People's Daily. The editorial, published after Ma's successful re-election, argued that "'deterring Taiwan independence' and 'compelling reunification' are related, but at the same time they are remotely separate…In cross-strait relations, we must not force the issue (reunification)…we have to give ourselves some strategic flexibility."[35]

W., "The Trouble with Carrots: Transaction Costs, Conflict Expectations, and Economic Inducements," *Security Studies*, Vol. 9, No.1-2 (1999), pp. 188-218.

35 〈環球時報：未來四年兩岸應有新格局〉，《新浪新聞》，2012 年 1 月 16 日，<http://news.sina.com.cn/pl/2012-01-16/075123806931.shtml>。

III. Variables That May Impact on China's Economic Statecraft toward Taiwan

Following George and Simons' discussion of coercive diplomacy, I analyze two kinds of variables that may be relevant to the success or failure of coercion: contextual variables and negotiation process-specific variables.[36]

Some contextual variables that are omitted from the simple model of China's economic compellence toward Taiwan may nevertheless influence the sequential dynamics of China's economic engagement, deterrence, and compellence. First, China's economic inducements to Taiwan (mainly tourism and purchase missions) are predicated on Taiwan's willingness to adopt the "1992 consensus" over the diametrically opposed sovereignty claims across the Taiwan Strait. Since Taiwan is a democracy, change of government is inevitable in the long run. Should a new administration in Taiwan deviate from the "1992 consensus" formula as formulated by the current Ma administration, and move Taiwan towards independence, then China is likely to oppose Taiwan's new position. The reason being that this allows China to maintain its credibility and avoid being outmaneuvered by Taiwan—i.e., successive Taiwan administrations may try "salami tactics" that push against the precedent set by the prior administration, hence driving Taiwan further away from China's "one China policy" (aka One-China "Framework"). Should this scenario pan out, China is likely to pursue a tit-for-tat tactic, i.e., punishing Taiwan such as suspending tourism to the island. If Taiwan retaliates by pursuing actions that are highly politically symbolic, e.g., applying for membership in the UN under the name of Taiwan, we can expect the end to the current cross-strait rapprochement.

---

36 Alexander L. George and William E. Simons, eds., *The Limits of Coercive Diplomacy*, 2nd Edition (Boulder, CO: The Westview Press, 1994). A litany of variables that may bear upon the success or failure of coercion ultimately depends on the subject matter of study at hand. George and Simon give a list of 14 variables, while other researchers offer different sets of variables. See, for example, the different case studies edited by Freeman, Lawrence, *Strategic Coercion: Concepts and Cases* (Oxford University Press, 1998).

Secondly, even if future administrations in Taiwan adhere to the formula of the "1992 consensus," China may change its current position by compelling Taiwan toward reunification. That is, China may get impatient. For example, Luo Yuan, a retired PLA general regarded by many as interlocutor for the Chinese military, stated in a high-profile speech that, "Although the mainland had released a great deal of goodwill to Taiwan, the proportion of those who support reunification with China had not risen, and the proportion for Taiwan independence not declined....Ma, by keeping China at arm's length, is sacrificing 'reunification' to achieve 'incremental secession'."[37] Interlocutors from various Chinese think tanks also expressed criticism at Taiwan's seeming reluctance to negotiate with China on political issues. If the new Chinese leadership (fifth-generation and beyond) are dissatisfied with the status quo and interpret it as a lack of progress toward reunification, rather than progress toward "peaceful development" as under former PRC President Hu Jintao, then economic leverages can be instrumental to compelling Taiwan into political talks. The possible scenarios under which the Chinese leadership may display greater impatience toward the pace of cross-strait relations include a more assertive PLA in China's political system,[38] or a wider "selectorate" for the new-generation leadership in which the winning coalition is strongly nationalistic,[39] or the political inclination of new leaders whose formative years dovetail the rise of China, hence harbor a strong sense of entitlement. Furthermore, if China begins to democratize, cross-strait relations may not necessarily benefit. As Mansfield and Snyder amply demonstrate, ruling elites in a democratizing country

---

37 Luo Yuan, "On Using Force to Solve the Taiwan Issue," Keynote Speech at Conference on Chinese Economic Growth and Economic Security Strategy, Beijing, November 21, 2009. What is significant is that Luo Yuan was still an active serving PLA general when he made the speech. The wording by Lo Yuan hints at the Anti-Secession Law the PRC passed in 2005 to give mainland a legal basis for using force against Taiwan.

38 Assessments vary with regard to PLA's political clout in China's political system.

39 The term "selectorate" is from de Mesquita, Bruce Bueno, Alastair Smith, Randolph M. Siverson, and James D. Morrow, *The Logic of Political Survival* (Cambridge, MA: MIT Press, 2003).

tend to agitate nationalistic feelings to coalesce its supporters, fencing off competition from new opposition.[40] The pent-up nationalism in the general populace and netizens in particular, can provide fertile ground for this tactic.[41]

The third contextual variable of China's economic statecraft is the development of interest groups in Taiwan that have an economic stake in China's economy. Albert Hirschman's ground-breaking study on the political effect of asymmetrical trade structure addresses this issue. In Hirschman's words,

"What we have called the influence effect of foreign trade derives from the fact that the trade conducted between country A, on the one hand, and countries B, C, D, etc., on the other, is worth *something* (italic original) to B, C, D, etc., and that they would therefore consent to grant A certain advantage—military, political, economic—in order to retain the possibility of trading with A. If A wants to increase its hold on B, C, D, etc., it must create a situation in which these countries would do *anything* (italic original) in order to retain their foreign trade A."[42]

Theoretically, the asymmetrical trade structure is not necessarily a source of bargaining power for the stronger in the trade dyad. This is because the weaker side may attach more value to the issue under negotiation than the losses suffered as a result of punishment from the stronger side.[43] In other words, for Taiwan, benefiting from trade with China is one thing, putting its political future on the negotiation table is quite another. However, empirical case studies

---

40 Edward D. Mansfield, and Jack Snyder, *Electing to Fight: Why Emerging Democracies Go to War* (Cambridge, MA: Harvard University Press, 2005).

41 For Chinese nationalism in general, see Zhao, Suisheng, *A Nation-State by Construction: Dynamics of Modern Chinese Nationalism* (Palo Alto, CA: Stanford University Press, 2004). For nationalism expressed on the internet, see Wu, Xu, *Chinese Cyber Nationalism* (Lanham, MD: Lexington Books, 2007).

42 Hirschman, p.17.

43 Wagner, R. Harrison, "Economic Interdependence, Bargaining Power, and Political Influence," *International Organization*, Vol.42, No.3 (Summer 1988), pp. 465-475.

have shown that if the economic stakeholders with interests in the stronger state attain significant political presence in the target state's domestic politics, then national interests of the target state can be redefined.[44] It is therefore not entirely inconceivable that China may someday succeed in coercing (or cajoling then) Taiwan to sit at the negotiation table, if Taiwan's ruling coalition at that point values trade with China more than its political future.

In addition to contextual variables, there are certain process-specific variables that may also influence the success and failure of China's statecraft. These process variables may include, as Schelling, in his insightful analysis of compellence, argues, timing, the challenger's skill at communicating expectations to its adversary, assurance guarantees, and the nature of compliance. In terms of timing, Schelling elaborates,

"compellence has to be definite: We move, and you must get out of the way...there has to be a deadline, otherwise tomorrow never comes. If the action carries no deadline it is only a posture, or a ceremony with no consequences. Compellence, to be effective, can't wait forever. Still, it has to wait a little; Collision can't be instantaneous...Too little time, and compliance becomes impossible; too much time, and compliance becomes unnecessary."[45]

Therefore, if China fails to set a firm deadline for Taiwan's compliance, then Taiwan may foil China's coercive attempt by procrastinating. If China sets a deadline, Taiwan will still procrastinate to test China's determination.[46]

With regard to communicating expectations, the initiator can also

---

44 Abdelal, Rawi, and Jonathan Kirshner, "Strategy, Economic Relations, and the Definition of National Interests," *Security Studies*, Vol.9, No. 1-2, pp. 119-156. Abdelal, Rawi, *National Purpose in the World Economy* (Ithaca, NY: Cornell University Press, 2001).

45 Thomas C. Schelling, *Arms and Influence* (New Haven, CT: Yale University Press), p.72.

46 Even ultimatums, which are the most forceful form of communicating a state's determination to another state, frequently are dismissed by the target state. See Lauren, Paul Gordon, "Ultimata and Coercive Diplomacy," *International Studies Quarterly*, Vol. 16, No. 2 (June 1972), pp.131-165.

encounter difficulties. Schelling argues that "a compellent advance has to be *projected* as to destination, and the destination can be unclear in intent as well as in momentum and braking power."[47] Hence, any demands from China for political negotiation will make Taiwan highly wary of the potential ramifications, such as inadvertently binding Taiwan to greater demands in the future or opaque commitments.

In respect to the assurances that the challenger state can guarantee the target state for its compliance, Schelling once again offers insight into the subject:

"Actually, any coercive threat requires corresponding *assurances*; the object of a threat is to give somebody a choice...They are, furthermore, confirmed and demonstrated over time...The assurances that accompany a compellent action...are harder to demonstrate in advance, unless it be through a long past record of abiding by one's own verbal assurances...[B] oth sides of the choice, the threatened penalty and the proffered avoidance or reward, need to be credible...[T]he assurances are a critical part of the definition of the compellent threat."[48]

In analyzing the game tree above, this author has argued that China will find it difficult to offer credible assurances to Taiwan affirming that it will *not* make further demands on Taiwan to engage in reunification talks should it agree to initial talks over "political issues." Furthermore, economic inducements are likely to be more effective as a strategy of deterrence than compellence. With deterrence, the threat of punishment in the event of noncompliance carries with it an underlying assurance of reward in the event of compliance. Hence, the threat of punishment should Taiwan's voters elect a candidate unfavorable to Beijing is accompanied by the promise of reward, i.e., continued economic favors should Taiwan voters elect a candidate supportive of Beijing. In contrast, with compellence, noncompliance leads

---

47　*Ibid.*, p.73.

48　*Ibid.*, pp. 74-75.

to punishment but compliance leads to further demands, such as China demanding further engagement in political talks. As a result, under the scenario of compellence, Taiwan can only choose noncompliance.

The nature of compliance as a result of compellence may also impact the outcome of the strategy. Compliance under the condition of compellence is "more conspicuously compliant, more recognizable as submission under duress, than when an act is merely withheld in the face of a deterrent threat."[49] In other words, compliance under compellence is tantamount to losing face. One can imagine that the ruling party of Taiwan can simply "publicize" the compellent threat to leverage the negative reaction from Taiwan's general public against Beijing's pressuring. A "losing face" tactic can prove effective to undermine a threat of compellence.

IV. Conclusion

This paper describes China's economic statecraft toward Taiwan. While most of the research on this topic provides strong descriptive statistics on the economic interdependence between Taiwan and China, they do not attempt to specify the conditions under which China exercises its economic clout over Taiwan. In this paper I argue that since 2008 China has greatly increased its economic inducements toward Taiwan. The economic inducements, i.e., Chinese tourism and high-profile purchase missions in particular, can serve as the basis of China's statecraft in economic deterrence and compellence. Based on Baldwin's elaboration on Hirschman,[50] I argue that China may make deliberate efforts to strengthen the supply effect in Taiwan (that is, Taiwan will benefit from its trade with China and hence enhance its own national power.) But at the same time, China can create an influence effect in Taiwan to make Taiwan more subservient to China's interests. The

49 *Ibid.*, p. 82.
50 Baldwin, *op.cit.*, 1985, pp.210-216.

influence effect makes economic deterrence possible, as illustrated in the 2008 presidential election in Taiwan. In contrast, economic compellence, i.e., China's use of its economic power to extract political concessions from Taiwan, may prove difficult to accomplish because of interactive dynamics embedded in a compellence game. If the current trend in cross-strait trades continues, then those in Taiwan with economic stakes in China may steadily grow. And if in the future these stakeholders form a ruling coalition in Taiwan, China's economic statecraft may prove more effective.[51]

---

51 The success of Hirschmanesque influence effect depends a lot on the domestic institutions of the target state. For a general model of trade and domestic politics, see Rogowski, Ronald, *Commerce and Coalitions* (Princeton, NJ: Princeton University Press, 1989). For a more specific elaboration on trade sanctions, both positive and negative, and domestic politics, see Allen, Susan Hannah, "Political Institutions and Constrained Response to Economic Sanctions," *Foreign Policy Analysis*, 2008, No.4, pp.255-274. My former colleagues at Taiwan's National Chengchi University also did research on the impact of cross-strait commerce on Taiwan's political coalition. See Keng, Shu, and Lu-Huei Chen, "Cross-strait Trade and Taiwan's Political Blocs," (in Chinese), *Wenti-yu-Yenju*, Vol.42, No.6 (November 2003), pp.1-27.

Implications of China's "One Belt One Road" Initiative on Taiwan in the Geopolitical Setting

Chih-Chieh Chou[*]

I. Preface: PRC's 'One Belt One Road' Initiative and Taiwan

Since the year of 2012, Chinese government has initiated two strategic projects, the Silk Road Economic Belt and the Maritime Silk Road, as well as called the One Belt, One Road plan. Some argues that great geopolitical changes might be coming with Beijing's such initiatives, which demonstrates pro-action, financial capabilities and assertiveness. There is no doubt that China's place among global powers is rising every day as its economic power, but there are many speculations about the extent of their ability and the nature of their intentions. The reactions from countries included in the plan and from influenced parties very greatly, their response will also shape the future of this policy.

A map published by China's Xinhua news agency shows 14 "stops" on the land-based silk road through Central Asia, and another 14 on its maritime counterpart, and Beijing is still expanding its list of potential partners and the plan is still in development. The so-called Silk Road Fund with $40 billion to support infrastructure investments in countries involved in this plan, and recent proposal is in addition to the Asian Infrastructure Investment Bank (AIIB) proposal that 21 countries have already joined. Actually, China had already put vast sums of money behind investments in those countries, even without this comprehensive term being invented. It is possible that a more coherent approach and concrete policies over the One Belt, One Road policy may emerge in 2015. If this plan is realized, it would create the most

---

*   Professor, Graduate Institute of Political Economy National Cheng Kung University.

promising economic region, directly benefiting 4.4 billion people or 63 percent of the global population, with a collective GDP of 2.1 trillion U.S. dollars that is 29 percent of the world's wealth.[1] It is more likely that China will offer aid bilaterally, thus more directly benefiting Chinese companies and providing much-needed burnishing of China's reputation abroad. This development aid likely will go to countries with large domestic markets or commodity resources.

For Taiwan, theoretically, through a trade pact with China Taiwan can have access to new markets and also opportunities for investment, especially in southern Chinese provinces, which are also included in the belt. The Chinese president, Xi Jinping, who combined a profound knowledge of Fujian and a deep understanding of the Taiwan issue, is offering Taipei an opportunity to benefit from his grand strategy and a space for regional economic integration besides the Asia Pacific Economic Cooperation (APEC). Actually, Taiwan's tremendous construction capabilities and creativities in service and labor capital are quite well known. Taiwan is more than capable of taking some parts in the One Belt, One Road plan. However, Taiwan's inner situation is complicated and reactions to closer economic relations with China are not positive. If the One Belt, One Road plan and the proposed FTAAP turn out to be a success and if Taiwan is excluded, it would mean greater isolation for the island. Some claim that Taiwan's economic strategy could fall hostage to an anti-China mindset, as was the case during the Sunflower Movement in March 2014. Even the cross-Taiwan Strait relation is still interdependent economically and rival politically, people in Taiwan might treat the China's threat as a constant find a way to ride on China's wings.

---

1   Wendell Minnick, "Modern-day Silk Road Effort Could Challenge US Influence in Asia, Africa, Mideast," *DefenseNews*, April 12, 2015, <http://www.defensenews.com/story/defense/2015/04/11/taiwan-china-one-belt-one-road-strategy/25353561/>

Unfortunately, the situation does not look very good for Taiwan. Some people and politicians in Taiwan seem to posit that since any rise of Chinese power threatens the island more and makes it more and more dependent on USA. Moreover, China is fighting Taiwan on other fronts too, such as ensuring diplomatic support and recognition from small pacific island countries. The grip is tightening more around Taiwan's neck as China can only become more powerful. Hence, taking balance between Washington and Beijing would be the crucial issue for Taiwanese leader, whoever is regarded as the pan-blue or pan-green camps.

II. PRC's Intentions on 'One Belt One Road' Initiative

China's intentions are clear. The crucial idea behind the phrase is to promote infrastructure development in Asia (and possibly beyond), thereby enabling deeper economic cooperation. Through this strategy, China can increase its regional influence as well as supporting its domestic economy by encouraging trade and investment and creating business opportunities overseas for Chinese companies. Firstly, the One Belt, One Road plan would boost China's trade with effectively the whole Eurasian continent. At the same time, if China pays for various infrastructures, the great trade network would convince relevant countries that China is a partner and benefactor rather than a threat. China can simultaneously promote its softer image building and strengthen its regional powers.

Additionally, this plan with its land and maritime route elements will make China better connect the Southeast Asia, Middle East, Africa and Europe through its landlocked neighbors in Central Asia and the states in Indo-China Peninsula and South Asia. It will decrease China's geographic and strategic vulnerabilities by diversifying access routes. Therefore, the system of ports, railways and roads will effectively help China to secure the transport of oil and gas and other essential goods needed to sustain China's economic development. It strengthens the country's energy and economic security and reduces the risks of transporting fuel and goods through unstable or unfriendly channels. For example, the proposed building of transport corridors via Pakistan, Myanmar and Thailand will shrink China's dependency on the Strait of Malacca. China has also taken over the major Gwadar port in Pakistan, enabling it to obtain oil from the Middle East while avoiding the Hormuz and Malacca straits, which are clogged with traffic and U.S.-controlled.[2] In other words, China is situated in a tough neighborhood, sharing a long contiguous land border with Russia and India and a common sea boundary with Japan. As such, this plan could possibly be seen as a strategy to prevent any encirclement or containment that a hostile power in concert with other states may undertake to harm China's interests.

Significantly, China's economic powers are rising and still growing. Beijing is naturally trying to take advantage of its financial situation to boost political influence. It is true that a rising global power intends to utilize its economic strengths to secure its foreign policy goals. Looking back to the history, the Marshall Plan in the end of WWII helped to establish the U.S. as a dominant power. China's plan might enable to do the same. Of course, some Chinese scholars have criticized the similarities between the two plans, and posited that the One Belt, One Road strategy has nothing to do with ideological intentions and a desire for being a hegemon. Furthermore, there are no political conditions in this plan which is open to all countries pursuing development and growth. In contrast to the Marshall Plan, the One Belt, One Road plan plays emphasis on mutual negotiation, joint efforts and sharing the fruits of development. Every country can decide whether or not to participate in this plan. China seems to understand the key desire of many developing countries: they want development first and they want development without the political strings imposed by the West.

More importantly, through linking the economies in Central Asia with western China, Beijing provides further development and stability to

2   Wendell Minnick, op. cit.

comparatively less-developed Xinjiang and Tibet. China intends to weaken any potential support that Uygur dissident groups may seek from kinship Muslims in Central Asia. Hence, this plan goes far beyond simply sharing economic prosperity. It has obvious political and security implications. Besides, this plan will also provide a strategic exit for Beijing at a time when the Pacific Ocean is being blocked by the U.S. As China is pushing for a Free Trade Area of the Asia Pacific region (FTAAP) to balance the U.S.-led Trans-Pacific Partnership (TPP), this strategy is an open statement that China will someday aim to share Washington leading position in the Asia Pacific.

III. Shifting Washington-Beijing Interplays in the Asia Pacific

On the one hand, some countries along the way have welcomed the idea as they perceive this plan as a great opportunity to comprehensively deepen economic and people to people relations. Simply cause smaller and less-developed countries need financial supports to establish new ports or related transport infrastructure or to upgrade existing facilities, they definitely welcome a willing new sponsor or financier. Especially Beijing's longstanding policy of foreign aid is non-intervening. Comparing to the "Washington Consensus" with political conditionality, "Beijing Consensus" without political requirement is more popular with states that have limited access to capital and technology because of foreign-imposed sanctions or stringent governance requirements set by regional or international lending institutions, such as the World Bank, IMF, and Asian Development Bank. This is one of the reasons Chinese help is so attractive.

On the other hand, some countries still consider Beijing as a major threat in national security, and they mistrust China's strategic objectives as more likely to wait and see what China take for this plan. To some degrees, China has fuelled its neighbors' suspicions by taking aggressive gesture on territorial disputes in recent years, repeatedly warning the possibility of military solutions to overlapping land claims with Japan, the Philippines, Vietnam and India. Central Asian states are fearful of replacing economic dominance from Moscow with Beijing. China's huge population also causes some fears that the vast Chinese immigrants in the region. As such, lots of countries expect the benefits of the One Belt One Road plan when they simultaneously look for offset their economic dependence on China by strengthening ties with other powers, especially the US. Considering soft power, Washington remains far more influential than Beijing in Asia. US' continue presence in the region is still crucial for most countries, in particular of security dimension.

Actually, China realizes that the world is closely watching how Beijing protects its sovereignty and territory and how it implements its so-called "harmonious development," "great power diplomacy" and "good neighbor diplomacy." So, Beijing will tend to balance between the doctrine of "peace development" rather than "hegemonization" and the perception of "sovereignty without compromise." China tends to facilitate the "Beijing consensus" and promote "democratization in international relations" in especially multilateral regimes and developing world. Therefore, China will treats Sino-US relations as a core in external relations, while it realized the US marks the rising China as a potential challenger. Much more Chinese elite acknowledges that China deserves a reasonable international status and role, given that China is a radically rise power in diverse dimensions. China defined it "core interests" both in external and internal aspects. China couldn't stay outside the partnership with Washington, simply cause China is still not strong enough to play as the rival polar of the "G2" against the US. The US is betting that China will go the other way to become the "responsible stakeholder" because it is in China's interests, not just the US's, that it does so.

For Washington, since the end of the Cold War, the US have faced a dilemma over how it should deal with China. A cottage industry has developed of academics and diplomats writing books and articles which evaluate the extent to which China is a "threat" to East Asia and the US.

As Harry Harding argues, "though China is willing to join the existing international order, it wants to play a larger role – as a rule-maker, not just a rule-taker."[3] These fears are fuelled by the concern that China's phenomenal economic growth over the past fifteen years will eventually translate into military power and a desire to exert its influence on the regional and - at some point - global stages. These fears are heightened by evaluations which indicate that China has greatly increased its military spending over the course of the past decade.[4] In terms of regional security, China's continuing conflict with Taiwan is the area with the greatest potential for an outright confrontation with the US. China also has active territorial disputes with several of its neighbors. China is in conflict with Japan and Taiwan over the Diaoyu/Senkaku Islands. China and several states in Southeast Asia dispute various parts of China's and Taiwan's claim to the islands chain in the South China Sea (Spratly Islands, Paracel Islands, Pratas Islands, and Macclesfeld Bank), as well as the South China Sea itself. Based on these disputes, most regional states are concerned that China will use its growing economic and military power to assert its claims at some point in the future. In this assessment, China is not satisfied with the status quo, and it will do what it can to change the status quo in the future.

As such, relations between China and the US were often strained in the early post-Cold War period. Japanese and American actions largely confirm the outlooks of Chinese hardliners, who have long argued that Japan is inherently militaristic and looking for the opportunity to reestablish itself as an independent power. China was deeply unhappy over the consolidating US-Japan security alliance. China's standard portrayal of the US is of a declining hegemon which, nonetheless, will remain the dominant global

---

3   Harry Harding, "China: Think Again!" *PactNet* (Pacific Forum CSIS) No.17, April 5, 2007.

4   Thomas J. Christensen. "Fostering Stability or Creating a Monster? The Rise of China and US Policy toward East Asia," *International Security* Vol. 31, No. 1 (2006), pp. 101-105.

power for the time being and must be handled carefully.[5] China remains concerned with how both the US and Japan exercise their power. The 1996 Taiwan Straits confrontation between the US and China and the collision between a US reconnaissance aircraft and a Chinese fighter in 2001 had a significant impact on China's perceptions of the US. This incident reinforced China's conviction that American global influence must be balanced and occasional operation of nationalism is benefited to the legitimacy of the Chinese Communist rule.[6]

In fact, there are two strategic approaches to China in Washington's strategic circle. A rising China threatens the preeminent role of the US in East Asia, and the American leading role, for a long term, has permitted the US to help shape regional politics in ways that directly serve US interests. During the Clinton administration, the policy toward China was one of "strategic engagement." The Americans argued that engaging China and gradually incorporating it into the international system through membership in the World Trade Organization and other international bodies would socialize China into accepting the basic norms of international conduct. The basic strategy was one of "entangling" China in alliances and structures, thereby moderating its behavior over the long term. However, the first term of the G.W. Bush administration is inclined to see China as a "strategic competitor."[7] It is the only single country that, in the foreseeable future, could emerge to challenge the US' economic domination of the world, and this economic power could eventually become military power.[8] Following

---

5   Fei-Ling Wang, "Self-Image and Strategic Intentions: National Confidence and Political Insecurity," in Yong Deng and Fei-Ling Wang (eds.), *In the Eyes of the Dragon* (Lanham: Rowman and Littlefield, 1999), p. 38.

6   Harry Harding, "China: Think Again!" *PactNet* (Pacific Forum CSIS) No. 17, April 5, 2007; Paul Bowles, "Asia's Post-crisis Regionalism: Bringing the State Back In, Keeping the (United) States Out," *Review of International Political Economy* Vol. 9, No.2 (2002), pp. 255-257.

7   The White House, *The National Security Strategy of the United States of America of 2002*, September, 2002, <http://georgewbush-whitehouse.archives.gov/nsc/nss/2002/>.

8   Thomas J. Christensen. "Fostering Stability or Creating a Monster? The Rise of China and

this approach, the G.W. Bush administration has also gone out of its way to antagonize China, particularly in its handling of US relations with Taiwan and its pursuit of NMD.

Nevertheless, there are many reasons to argue that interpretations of China's future intentions which depict China as a hegemon-in-waiting are premature. It is worrying that China insists that its sovereignty over disputed areas is indisputable, and it is this attitude that feeds much of the regional uncertainty around China's intentions. However, in most other respects, the evidence supporting the argument that China is a long-term regional threat is ambivalent. China has faced a dilemma. On the one hand, China has to sustain economic development in order to offset the social and political instabilities. On the other hand, socio-political problems are the product of its rapid economic development. China itself announces that it is following a "good neighbor" policy in its regional relations and insisting the "peaceful rising" path towards a modern state.[9] China's top priority is its own economic development. For the foreseeable future, that goal requires that China have a peaceful, stable, and economically prosperous regional environment in which to develop. It is not in China's interest to antagonize its neighbors, on whom it depends for investment and technology, or to create an environment of political instability. Taking all of these factors into account, it is difficult to argue that China is an imminent threat to East Asia.[10]

Thus, President Bush, since his second term, was gradually aware of China's irreplaceable status in cooperating with the US on issues as terrorism, nuclear proliferation, energy, and other transnational problems, if China keeps its promise of peaceful development.[11] The Bush Administration

US Policy toward East Asia," *International Security* Vol. 31, No. 1 (2006), pp. 96-97.

9   "Prospects on the Incoming Decade," *Xinhua News Agency*, May 4, 2005.

10   For further discussions, please see David Shambaugh, "China Engages Asia: Reshaping the Regional Order," *International Security* Vol.29, No. 3 (2004), pp. 64-99

11   The White House, *The National Security Strategy of the United States of America of 2006*, 2006, <http://www.whitehouse.gov/nsc/nss/2006>.

has adjusted its Chins policy to "return back to the normal track" through building a newly ambiguous concept of "stakeholder," rather than the existed "partner" or "competitor."[12] Accompanying with the radical growth and development of national economy, China became increasingly aware of the need for a multilateral cooperation regime in Asia Pacific so as to mitigate anxiety about the country's military build-up and economic rise, and at the same time, to check Japanese efforts on remilitarization and strategy at sustaining leading status in economic integration.[13] Accordingly, China has adopted a more flexible approach to resolving relevant trade and economic issues in the region through bilateral negotiation through signature of FTA with, say, the ASEAN, and has actively participated in community building like the RCEP and FATAAP.

Therefore, the Obama administration announced that it was "returning to Asia" since 2009, it is really about shaping the environment in which China will rise in ways that the US prefers. Washington thinks it still has a strong hand to play. Partners in the region are looking for Washington to demonstrate the sustainability of the "pivot" through not only words but actions, and not just in the military realm but across the breadth of US political, security, and economic interests in the region. It should continue to maintain a neutral gesture between China and Japan on the territorial dispute, and to press China and ASEAN to make progress toward a formal code of conduct for the South China Sea. Obama's strategy is to remind China that while it has lots of big trade partners, the US has lots of good friends as well as allies. It explains why the US has taken up the mantle of creating a proto

---

12 Ibid., the report addresses: "As China becomes a global player, it must act as a responsible stakeholder that fulfills its obligations and works with the United States and others to advance the international system that has enabled its success: enforcing the international rules that have helped China lift itself out of a century of economic deprivation, embracing the economic and political standards that go along with that system of rules, and contributing to international stability and security by working with the United States and other major powers."

13 Alastair Johnston, "Is China a Status Quo Power?," *International Security*, Vol. 27, No. 4 (2003), pp. 5-56.

Asia-Pacific free trade area through the TPP. However, Washington cannot contain Beijing and isn't trying to. It wants to continue to engage with China and worries it will need to hedge in case China's rise turns malign. But most of all, the US wants to shape China's rise, while China tend to rise in its own way, and most importantly, it respects the US-led but widely shared and co-defined "rules of the game" or "status-quo order."

To sum up, Washington's attitude has shifted toward China in the past two years, simply cause the US gradually acknowledge that China's economic interdependence with East Asian countries and the rest of the world is likely to prevent Beijing from military action unless major national interests are jeopardized. Moreover, the need for US to treat China as a strategic partner on some regional and global issues is also well taken by decision makers in Washington.[14] As China rises to the position of a major power in East Asia, Beijing is competing with Washington, the traditional regional powers, for dominance. However, the key task for the US and Japan is not "Beijing will use its military power to attack other countries, but rather that it will use its growing resources to shift the overall balance of power in China's favor."[15]

IV. Taiwan's Response to Regional Trend: Ma's Redirections on Cross-Strait Relations and Diplomacy

One could easily discover that issues of cross-strait relations always occupied the center of the attention in political arena and civil society in Taiwan. The crucial differences on cross-strait policy between the two major political parties are regarded as "conservativeness vs. openness" in

---

14 David Shambaugh, "China Engages Asia: Reshaping the Regional Order," *International Security*, Vol.29, No. 3 (2004), pp. 89, 93.

15 Harry Harding , "China: Think Again!," op. cit. Paul Bowles, "Asia's Post-crisis Regionalism: Bringing the State Back In, Keeping the (United) States Out," *Review of International Political Economy*, Vol. 9, No.2 (2002), pp. 255-257.

economy, and "separation vs. overlapping (of sovereignty across the Strait)" in politics. Taiwan successfully accomplished the regime change from the pro-independence camp to the pro-status quo camp in May 2008. After the President Ma Ying-jeou assumed office, the progress of cross-strait relation has moved faster in closer economic ties and greater political understanding. In his inaugural address of 2008, Ma posits that "under the principle of 'no unification, no independence and no use of force,' as Taiwan's mainstream public opinion holds it, and under the framework of the Republic of China (ROC) Constitution, we will maintain the status quo in the Taiwan Strait."[16] As such, based on the "1992 Consensus," negotiations between both sides across the Taiwan Strait resume soon, and cross-strait interplays forward to so-called the period of peaceful development.

The Ma administration tends to improve cross-strait relations, which in turn helps to improve Taiwan's international relations. In other words, Taiwan pursues its diplomacy with the precondition of maintaining friendly and cooperative relations with China. The Ministry of Foreign Affairs of the ROC declares that it has implemented this policy based on the principles of "dignity, autonomy, pragmatism, and flexibility."[17] This policy aims to allow Taiwan to forge ahead with its diplomatic work and find a modus vivendi for its diplomacy. Thus, the approach of so-called "viable diplomacy" is a product of such a discourse. In the past, Taipei and Beijing's decades-long competition to win over diplomatic allies had left cross-strait interactions at an impasse and isolated Taiwan from the world stage. Under the viable diplomacy approach, Taiwan seeks to enlarge its international space and reduce cross-strait tensions. As such, Taiwan bolsters relations with its diplomatic allies as well as important non-diplomatic partners, and pursues meaningful participation in international organizations.

---

16 Taipei Economic & Cultural Office in HO Chi Minh City, *President Ma's Inaugural Address of 2008*, 2008, < http://tecohcm.org.vn/en/data/president-ma.pdf>.

17 See Mainland Affairs Council, Republic of China (Taiwan), *Mainland Policy and Work*, December, 2012, <http://www.mac.gov.tw/ct.asp?xItem=102566&ctNode=6607&mp=3>.

In the realm of political trust, the Ma administration advocates "mutual non-recognition of sovereignty and mutual non-denial of governing authority (jurisdiction)" based on "1992 Consensus" (one China, two different definitions) calling on both sides to end hostile competition, pursue reconciliation in the international sphere and cease squandering valuable resources. The concept of "mutual non-recognition of sovereignty and mutual non-denial of authority to govern" is a pragmatic reflection of the status quo. It is based on the ROC Constitution, because according to the Constitution, the government cannot recognize the existence of another sovereign state on the Chinese mainland. The government thus denies the sovereignty of the People's Republic of China (PRC), and not its own sovereignty. In 1992, the ROC government reaffirmed its sovereignty over the Chinese mainland in accordance with the Constitution, while acknowledging that it no longer exercises jurisdiction over the mainland. Thus, cross-strait relations are not state-to-state but represent a "special relationship."[18] In other words, Taiwan and China do not recognize each other's sovereignty and they also do not repudiate each other's jurisdictions. Under such an understanding, two sides have engaged each other and have signed binding agreements. For President Ma, it is the best strategy for defining the status of the cross-strait relationship and providing an opportunity for Taiwan's international participation.

Actually, Taiwan realizes China's rising power and influence in the world. It will be difficult for it to develop diplomacy without reducing China's suppression. Reducing cross-strait tensions can allow Taiwan to avoid spending unnecessary resources in pursuing Taiwan's diplomatic interests by stopping diplomatic race with China. As such, Taiwan's interactions with the mainland and the international community have grown into a virtuous cycle. More importantly, it has helped restore mutual trust

---

18 Ma Ying-jeou, President of the Republic of China, Remarks in *2011 International Law Association Asia-Pacific Regional Conference*, May 30, 2011, <http://www.cils.nccu.edu.tw/Opening%20Address%20of%20President%20Ma%20Ying-jeou.pdf>.

between Taiwan and other countries, especially the US, as well as creates additional avenues for Taiwan's future diplomatic work. As Kin Moy noted that "it is very much in our interest to see improvements in cross-Strait relations. We commend the progress that has been achieved in recent years and we encourage both sides to continue these efforts. The reason is straightforward: maintenance of cross-Strait stability is essential to the US goal of promoting peace and prosperity in the Asia-Pacific region."[19]

It is fair to say that the cross-strait peaceful development and viable diplomacy is a triple-win policy. Taipei, Washington and Beijing all benefit from it. Diplomatic truce and peaceful interactions across the Strait is helping Taiwan to further strengthen its substantive relations with countries in the Asia Pacific, thus raising the prospect of Taiwan playing a more active role and yielding greater influence in the region. Especially in East Asian security, Taiwan wins praise from the international community and is considered as a peace-maker rather than a trouble-maker. Any successor of Taiwanese leader might not diverge from such an external strategy.

V. Concluding Remarks: Taiwan's Opportunities and Tasks

In general, the One Belt, One Road plan will spread China's influence on many sides. Massive and expensive project that however if finished, will definitely put China on a new level, greatly resembling the US. We will see a complex geostrategic interplay progressively undermining the hegemony of the US dollar as a reserve currency and the petrodollar. For all the immense challenges the Chinese face, all over Beijing it's easy to detect unmistakable signs of a self-assured, self-confident, fully emerged commercial superpower. For Taiwan, the peaceful development across the Strait expands Taiwan's international space and participation, including to

---

19 Kin Moy, "Trends in the U.S.-Taiwan Relationship," *Remarks in the Carnegie Endowment for International Peace*, October 3, 2013.

joining the AIIB and the One Belt One Road Initiative. Furthermore, Taiwan pursues its concrete interests without insisting on using formal titles in participating in international organizations. However, while considering the opportunities possibly provided by this initiative, further risks and tasks are also needed to face by Taiwan.

First, the Taiwan policy under the Xi Jinping administration seems to slightly transform from a "92 consensus" to a "one China framework", China intends to focus only on "Taiwan and mainland belong to one China" and ignore "the different definitions of 'China'."[20] Hence, especially since 2014, the cross-Strait relations and the issue of Taiwan's status have been hotly debated in Taiwan and the major announcements by President Ma, particularly his proclamation of Taiwan status as non-state-to-state special relations do provoke domestic debate that Taiwan might make unilateral compromise on its sovereignty. Therefore, Beijing needs to realize that no Taiwanese president will turn his back on the public that strongly identifies with the ROC and launch talks with China, with Taiwan being placed in an unjustified and diminished position. No matter how friendly relations are, or how much understanding and care is expressed, Chinese authorities can only truly win Taiwanese people's support by recognizing the political reality of both sides across the Taiwan Strait being governed separately and the existence of the ROC, as well as by respecting the ROC president.

The KMT and DPP in Taiwan understand the games authorities play in Beijing. Based on policy prescriptions of the CCP Small Leading Group on Taiwan, the CCP Propaganda Department seeks to manipulate perceptions that Taiwan is equal to a province in stature, thus expanding the sovereignty gap in China's favor. The diversity of Taiwanese society and the possibility of a change in the ruling party might both be a result of China adopting a cautious attitude towards political relations between the two sides. But why not think outside the box and look at the bigger picture? The peaceful

---

20 "One China Policy," *China Net*, <http://www.china.org.cn/english/taiwan/7956.htm>.

development of cross-strait ties will become the mainstream for Taiwanese society and pave the way for stable Taiwan-China relations. Hence, both sides across the strait should try to move the common political base from the concept of "mutual non-recognition of sovereignty and mutual non-denial of authority to govern" to the discourse of "mutual acceptance of co-sharing of 'Chinese statehood' (in international arena) and mutual recognition of co-existence of authority to govern (across the strait)."[21]

Second, for China's Taiwan policy, the 18th Party Congress Work Report suggests a continuation of policies to promote the mainland's gradual economic, cultural and political integration with Taiwan. So long as such trends can plausibly be interpreted by Beijing as progress toward laying the material foundations for eventual unification, the CCP leadership led by Xi may be satisfied with the "peaceful development" of cross-Strait ties. It seems that China attempts to institutionalize the existed diverse cross-Strait platforms in mutual dialogues and exchanges by focusing on promote four major forums: the Strait Forum (focus on social exchange: mainly inviting local NGO activists and local politicians), the KMT-CCP Forum (focusing on economic and cultural dimensions), the Entrepreneurs Summit (focusing on industrial cooperation), and the Peace Forum (focusing on political and military dialogues since 2013). Through these platforms, Taiwan has the responsibility to push forward freedom, democracy, human rights and the rule of law as core values in the cross-strait relation. However, it is also true

---

21 For the discourse about the both sides "mutual acceptance of co-sharing of 'Chinese statehood' (sovereignty) and mutual recognition of co-existence of authority to govern," see Chih-Chieh Chou, "China Revises its Law to Identity Taiwan's Current Status," *Want Daily News*, 22 March, 2013, <http://www.want-daily.com/portal.php?mod=view&aid=67407>; Chih-Chieh Chou, "Establishing the Commission on Peaceful Development," *Want Daily News*, 21 June, 2013, <http://www.21stcentury.org.tw/02_research/03_detail.php?id=6&type=3&did=1144>; Chih-Chieh Chou, "Linking Taiwan's Inward-Looking Mind and External Tendency across the Strait," *Want Daily News*, 5 June, 2014, <https://tw.news.yahoo.com/%E9%80%A3%E7%B5%90%E5%85%A9%E5%B2%B8%E5%B0%8F%E7%A2%BA%E5%B9%B8%E8%88%87%E5%A4%A7%E5%BD%A2%E5%8B%A2-215049774.html>.

that the different paths towards modern societies between the two sides, which cannot be solved within a short period of time. Taiwan can be an appropriate lesson in terms of China's upcoming socio-political reform, as well as Cross-strait interplays in a spirit of mutual tolerance and mutual understanding.

Third, through a trade pact with China, Taiwan can have access to new markets and also opportunities for investment in Chinese. Xi Jinping, who combined a profound knowledge of Fujian and a deep understanding of the Taiwan issue, is offering Taipei an opportunity to benefit from his grand strategy and a space for regional economic integration besides the APEC. Actually, Taiwan's tremendous construction capabilities and creativities in service and labor capital are quite well known. Taiwan is more than capable of taking some parts in the One Belt, One Road plan. However, Taiwan's inner situation is complicated and reactions to closer economic relations with China are not positive. If the One Belt, One Road plan and the proposed FTAAP turn out to be a success and if Taiwan is excluded, it would mean greater isolation for the island. Some claim that Taiwan's economic strategy could fall hostage to an anti-China mindset, as was the case during the Sunflower Movement in March 2014. Even the cross-strait relation is still interdependent economically and rival politically, people in Taiwan might treat the China's threat as a constant and find a way to ride on China's wings.

Hence, on the one hand, considering the deepening and widening exchanges and ties across the Strait, and the geopolitical tendency faced by Taiwan, perhaps it is the time for Taiwan's to try to shift its strategic paradigm during the past 60 years (See Table 1). Cooperating with Beijing might be a rational option rather than an ideological thought. China could not be the only potential enemy for Taiwan. Both sides can cooperation in non-traditional security and maritime security. Furthermore, Taiwan may consider its own interests from PRC-ROC common interests rather than from US-led geopolitical view.

On the other hand, the situation does not look very good for Taiwan. Some people and politicians in Taiwan seem to posit that since any rise of Chinese power threatens the island more and makes it more and more dependent on US. The grip is tightening more around Taiwan's neck as China can only become more powerful. Hence, taking balance between Washington and Beijing would be the crucial issue for Taiwanese leader, whoever is regarded as the pan-blue or pan-green camps. Indeed, China's rise and activism within the region suggests a larger, longer-term struggle to define the nature of East Asian geopolitics. Many of China's initiatives promote a far more integrated Asia than currently exists. Such a future may seem unlikely; simply causing American strategic concerns. Other states' leaders appear torn between their long-term concerns over a bullying US and a rising China. As Muthaih Alagappa has argued, "the primary purpose of the state-centered regional security order in Asia is to consolidate the nation-state, enhance its international power and influence, and create a safe and predictable environment."[22]

Finally, the real task for Taiwan is to re-identify its geopolitical and geo-economic status in the setting of the Asia Pacific and across the Taiwan Strait. Taiwan is a de facto small island country in geographical terms, so doing some human insecurity and sustainable development issues such as rising sea levels is an urgent matter. More importantly, Most of Taiwan's diplomatic allies are less-developed island or coastal nations. Taiwan being perhaps the biggest and strongest among these small island nations, the government would be wise to help friendly countries find a solution, for their benefit and for Taiwan itself. Taiwan can establish its own 'blue belt' in the Pacific islands and other coastal allies. Taiwan could facilitate technology transfers to friendly island countries and help them build up disaster response capabilities that are similar to Taiwan itself. This would not just help Taipei's allies resolve practical problems, but would also establish a sense

---

22 Muthaih Alagappa, "Constructing Security Order in Asia," *Asian Security Order* (Stanford, CA: Stanford University Press, 2003), p. 79.

Table 1: Relative Power Changes among USA, PRC, and ROC

Self-Identity	Position(capacity)			Identity(Perception)
	Political	Military	Economic	
USA	⌣	⌢	⌣ ?	A (Friendly) Hegemon
PRC(China)	⌢	⌢	⌢	A Regional Power A Hegemon Challenger? A Responsible Civilized Power?
ROC(Taiwan)	⌣	⌣	⌣	An US "Buck-passing" Ally (or A Bandwagon)? A Member of Democratic Community? A Civilizational Leader in Chinese Societies?

Source: the figure made by the author.

of belonging to a community with a common destiny and thus cement our friendship with our allies in a meaningful way. Only if Taiwan's geopolitical orientation and diplomatic strategy are adjusted can it overcome obstacles and succeed in its flexible diplomacy.

Taiwan's FTA negotiative strategies after "ANZTEC and ASTEP"–An approach of neo-regionalism

Joyce Juo-Yu Lin[*]

Abstract

This paper will adopt "neo- regionalism" approach to analyze the future political and economic integration in East Asia. It will focus on the Taiwan FTA strategies after ANZTEC and ASTEP. Following two years of negotiations, the 12 members of TPP (The Trans-Pacific Partnership) have had 19 rounds meeting and will be concluded in next March 2014. Also, RCEP (The Regional Comprehensive Economic Partnership) the 16 members of RCEP will finish negotiations and be concluded by the end of 2015.

In 2013, Taiwan and New Zealand signed ANZTEC, Taiwan and Singapore signed ASTEP. These two nations are membership of TPP and RCEP. What kind FTA strategies are advantageous for Taiwan to adopt if Taiwan signed more bilateral then it will benefit for Taiwan's entry into RECP? How will great powers (China and the U.S.) influence the Political and Economic integration in East Asia? Taiwan wants to avoid being economically marginalized during the process of future Asia-Pacific and East Asia political and economic integration.

[*]   Associate Professor, Graduate Institute of Asian Studies, Tamkang University.

Preface

Taiwan is East Asia's fourth largest economy and possesses one of the region's most dynamic and innovative business communities. Taiwanese firms are at the cutting edge of East Asia's information and communications technology (ICT) sector. The Taiwanese economy also fared the storm of the 1997/98 financial crisis better than any other, recording 6 percent economic growth in 1998 while most East Asian economies experienced a fall in their gross domestic product. Taiwan has a well-educated, enterprising, and prospering people, and is plugged into many important regionalization processes in East Asia, such as ICT and electronics sector international production networks.

I. TPP: Trans-Pacific Partnership Agreement

The 2005 Trans-Pacific Strategic Economic Partnership Agreement (TPSEP or P4) is a free trade agreement among Brunei, Chile, New Zealand, and Singapore. It aims to further liberalize the economies of the Asia-Pacific region.[1] TPP is a multilateral free trade agreement among APEC forum member economies, New Zealand, Chile, Singapore and Brunei (P4, 2006). TPP has enlarged to P9 (add Australia, Peru, and Vietnam 2008) and then will be P10. It is the only trans-regional trading agreement that builds new strategic and economic links between Asian and Latin American states. Originally, it hasn't aroused sufficient attention after its taking effect in 2006. However, following the initial U.S. decision to join the negotiations in September, within the 21-member APEC forum to forge a Free Trade Agreement of the Asia Pacific.

---

1   The 2005 Trans-Pacific Strategic Economic Partnership Agreement, TPP Retrieved on January 28, 2012.

TPP was formed by four APEC economies of Brunei, Chile, New Zealand, and Singapore in 2006. Its objective in Article 1 states that it aims to establish a Trans-Pacific Strategic Economic Partnership among the parties, based on common interest and deepening of the relationship in all areas of application'. It has taken a "WTO plus", covering not only commodity and services trade but also such facilitation areas as rules of origin, customs procedures, trade remedies, technical barriers to trade, competition policy, intellectual property, government procurement, and dispute settlement. (TPP 2006).

At APEC 2010 Yokohama Leaders clearly declared to continue TILF as a core activity of APEC for another decade and symbolized the FTA in the Asia Pacific (FTAAP) as its concrete target. FTAAP was proposed to APEC Leaders by ABAC in 2006 aiming at a greater FTA covering the whole APEC economies (ABAC 2006). It promotes the integration and conglomeration of all FTAs mushroomed in the APEC region for the past decade and thus creating a greater single market achieving the maximum scale economy. ABAC/PECC joint report of the same year (ABAC/PECC 2006) included both pros and cons of the FTAAP. Fred Bergsten, Director of Peterson Institute of International Economics, Washington D.C., expressed his concern about the stumbled negotiation of the WTO/DDA and recommended FTAAP as a "Plan B" in preparation for the failure of the DDA and resulting vacuum of liberalization momentum in the region (Bergsten 2006). He served as the chair of APEC/EPG for 1993-1995 and led actively the liberalization momentum within APEC then.

The momentum heightened to the Bogor Declaration in 1994 and he planned to achieve it by negotiating an FTA. However, in the following year the Japanese host invented the concept of "Concerted Unilateral Liberalization" within the Osaka Action Agenda, which disappointed many Americans including Bergsten. The author conjectures he resumed his original proposal together with American ABAC members after ten years. On the other hand, Charles Morrison, the American Chair of PECC, represented a majority view of PECC academics, indicating practical difficulty with conducting liberalization negotiation within APEC and insisting the pragmatic strategy along the Busan Roadmap (Morrison 2006).

Nevertheless, the current studies of FTAAP have not gone into concrete procedures of achieving it. Academic studies focused on the CGE model calculation under specific assumptions, which results in a greater welfare gains of FTA of a greater geographical coverage. Sangkyom Kim (2009) reported that, under the assumption of all tariffs abolished, 10% reduction of services barriers, 5% reduction of transaction cost through trade facilitation, and simplified rules of origin, all APEC economies would gain and APEC's real GDP increase by 1.13%, while the real GDP of EU would decrease by 0.08% and that of rest of the world decrease by 0.06%. Since welfare gains is in the order of 0.1% or less for smaller FTAs, FTAAP would give a greater trade creation but less trade diversion effects. (see Table 2 "ASEAN+N" VS. "TPP"—Market Liberalization).

Having been making efforts since 2010, Taiwan finally signed the Agreement between Singapore and the Separate Customs Territory of Taiwan, Penghu, Kinmen, and Matsu on Economic Partnership (ASTEP) on November 7, 2013. The ASTEP negotiations were carried out under WTO rules, and the resulting agreement is Taiwan's first such with a Southeast Asian country.

The new agreement requires Singapore to cut import tariffs on all Taiwan goods to zero immediately. Taiwan is required to lower tariffs on 99.48% of all Singapore goods, following five different timetables depending on the sensitivity to liberalization: immediate, 5 years, 10 years, 15 years, and partial reduction (a reduction to 80% of the original tariff within five years). It helps set the stage for Taiwan's entry into the Trans Pacific Partnership (TPP), Regional Comprehensive Economic Partnership (RCEP), and other forms of regional integration.

The TPP is currently being negotiated by the U.S. and 11 other countries —New Zealand, Chile, Singapore, Canada, Brunei, Australia, Peru, Malaysia, Vietnam, Mexico and Japan. Following two years of negotiations, the 12 members of TPP have had 20 rounds meeting and will be concluded in March 2014. Also, the 16 members of RCEP will finish negotiations and be concluded by the end of 2015. The RCEP is a trade group planned to start operations by the end of 2015. Present talks include the ten members of the Association of Southeast Asian Nations (ASEAN), and other 6 countries in EAST Asia- China, Japan, South Korea, India, Australia and New Zealand. It is so called "ASEAN plus 6".

These two mechanisms both are very crucial. In 2013, Taiwan and New Zealand signed ANZTEC, Taiwan and Singapore signed ASTEP. These two nations are overlapping membership of TPP and RCEP. This is expected to create mutual prosperity and enhance collaboration between Taiwan and the two countries. As Singapore is not only a key trading partner of Taiwan but also a member state in the TPP and RCEP, the ASTEP shows to international community that Taiwan is ready to ink similar pacts with other countries and participate in the economic integration of the Asia-Pacific region

It seems likely if Taiwan signed more bilateral FTA then it will benefit for Taiwan's entry into TPP and RECP. What kinds of FTA strategies are advantageous for Taiwan to adopt and how will great powers (the PRC and the U.S.) influence Political and Economic integration in East Asia? How can Taiwan avoid being economically marginalized during the process of future Asia-Pacific and East Asia integration. These two bilateral FTAs have the most important implications since Taiwan has been worrying economic marginalization during the FTAs trend in East Asia. Definitely Joining TPP and RCEP is a must for Taiwan to compete with players like South Korea, avoid disrupting local production chain and promote systemic transformation. But if the nation is to win the trust of the members of these two major free trade blocs and their support for Taiwan's entry, apart from the preparatory work of domestic liberalization, Taiwan to seek U.S. support for TPP bid at TIFA. The TIFA talks will be an opportunity for Taiwan to reiterate its efforts to seek entry into the U.S.-led trade bloc and seek Washington's support. Taiwan and the U.S. resumed the TIFA talks last March. The agreement was signed in 1994 as a framework for Taiwan-U.S. dialogue on trade-related issues in the absence of diplomatic ties, but talks had been suspended since 2007, largely due to controversy over U.S. beef imports. Taiwan is expected to use the TIFA talks to seek U.S. support for its bid to join the TPP, a proposed U.S.-led Pacific Rim trade bloc.

In recent FTAs, including KORUS FTA, the United States has made market access of express delivery services a priority, which could also be the case in its negotiations on the TPP. Of particular concern are cases where a government-owned and operated postal system provides express delivery services competing with private sector providers. The KORUS FTA stipulates that the postal system cannot use its monopoly power in providing postal services to give an express delivery subsidiary an unfair advantage. Nor should it divert revenues from its postal services to subsidize its express delivery services to the disadvantage of other providers.

Ever since Japan joined the talks in 2013, the TPP has attracted increasing interest in the rest of East and Southeast Asia (South Korea, Taiwan, Thailand, Philippines), and South Asia (India), and to a degree even in China. President Obama has mentioned, for two long decades, the U.S. has failed to participate in Asia's rapid growth. It is also supported by a strategic quest to move U.S. military presence from the transatlantic axis to the trans-Pacific. Finally, the talks have been pushed by President Obama's pledge to double U.S. exports to rejuvenate American economy.

Also, Taiwan wants to have Japan's help in terms of entry into TPP. Economic ties continue to deepen between Taiwan and Japan, and the two countries signed five new bilateral agreements on November 5, 2013 which was following recent investment and fishery pacts. In the future the two sides will carry out ongoing talks on financial supervision, taxation, customs, and trade in services with the aim of establishing a solid foundation for the signing of a comprehensive economic and trade agreement. The five newly signed documents include an agreement for cooperation in the fields of ecommerce, a memorandum of understanding (MOU) on cooperation in priority document exchange (PDX), a framework agreement on cooperation.

Taiwan and Japan will create an open, secure, and stable Internet transaction environment by, among other things, promoting transparent, reasonable, and fair e-commerce regulations and measures, and by reducing obstacles to cross-border trade. The two sides will work together to prevent commercial fraud on the Internet and, in accordance with their own regulations, to protect the personal information of e-commerce users and upgrade the security of Internet transactions.

Taiwan's President Ma Ying-jeou has reiterated his government's determination to join the TPP and the proposed Regional Comprehensive Economic Partnership (RCEP). He had indicated that Taiwan is earnestly seeking support from its trade partners for its bid into the trade blocs. He perceives that mainland China's attitude and position is also a crucial factor. Mainland China has become a major trade partner for many countries in the Asia-Pacific region, and economic clout is of prime importance in international relations. If supporting Taiwan were to impact these countries' economic and trade opportunities with mainland China, they will naturally act from self-interest. Some international observers will defend that China has not joined the TPP, due to TPP is too high quality for China to fulfill. From the PRC's perspective the TPP is also the rule-making competition between U.S.-led deep-integration TPP and China's shallow-integration approach (ASEAN+N) is inevitable but good (competitive liberalization). It seems likely that this competition will be more crucial and then China will be on the TPP negotiation table eventually

From the U.S.'s Strategic Thinking on TPP, TPP would be a Regional institution-building which hold multilateral trade negotiation, companies the effect of export promotion. Besides, TPP will emerge direct effect – hybrid approach to seek market expansion of new partners and indirect effect. There would be some competitions between TPP members and non-TPP members. Also, the U.S. will benefit from the alliance broadening, it is bringing new partners through TPP (as Vietnam, Malaysia and New Zealand). If you asked about the U.S. attitude toward Taiwan's TPP bid, Washington always responds welcome Taiwan's interest in the TPP.

What is the future scenario for Taiwan's entry into TPP? Based on difference in tariffs (IDB, CIER), the winners would be Petrochemical, Machinery, Pulp and Paper, Steel (main beneficiaries), Textile, Bicycle; the losers will include Food Processing, Auto Parts, Agriculture (beef, diary). Currently tariff exceeding 10% fall in items covering: animal(16%), vegetable(11%), Fats, Oil, Wax(12%), food stuff(16%); those exceeding 5%: textile (8%), glass (6%), transportation(8%).

Current China's evaluation on TPP would be some skeptics: for example—TPP is difficult to succeed, TPP escalates competition in rule-making and TPP interferes in regional production chain. In the past 2-3 years, China has cautioned that TPP offers more market-opening, TPP is the way to go through the U.S. and 11 countries efforts and Vietnam is the test case for the PRC to consider the TPP's future function.

The current state of affairs, where mainland China's making no move to join TPP is practically blocking Taiwan from moving forward, is certainly far from what Taiwan desires. To iron out the problems requires a continuation of cross-strait dialogue, and Beijing needs more innovative thinking, so that a mutually beneficial solution for both sides can be found.

Taking a closer look at the precedence issue, Taipei and Beijing's positions appear to be contradictory, but the discrepancy is caused by progress on the trade in services and trade in goods agreements and the dispute resolution mechanism. The faster these accords are completed the smaller this discrepancy will be. Put another way, the longer such negotiations drag out, the greater their impact will be. The next wave of accessions to the TPP and RCEP is projected for 2015 and 2016, it is probably building pressure on Taiwan's concluding the next batch of cross-strait agreements.

Since 2010, negotiations have been taking place[2] for the Trans-Pacific Partnership (TPP), a proposal for a significantly expanded version of TPSEP. The TPP is a proposed free trade agreement under negotiation by (as of December 2012) Australia, Brunei, Chile, Canada, Malaysia, Mexico, New Zealand, Peru, Singapore, the United States, and Vietnam.[3] Japan has expressed its desire to become a negotiating partner,[4] but not yet joined negotiations as the TPP became a major issue in Japan's 2012 election.[5] South Korea was asked by the U.S. to consider joining the TPP[6] but declined for the time being.[7]

The TPP is ostensibly intended to be a "high-standard" agreement specifically aimed at emerging trade issues in the 21st century.[8] These

2   *"On-going Negotiations at a Glance: TPP (Trans-Pacific Partnership),"* Singapore Government; Formal negotiations started in March 2010, and there has been 10 rounds of negotiations as of January 2012.

3   Agence France-Press, "Protests turn violent at trade talks in New Zealand," *MSN News*, Dec. 8, 2012, <http://news.malaysia.msn.com/regional/protests-turn-violent-at-trade-talks-in-new-zealand-2>.

4   ANDY HOFFMAN, "Japanese PM Looks to Join TPP," *The Globe and Mai*, Nov. 11, 2012, <http://www.theglobeandmail.com/report-on-business/international-business/japanese-pm-looks-to-join-trans-pacific-partnership-trade-deal/article5186241/>.

5   MAI IIDA, "Major parties give themselves wiggle room on thorny TPP," *The Japan Times*, Dec. 12, 2012, <http://www.japantimes.co.jp/news/2012/12/12/business/major-parties-give-themselves-wiggle-room-on-thorny-tpp/#.VWG8TE-qqko>.

6   "U.S. Requests Korea Join of regional FTA," *THE DONG-A ILBO*, Dec. 18, 2010, <http://english.donga.com/srv/service.php3?biid=2010121816208>.

7   REUTERS, "S. Korea prioritizes Asia trade pacts over Pacific partners," *The Jerusalem Post*, May 17, 2012, <http://www.jpost.com/Breaking-News/S-Korea-prioritizes-Asia-trade-pacts-over-Pacific-partners>.

8   Office of the United Trade States Trade Representative,"*The U.S. and the TPP*," <https://ustr.gov/tpp>.

ongoing negotiations have drawn criticism and protest from the public, advocacy groups, and elected officials, in part due to the secrecy of the negotiations, the expansive scope of the agreement, and a number of controversial clauses in drafts leaked to the public.

The negotiations initially included three countries (Chile, New Zealand and Singapore), and Brunei subsequently joined the agreement. The original TPSEP agreement contains an accession clause and affirms the members' "commitment to encourage the accession to this Agreement by other economies."

In January 2008 the United States agreed to enter into talks with the P4 members regarding liberalization of trade in financial services. Then, on September 22 2008, U.S. Trade Representative Susan C. Schwab announced that the United States would begin negotiations with the P4 countries to join the TPP, with the first round of talks scheduled for early 2009.[9]

In November 2008, Australia, Vietnam, and Peru announced that they would be joining the P4 trade bloc.[10] In October 2010, Malaysia announced that it had also joined the TPP negotiations.[11]

In June 2012, it was announced that Canada and Mexico would join TPP negotiations.[12] Mexico's interest in joining was initially met with concern among TPP negotiators about its customs policies. Two years earlier, Canada became an observer in the TPP talks, and expressed interest

---

9 Office of the United States Trade Representative *"Trans-Pacific Partners and United States Launch FTA Negotiations*," Sep. 2008, <https://ustr.gov/trans-pacific-partners-and-united-states-launch-fta-negotiations>.

10 Johnny C. Chiang, "The challenges of regional bodies," *Taipei Times*, Dec. 17, 2008, <http://www.taipeitimes.com/News/editorials/archives/2008/12/17/2003431334>.

11 The White House, *"Trans-Pacific Partnership Leaders Statement*," Sep 9, 2012, <http://www.ustr.gov/about-us/press-office/press-releases/2012/september/tpp-leadership-statement>.

12 Office of the United States Trade Representative,*"U.S. Trade Representative Kirk Welcomes Mexico as a New Trans-Pacific Partnership Negotiating Partner*," June 18, 2012, <https://ustr.gov/about-us/policy-offices/press-office/press-releases/2012/june/ustr-mexico-new-tpp-partner>.

in officially joining,[13] but was not committed to join, purportedly because the United States and New Zealand blocked it due to concerns over Canadian agricultural policy—specifically dairy—and intellectual property rights protection.[14] Several pro-business and internationalist Canadian media outlets raised concerns about this as a missed opportunity. In a feature in the Financial Post, former Canadian trade negotiator Peter Clark claimed that the Harper Government had been strategically outmaneuvered by the Obama Administration, Wendy Dobson and Diana Kuzmanovic for The School of Public Policy, University of Calgary, argued for the economic necessity of the TPP to Canada.[15]

Canada and Mexico formally became TPP negotiating participants in October 2012, following completion of the domestic consultation periods of the other nine members.[16]

South Korea expressed interest in joining in November 2010,[17] and was officially invited to join the TPP negotiating rounds by the United States after the successful conclusion of the U.S.-South Korea FTA in late December.[18] The country already has bilateral trade agreements with other TPP members, thus making any further multilateral TPP negotiation less complicated.[citation needed]

---

13 "Tories consider joining Trans-Pacific trade group," *CBC News*, Nov 16, 2010, <http://www.cbc.ca/news/canada/tories-consider-joining-trans-pacific-trade-group-1.881614>.

14 U.S. Trade, "*TPP Countries Say Canada Not Ready To Join Talks, Press Vietnam To Decide,*" Jan. 28, 2012.

15 Embassy warned that Canada's position in APEC could be compromised by being excluded from both the U.S.-oriented TPP and the proposed China-oriented ASEAN +3 trade agreement (or the broader Comprehensive Economic Partnership for East Asia).

16 Government of Canada, "*Canada Formally Joins Trans-Pacific Partnership,*" Oct 9, 2012 ,<http://www.international.gc.ca/media_commerce/comm/news-communiques/2012/10/09a.aspx?lang=eng>.

17 Nishikawa, Yoko, "South Korea mulling U.S.-led TPP trade initiative: report," *Reuters*, Nov. 13, 2010, <http://www.reuters.com/article/2010/11/14/us-apec-korea-idUSTRE6AD05L20101114>.

18 "U.S. Requests Korea Join of regional FTA."

Japan joined as an observer in the TPP discussions that took place 13–14 November 2010, on the sidelines of the APEC summit in Yokohama.[19] Japan is regarded as a potential future member but it would have to open its agricultural market in a way it refused to do in previous trade negotiations such as the Doha Development Round. Autos and insurance are also issues of contention. On November 11, 2011, Japanese Prime Minister Yoshihiko Noda announced his nation's interest in joining the treaty negotiations.[20] However, as of mid-2012, Japan was still only an observer, and had not yet formally entered the negotiations. Japan declared its intent to join the TPP negotiations on March 13, 2013 and an official announcement was made by Prime Minister Shinzō Abe on March 15, 2013.

Other countries that have expressed interest in TPP membership are Taiwan,[21] the Philippines, Laos, Colombia, and Costa Rica. On 20 November 2012, Thailand's government announced that it wishes to join the Trans-Pacific partnership negotiations during a visit by President of the United States Barack Obama and if it follows the process for Canada and Mexico, Thailand will be in the extraordinary position of having to accept any existing agreed text, sight unseen.

Trans-Pacific Partnership (TPP): 17th Round of TPP Negotiations Set for Lima, Peru -May 15-24, 2013.[22]

---

19 "U.S. Government: Japan PM Kan Attended TPP Talks As Observer," *NASDAQ*, Nov. 12, 2010, <http://www.nasdaq.com/aspx/stock-market-news-story.aspx?storyid=201011132 333dowjonesdjonline000254&title=us-governmentjapan-pm-kan-attended-tpp-talks-as-observer>.

20 Rick Wallace, "Trade boost for Australia as Japan agrees to free-trade negotiations," *The Australian*, Nov. 12, 2011.

21 "Taiwan aims to join Trans-Pacific Partnership: minister," *FOUCS TAIWAN*, Nov. 10, 2010, <http://focustaiwan.tw/news/aall/201011100039.aspx>.

22 "Trans-Pacific Partnership (TPP)," Office of the United States Trade Representative, <http://www.ustr.gov/tpp>.

II. RCEP competes with the TPP?

Competition appears likely to emerge between ASEAN's Regional Comprehensive Economic Partnership (RCEP), an agreement to launch negotiations for which was reached at the East Asia Summit (EAS) in Phnom Penh on November 22, and the Trans-Pacific Partnership (TPP).

The two regional trade pacts have quite similar objectives trade liberalization and economic integration and competition between the two to be Asia's predominant economic arrangement has the potential to divide the ASEAN countries.

In 2011, the total GDP of TPP countries was U.S.$20 trillion, with the U.S. accounting for three quarters of this. In line with its pivot toward Asia, the U.S. has led the expansion of the TPP and encouraged other APEC countries to join the negotiations. The U.S. argues that the TPP needs to be broadened in order to cover relevant elements of economic cooperation and to meet the economic challenges of the 21st century. The TPP countries have negotiated on which areas should be covered by the agreement; these now include trade in goods and services, investment, intellectual property rights (IPRs), environmental protection, labour, financial services, technical barriers and other regulatory issues. The 16th TPP negotiations will be held in Auckland, New Zealand in early December 2012.

RCEP has a different origin to the TPP. ASEAN has FTAs with non-ASEAN countries, such as China, South Korea, Japan, India, Australia and New Zealand, which are separate from one another. The ASEAN framework for RCEP is an ASEAN initiative to gather all these FTAs into an integrated regional economic agreement. However, it will establish deeper economic cooperation than the existing FTA agreements. RCEP will open up more trade in goods and services, eliminate trade barriers, and gradually liberalize services and provide for greater foreign direct investment in ASEAN and its external trading partners. The GDP of the ASEAN and non-ASEAN negotiating parties is U.S.$17 trillion.

Given the similarities between the two agreements, RCEP may pose a challenge to the TPP. The TPP calls for deeper integration than RCEP, promoting trade in goods, services and investment, as well as tackling other issues (for example, IPRs). RCEP will be a partial WTO-plus arrangement, which focuses on trade in goods, several types of services and investment. However, the TPP and RCEP may come into conflict due to the tension between the U.S. and China, as each wants to shape economic cooperation in the Southeast and East Asian regions in order to secure its economic interests. Consequently, rivalry between the U.S. and China might become the predominant factor in how the regional economic architecture develops.[23]

Any competition between these two agreements may divide the ASEAN members. Singapore, Malaysia and Vietnam may be likely to focus on promoting the TPP to other Southeast and East Asian countries, while the rest of the ASEAN countries will likely aim to develop RCEP, so that it is at the centre of economic cooperation in the region. (see Figure 1- the Regional Economic Integration)

Such division will profoundly influence the centrality of ASEAN. ASEAN aims to preserve its centrality to economic co-operation within Southeast and East Asia through initiatives such as the EAS and ASEAN+3. If ASEAN does not respond effectively to any potential competition between the TPP and RCEP, ASEAN's role as a driving force in the various regional arrangements is more likely to decline. The rivalry between the U.S. and China could also undermine the crucial role that ASEAN plays.[24] (see Table 3 Trade partnership competition: TPP vs RCEP)

---

23 Beginda Pakpahan, "Will RCEP compete with the TPP?," *EAST ASIA FOUR*M, Nov. 28, 2012, <http://www.eastasiaforum.org/2012/11/28/will-rcep-compete-with-the-tpp/>.

24 Mark Thomson ,"Trade partnership competition: TPP vs RCEP," *ASPI*, Apr. 16, 2013, <http://www.aspistrategist.org.au/trade-partnership-competition-tpp-vs-rcep/>.

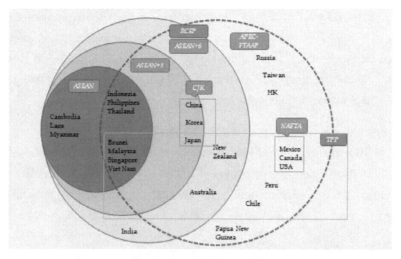

Figure 1: The Regional Economic Integration

Resourse:2015, The ADB Razeen Sally, REGIONAL ECONOMIC INTEGRATION IN ASIA: THE TRACK RECORD AND PROSPECTS <http://www.ecipe.org/app/uploads/2014/12/regional-economic-integration-in-asia-the-track-record-and-prospects.pdf>.

Table 1: Trade partnership competition: TPP vs RCEP

Trans-Pacific Partnership	Regional Comprehensive Economic Partnership
APEC	East Asia Summit
Australia	Brunei
Brunei	Cambodia
Canada	Indonesia
Chile	Laos
Japan	Malaysia ASEAN
Malaysia	Myanmar
Mexico	Philippines
New Zealand	Singapore
Peru	Thailand
Singapore	Vietnam
Vietnam	China
United States	Japan
	South Korea ASEAN+3
	Mexico
	Australia
	India ASEAN+6
	New Zealand

So, in order to maintain its centrality, ASEAN must focus on the creation of RCEP while furthering its regional consolidation through the ASEAN Community. If it does not do this, ASEAN may find that its role as a proactive, central player in fostering political and economic arrangements in East and Southeast Asia declines.

From the United States under the auspices of APEC, the proposed Trans-Pacific Partnership (TPP). From the East Asia Summit (EAS), with ASEAN in the lead, the proposed Regional Comprehensive Economic Partnership (RCEP). Those countries presently involved in negotiations on each are listed below. (see Table 1. Trade partnership competition: TPP vs RCEP)

III. The ASEAN's Regional Economic Strategies

As an economic project, the ASEAN Economic Community (AEC) is expected to achieve its objective of a single market by this end of 2015. Although ASEAN has achieved about 82.1 % of its targets, it has not yet reached its end-goal since both border and beyond-the-border restrictions continue to prevail in the region. The elimination of such restrictions is likely to be the most important task if ASEAN intends to move towards a single market space in the future.

1. Strategic Engagement

The ten Southeast Asian nations and their concrete 'deliverable' of an ASEAN Economic Community (AEC) on 31 December. Understandably, questions have been raised as to whether the AEC can be successfully achieved. This paper tries to provide an answer to this by arguing that one should not judge the AEC solely by its economic outcomes and the issue of whether the AEC can be attained in its entirety by the deadline. Rather, one should also evaluate the AEC against its ability to serve the region's strategic goals of economic coherence in dealing with the international community as well as maintaining ASEAN centrality.[25]

The AEC is said to have achieved 82.1% of the stipulated targets mentioned in the 2007 Blueprint.[26] This achievement can be considered a significant beginning for ASEAN (Table 1). Under trade in goods, tariffs have been lowered, the ASEAN Single Window is ready, key agreements like the ASEAN Trade in Goods Agreement (ATIGA) and the ASEAN Comprehensive Investment Agreement (ACIA) are in place. In addition, the Master Plan for ASEAN Connectivity (MPAC) has been adopted to reduce business transaction cost as well as time and travel costs in the region. Mutual Recognition Arrangements (MRAs) for seven professions have been signed. These include engineering and architecture, nursing, accountancy and surveying services, medical and dental profession.

2. Pragmatic Security Thinking

Furthermore, disparity in per capita income among members has been reduced. Since the beginning of 2000, ASEAN has engaged its major trading partners through Free Trade Agreements (FTAs), and a limited number of private sector firms to benefit from ASEAN's initiatives of liberalization and facilitation.[27]

The ASEAN Trade Facilitation Joint Consultative Committee will be reactivated, as will be the ASEAN Consultation to Resolve Trade and Investment Issues (ACT), which is basically an internet- based "complaint box" for companies to raise AEC issues anonymously with the ASEAN

---

25 ASEAN Centrality implies that ASEAN, instead of the bigger economies like those of China, Japan, the U.S. or India, should be the hub of developing a wider Asia-Pacific regional architecture. See Amitav Acharya, "The End of ASEAN Centrality?," *Asia Times Online*, August 8, 2012.

26 ASEAN Secretariat (2014), Chairman's Statement of the 25 the ASEAN Summit: "Moving Forward in Unity to a Peaceful and Prosperous Community," November 12, 2014.

27 ASEAN Community Progress Monitoring System, The ASEAN Secretariat, 2012; Economic Research Institute for ASEAN and East Asia (ERIA), 2012, "Mid-term Review of the ASEAN Economic Community Blueprint"; discussion with ASEAN Secretariat officials.

Table 2: Progress towards the ASEAN Economic Community

Selected Indicators	Year	Value	Year	Value	Trend
	Early Year		Latest Year		
Intra-ASEAN Trade, U.S.$ billion	2000	166.1	2012	602.0	Increasing
Intra-ASEAN trade share (%)	2000	22.0	2012	24.3	Increasing
Intra-ASEAN FDI Inflows, U.S.$ billion	2000	1.2	2012	20.1	Increasing
Intra-ASEAN FDI share (%)	2000	5.1	2012	18.3	Increasing
Intra-ASEAN Trade in Services, U.S.$ billion	2005	21.3	2011	44.4	Increasing
Intra-ASEAN services trade share (%)	2005	8.1	2011	8.4	Increasing
ASEAN GDP per capita (PPP$), averagea	2000	4187	2012	8394	Increasing
ASEAN average of WEF Competitiveness index (as % of the first ranked country)	2000	77.7	2011	80.6	Increasing
ASEAN average of Human Development Index	2005	0.635	2013	0.690	Increasing

Note: a- the per capita average is calculated based on IMF world economic outlook database and excludies the figures for Brunei and Singapore (their GDP per capita in PPP term is more than $75,000 in 2012).

Source: Author's modification, using ASEAN Community Progress Monitoring System, The ASEAN Secretariat, 2012

Secretariat (reportedly the previous ACT system was inoperable for months or years due to internet security issues). GOASEAN, a 24-hour ASEAN travel channel, was also launched. The Summit statement discussed the Initiative for ASEAN Integration, which deals with the economic development gaps in the region, but did not mention the Asian Infrastructure Investment Bank, newly funded by China.

3. Strategic Hedging: TPP and RCEP

Despite these outcomes, ASEAN is far from its goal of attaining a single market and production base.[28] There are a number of hurdles as the followings:

First, non-tariff barriers (NTBs) in the form of non-automatic licensing, technical regulations and quality standards continue to prevail in the region. Second, the region continues to suffer from infrastructure deficiency. These two factors together negate the full benefit from tariff liberalization. Third, despite negotiations over the past fifteen years, there is only a marginal liberalization in the services sector. This is attributed to the lack of policy alignment between the regional and domestic economies. For example, although MRAs for seven professions have been signed, many countries impose domestic restrictions on foreign nationals or nonresidents working as professionals. Fourth, the region continues to experience difficulties from the development gaps among its member economies.

The ASEAN states represent a 600 million-strong market that has relatively stable political institutions, young and cheap labor sources, and a longstanding relationship based on cultural, educational, and economic exchanges supported by ODA, JIAC, and other Japanese institutions. Importantly, it is a part of the world that "likes" us. The cost of doing business in China keeps rising. It's too big of a market not to be a part of, but the recent anti-Japanese riots and growing nationalism are compelling us to look to "friendlier" markets like those in Southeast Asia. The Japanese government since PM Abe's election in December 2012 has also aggressively courted ASEAN nations through expanded ODA, norm-based multilateral agreements, and the elicitation of a commitment to settle disputes in multilateral forums. With a total of five visits to ASEAN states in

---

28 Sanchita Basu Das, "Can the ASEAN Economic Community be Achieved by 2015?," *ISEAS Perspective*, Oct 11, 2012, <http://www.iseas.edu.sg/documents/publication/ISEAS-Perspective_07_11oct121.pdf>.

2013, the Japanese government was able to meet each member of ASEAN and ramp up its strategic hedging, while continuing to engage in China-Japan relations by taking a "where they can" approach.[29]

Similarly, the U.S. has thought it necessary to distribute some of its financial investments and geopolitical commitments in the region by broadening trade, political, and security relations. For example, the amelioration of Myanmar-U.S. relations is an illustrative case. Long isolated from the U.S., beginning in 2012 the U.S. began to court the Myanmar leadership starting with low-level diplomatic challenges to eventually reestablish an embassy there.[30]

4. ASEAN Centrality?

The RCEP (Regional Comprehensive Economic Partnership) and Trilateral Summit (TLS) are also examples of strategic engagement along apolitical, economic lines. In the case of the RCEP, this regionally inclusive agreement includes China, Japan, and South Korea, among other nations. It aims to create a free-trade area that encompasses most of East Asia. It further tethers the regional economies together, fostering deeper economic integration. The lack of ideological barriers and qualitative limitations means that all nations in the region can and will participate. This contrasts with the TPP, as we will see in the discussion below.[31]

---

29 "With visits to all 10 ASEAN nations, Abe's China containment strategy complete," *The Asahi Shimbun*, Nov. 13, 2013, <https://ajw.asahi.com/article/behind_news/politics/AJ201311180082/>.

30 Bureau of East Asian and Pacific Affairs, *U.S. relations with Burma*, fact sheet, Aug. 13, 2013, <http://www.state.gov/r/pa/ei/bgn/35910.htm/>.

31 Balancing Trade and Security Relationships in the Asia Pacific: The Advent of a Trilateral Seikei Bunri Relationship between Japan, China, and the U.S.

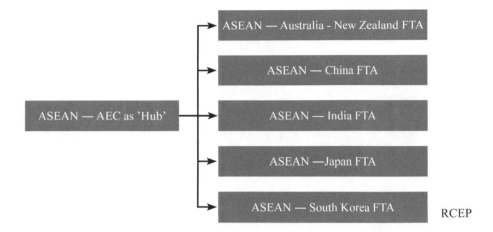

Figure 2: ASEAN as a 'Hub' in the Bigger Regional Architecture

IV. Taiwan's Economic Strategies in the Regional Integration between Asia-Pacific and East Asia

Taiwan's engagement with East Asia's micro-level regionalization is deep, and its economic integration with mainland China is well developed (particularly in the past 2 years). This has posed various economic security predicaments for Taiwan's policymakers. While deepening Cross-Strait economic ties have permitted Taiwanese businesses to remain internationally competitive, it has also made Taiwan increasingly dependent on a singular and diplomatically. Both the RCEP and TPP regional frameworks have to date proved disappointing as mechanisms for collective action in dealing with the current global financial crisis. Despite these failings, it remains in Taiwan's longer term strategic interests to seek APT and EAS membership, not because of any current imperatives but rather because of how these regional frameworks and their agendas are likely to evolve in the future.

Notwithstanding the scope for transnationalized Taiwanese firms to mitigate and mediate the trade diversion effects of FTAs signed by other countries in the region, Taiwan's business associations have long pressed the government to enter into an agreement with China that could unblock the diplomatic constraints facing Taiwan's FTA policy generally, as well as provide a competitive fillip to the island economy.

The Ma Ying-jeou administration started talks with Beijing on an FTA styled Economic Cooperation Framework Agreement (ECFA) has thus been welcomed by the business community but viewed with great caution by the opposition party DPP, labor groups, the farming lobby, and many social welfare organizations on account of the potential threats such an opening up to China this may pose to Taiwan's society. ECFA has been signed in June 2010, it would significantly change the calculus of Taiwan's position in East Asia's regional political economy, albeit it in mostly unpredictable ways. It primarily depends on what kind of ECFA, and whether this would be a precursor to other subsequent developments in Taiwan's bilateral and regional economic diplomacy.

Conclusion

Taiwan's omission from RCEP is more a concern for Taiwan than its omission from EAS. This is not just because RCEP has developed a much stronger diplomatic apparatus for regional co-operation but also because it is the more likely to be the vehicle for advancing East Asia's future regional integration owing to two fundamental factors: (i) the RCEP group possesses a much stronger degree of regional economic coherence than the EAS group, and thus a firmer basis of existing regionalized linkages on which to build deeper integration; (ii) regional groups with smaller memberships tend to have a smaller range of national interests to reconcile, and are therefore able to secure a basis for collective action on regional integration, which requires deeper policy-related commitments than regional co-operation.

And, the harmonization of the Cross-strait economic relationship with mainland China, especially Taiwan has had ANZTEC and ASTEP signed with New Zealand and Singapore, and other bilateral agreements under negotiation. It will be building consensus and support with stakeholders.

In sum, Taiwan's marginalization regarding the expansion of FTA activity among East Asian and Asia-Pacific states has been of greater concern for Taipei than its non-participation in both China-led & the U.S.-led regional financial schemes. Either RCEP or TPP which Taiwan may adopt under the currently competitive circumstances, Taiwan would not take sides and hope to join the RCEP or TPP any FTA approach.

Analysis on China's Economic Integration into Asia

Andrea, Pei-Shan Kao[*]

Abstract

If one compares China's participation in international organisations, he will find that China now is much more active than before. In the past few decades, China was not willing to join too many international regimes as it considered their design for the aims of the United States foreign policy for controlling and leading the world. However, after the rise of its Comprehensive National Power (CNP), especially its economic power, China now not just actively joins international regimes but also tries to promote, invent and create organisations based on its interests, such as the Shanghai Cooperation Organisation (SCO) or the Asian Infrastructure Investment Bank (AIIB). After his rapid consolidation of political power, Xi Jinping is moving to put his own stamp on China's foreign policy. He proposed a "New Model of Great Power Relations" with the United States, "Great Power Diplomacy" with other powers, and a "Good Neighbor Policy" with Southeast Asian countries. On China's economic development, Southeast Asian countries play a critical role no matter on Xi's strategic planning of the "Belt and Road" initiatives or the establishment of the AIIB. China's new strategies hence have caused the U.S. the greatest concern. Therefore, this paper wants to first examine the adjustment of China's Southeast Asian policy, especially its economic integration with the Association of Southeast Asia Nations (ASEAN) member countries.[1] Then it will discuss its impacts

---

*   Assistant Professor, Department of Bordering Police, Central Police University.

1   The Association of Southeast Asian Nations (ASEAN) was established in 1967 in Bangkok, Thailand, with the signing of the Bangkok Declaration by the founding members of ASEAN, namely Indonesia, Malaysia, Philippines, Singapore and Thailand. Brunei

and implications for President Barack Obama's the Asia-Pacific region and their struggle for power in this region hence conclude with some suggestions.

I. China's Southeast Asia Policy and Development of China-ASEAN Relations

In general, China's foreign policy in Southeast Asia can be divided into five periods: (1) before the reform and opening up; (2) U.S.-China rapprochement during the 1970s; (3) reform and opening up in the 1980s; (4) China's economic rise in the 1990s; (5) China's rise as a global power since 2000 until present. In the early period, as most of Southeast Asian countries did not establish yet diplomatic relations with China and due to the opposition between the U.S.-led capitalist camp and the Soviet side of socialist group during the Cold War, China had negative, hostile and unfriendly views to these countries. In the strategic triangle (comprising the United State, the Soviet Union and the People's Republic of China), China pursued a policy of strategic independence; that is to say, China's role in world politics at this period was one of balance. On regional politics, China's foreign policy was full of communist ideology; in addition to developing relations with Southeast Asian countries based "on party-to-party" contacts, China also tried to enhance relations with regional communist countries by providing capital, weapons, and military equipment. Following with its opposition to the United States and the Soviet Union at the same time, China could not develop well its relations with Southeast Asia. However, since the deepening of the Soviet threat, China decided to adopt a strategy to make alliance with the United States; its relations with Southeast Asian countries there could be improved. Since China adopted economic reform and opening up policies in 1979, its foreign policy was adjusted to an open and pragmatic

---

then joined in 1984, Vietnam in 1995, Lao and Myanmar in 1997, and Cambodia in 1999. About the aims and purposes of the ASEAN, can see the official website, *ASEAN*, <http://www.asean.org/>.

direction under the leadership of Deng Xiaoping. It then tried to dilute and alleviate past ideological views and style hence emphasised peaceful coexistence and economic cooperation with Southeast Asian countries.

Throughout the 1980s, China made many efforts to improve its relations with Southeast Asian countries; however, due to the occurrence of the June 4 incident in 1989, namely the Tiananmen Square incident, China's reputation in international society was seriously damaged. China was isolated by the Western countries, it could only improve its relations with neighboring countries by economic and trade exchanges. It then pursued an active diplomatic strategy from previous passive stance. In addition to adopting a "good-neighborly foreign policy" to develop relations with Southeast Asian countries, China also promoted its economic and trade contacts with these countries, and actively participated on regional affairs. From this period, Southeast Asian countries also started to recognise the benefits for a collective policy to enhance their importance and bargaining chips, as well as the role they could play in world politics. The Chinese government gradually improved and successfully established formal diplomatic relations with Southeast Asian countries. It then eventually joined the Asia-Pacific Economic Cooperation (APEC) in 1991,[2] and also launched the China-ASEAN dialogue. To focus on China's national development, in the early 1990s, Den Xiaoping put forward the "24 character strategy", namely "observe calmly, secure our position, cope with affairs calmly, hide our capacities and bide our time, be good at maintaining a low profile, and never claim a leadership".[3] Therefore, on its relations with ASEAN, it adopted "Economic Diplomacy" and a policy of "Good-Safe-and-Rich-

---

2   The APEC is a regional economic forum founded in 1989 to leverage the growing interdependence of the Asia-Pacific. It now has 21 members to create greater prosperity for the region by promoting balanced, inclusive, sustainable, innovative and secure growth and by accelerating regional economic integration. About the introduction of the APEC, see *APEC*, <http://www.apec.org/>.

3   "Deng Xiaoping's '24-Character Strategy'," *Global Security*, <http://www.globalsecurity. org/military/world/china/24-character.htm>.

Neighborliness".[4] That is to say, China has downplayed its hard power in this region; its foreign policy to its neighboring countries was based on harmony, security and prosperity, Good-Neighborliness Policy.

In 1996, China became ASEAN's full dialogue partner, and the two established in 1997 a partnership of "good-neighborliness and mutual trust".[5] This was upgraded in 2003 to a "strategic partnership for peace and prosperity", China therefore became the first to establish strategic partnership with ASEAN. In addition, China was also the first to join the "Treaty of Amity and Cooperation in Southeast Asia" (TAC). The two have also formulated the "Declaration on the Conduct of Parties in the South China Sea",[6] and signed it in 2002. Chinese leaders and high-level officials actively and intensively visited the ASEAN countries to strengthen their economic, political, military and cultural contacts and exchanges.[7]

---

4   "Economic diplomacy" is a central part of China's foreign policy. Since the rise of its economic power, China has used economic diplomacy mainly by trade as "carrots" to develop its relations with developing countries. Following with it rise as a global power, many scholars and observers consider that economic diplomacy has become a coercive means for China to achieve its goals of foreign policy. About the comments on China's coercive economic diplomacy, can see Bonnie Glaser, "China's Coercive Economic Diplomacy," *The Diplomat*, July 25, 2015, <http://thediplomat.com/2012/07/chinas-coercive-economic-diplomacy/>.

5   On the development of China-ASEAN relations, can see Wang Yi's speech at the Boao Forum for Asia Annual Conference 2015. *Ministry of Foreign Affairs of the PRC*, Mar 28, 2015, <http://www.fmprc.gov.cn/mfa_eng/wjb_663304/wjbz_663308/2461_663310/t1252648.shtml>.

6   On the content of the Declaration, can see *ASEAN*, <http://www.asean.org/asean/external-relations/china/item/declaration-on-the-conduct-of-parties-in-the-south-china-sea>.

7   The ASEAN was built in August 1967 in Bangkok, Thailand, with the signing of the ASEAN Declaration, namely the Bangkok Declaration by Indonesia, Malaysia, Philippines, Singapore and Thailand. Brunei then joined in 1984, Vietnam joined in 1995, Lao and Myanmar joined in 1997, and Cambodia in 1999. So now the ASEAN has 10 member states. The aims and purposes of ASEAN can see the official website, *ASEAN*, <http://www.asean.org/asean/about-asean>.

II. China's Regional Strategy in Southeast Asia

This paper considers that the reason why there is a great change and adjustment of China's foreign policy to Southeast Asia can be explained from the change of international situation, the need of China's economic development, China's consideration to prevent the occupation and invasion of the influence of the United States and Japan in this region; and most importantly, the great role Southeast Asian countries could play not just on Asia-Pacific affairs but also on world politics. The ASEAN countries not only have played a very important role in the Asia-Pacific economies, but have also established many regional regimes to contribute to regional peace and cooperation. For instance, the ASEAN Ministerial Meeting (AMM), the ASEAN Economic Official Meeting (AEM), the ASEAN Dialogue Partners, the ASEAN Regional Forum (ARF), the East Asia Summit (EAS), and the (Asia-Europe Meeting (ASEM),[8] etc. Compared with other countries, ASEAN also has brilliant economic performance. To response the trend of economic integration under globalisation, ASEAN now is making great efforts to sign trade agreements and pacts with many countries. China is ASEAN's biggest neighbor connected by land and sea.[9] They share the borders of sea and land with China and they have a common land boundary of over 4,000 kilometers. Therefore, for China, to expand its influence in the region of Asia-Pacific, it is of importance to enhance its relations with ASEAN. In fact, not just China, the United States, Japan and South Korea also have actively and greatly developed their relations with ASEAN.

---

8   On the different meeting, institutions, and programs under the ASEAN, please see "ASEAN Institutions," ASEAN, <http://www.asean.org/news/item/asean-institutions>, and "The Brief Introduction of the Development of the ASEAN", Taiwan ASEAN Studies Centre, <http://www.aseancenter.org.tw/ASEANintro.aspxChung-Hua Institution for Economic Research>.

9   China is connected with Myanmar, Laos, and Vietnam, and faces other ASEAN countries across the sea.

Since the rise of China's economic power, it has accumulated and obtained many bargaining chips when dealing with ASEAN. Now China has expanded and deepened its relations with ASEAN into many levels and areas. For example, China signed the framework agreement in November 2002 in Phnom, Penh, Cambodia with ASEAN to establish a free trade area; that is, the China-ASEAN Free Trade Area (CAFTA),[10] which came into effect in January 2010 and is the largest free trade area in terms of population. It is comprised of 1.9 billion people ranking the third largest free trade area in the world in terms of nominal GDP (U.S.$6,000 billion) and trade volume (U.S.$4,500 billion) after the European Union (EU) and the North American Free Trade Area (NAFTA).[11] The CAFTA occupies 13.4% of world trade amounts. What is most important is that the average taxes of Chinese products exporting to ASEAN will decrease from 12.8% to 0.6%; and those from ASEAN countries to China will be 0.1% from 9.8%.[12] Now the taxes of 93% of all products, about 7,000 items on bilateral trade, have reduced to zero. Since the importance and close relations of their two-way trade, China suggested and proposed in 2013 to establish an upgraded version of the CAFTA, that is the so-called "China-ASEAN Free Trade Area version 2.0".[13] This clearly indicates that following with the rise of the ASEAN's economic power, and the improvement of its

---

10 The CAFTA is also the largest free trade area established by developing countries. See *China FTA Network*, <http://fta.mofcom.gov.cn/topic/chinaasean.shtml>.

11 Song Jenn-Jaw, "Political and Economic Impacts of the Implementation of the CAFTA: Taiwan's Response and Thinking," *Haixian Information*, Vol. 230 (February 2010), <http://www.haixiainfo.com.tw/230-7795.html>.

12 台商南進布局 (Tai Shang Nan Jin bu Jiu), *Trade Magazine*, Vol. 230, Nov., 2010, p. 11, <http://www.ieatpe.org.tw/magazine/ebook233/b0.pdf>。

13 When giving a keynote speech in Nanning on September 3, 2013 at the opening ceremony of the 10th China-ASEAN Expo (CAEXPO), Chinese Premier Li Keqiang gave a five-point suggestion to create an "upgraded version" of the CAFTA. Li suggested further lowering tariffs, improving connectivity, and communications, strengthening financial cooperation, expanding maritime cooperation and promoting cultural exchanges. See Cheong Chua Guan, "China proposed a CAFTA version," *The Brunei Times*, <http://archive.bt.com.bn/news-national/2013/09/04/china-proposes-cafta-version-2-0>.

infrastructure, ASEAN has become a potential regional and world market. This has been greatly enhanced by its important strategic position and a comfortable climate. The economic performance and growth of ASEAN not just helps to promote economic development of this region but can also contribute to global economic growth. The initiatives for establishing the ASEAN Economic Community (AEC), which is comprised of a population of 0.57 billion, or the ASEAN plus three Cooperation (ASEAN plus China, Japan and South Korea), and then ASEAN plus six,[14] all have explained the expansion of closer trade and economic cooperation among Asian countries in this region. This certainly will help the flow of capital, services, products and labors among Asia-Pacific countries.

On bilateral trade between China and the ASEAN countries, China now is the largest trading partner of ASEAN (See Table 1); the United States ranked fourth after the European Union (EU) and Japan. ASEAN is China's third largest trading partner, the fourth largest export market and the second largest source of imports.[15] Although the data from different sources are discrepant as Table 2 showed,[16] the bilateral trade did grow sharply.

---

14 In addition to the ASEAN plus China, Japan and South Korea (the ASEAN plus three group), the ASEAN plus six is comprised additionally of New Zealand, Australia, and India. On the implication and works of the ASEAN plus 6 group, can see Shujiro Urata, "An ASEAN +6 Economic Partnership: Significance and Tasks," *Asia Research Report 2007*, February 2008, <https://www.jcer.or.jp/eng/pdf/asia07.pdf>.

15 〈2013 年 1 至 7 月中國大陸東協雙邊貿易額達 2,477.23 億美元〉,《台灣經貿網》, 2013 年 8 月 27 日, <http://www.taiwantrade.com.tw/CH/bizsearchdetail/7234258>。

16 According to the research of Kevin Chua, Ronald U. Mendoza and Monica Melchor, the discrepancy of statistic numbers is caused by some reasons: (1) Hong Kong as trade entrepot, on transiting Hong Kong, export goods are added value due to further processing or re-packing; (2) Chinese goods are recorded as exports to an intermediary country because it is the last known destination by the exporters even if the goods are destined to a third country; (3) differences in values declared by Chinese customs at time of exportation and values declared to U.S. customs at time of importation. See Kevin Chua, Ronald U Mendoza and Monica Melchor, "An Analysis of the Evolving ASEAN-China Trade Linkages," paper presented at the Philippine Economic Society (PES) 52nd conference, November 14, 2014.

Table 1: ASEAN's Trade with Major Trade Partners (In U.S.$ billions)

Partner country/ region		2000	2005	2010	2013
ASEAN	Export	98.2(23%)	165.4(25%)	263.0(25%)	330.5(26%)
	Import	84.3(22%)	154.3(26%)	236.4(25%)	288.0(23%)
	Total-Trade	182.5(23%)	319.7(25%)	499.4(25%)	618.5(25%)
China	Export	16.5(4%)	53.7(8%)	113.7(11%)	153.2(12%)
	Import	20.2(5%)	63.0(10%)	127.2(13%)	205.0(16%)
	Total-Trade	36.7(5%)	115.7(9%)	240.9(12%)	358.2(14%)
EU	Export	63.9(15%)	84.2(13%)	116.2(11%)	128.5(10%)
	Import	41.9(11%)	60.8(10%)	89.1(9%)	117.9(9%)
	Total-Trade	105.8(13%)	145.0(12%)	205.3(10%)	246.4(10%)
Japan	Export	57.9(14%)	73.1(11%)	103.2(10%)	122.9(10%)
	Import	74.0(19%)	83.6(14%)	115.8(12%)	113.1(9%)
	Total-Trade	131.9(16%)	156.7(12%)	219.0(11%)	236.0(9%)
U.S.	Export	80.9(19%)	94.3(14%)	100.6(10%)	115.1(9%)
	Import	51.9(14%)	61.1(10%)	82.2(9%)	90.7(7%)
	Total-Trade	132,8(16%)	155.4(12%)	182.8(9%)	205.8(8%)
World	Export	426.8(100%)	654.5(100%)	1,52.4(100%)	1,269.6(100%)
	Import	380.0(100%)	602.7(100%)	952.9(100%)	1,244.9(100%)
	Total-Trade	806.8(100%)	1,257.3(100%)	2,005.3(100%)	2,514.5(100%)

Source: Nonoy Oplas, "Government and Taxes," March 20, 2015. <http://funwithgovernment.blogspot. tw/2015/03/china-asean-3-trade-and-investment.html>.

Figure1 showed that except for 2009, due to the global financial crisis, the bilateral trade between China and ASEAN has quickly increased from U.S.$36.7 billion in 2000 to U.S.$358.2 billion in 2013. Among the ASEAN member countries, Singapore, Thailand and Malaysia are the three countries with the highest trade volumes with China in 2013.[17] If one uses the data from the Chinese statistical yearbook as Table 2 showed, China-ASEAN two-way trade has already reached to U.S.$400 billion in 2012. In 2013, the

---

17 Nonoy Oplas, "Government and Taxes," March 20, 2015, <http://funwithgovernment. blogspot.tw/2015/03/china-asean-3-trade-and-investment.html>.

Table 2: Data Base Comparison of China-ASEAN Bilateral Trade (In U.S.$ billions)

Year	ASEANstarts Database				China Statistical Yearbook				UNCTADstat Database			
	Export	Import	Net Balance	Total Volume	Export	Import	Net Balance	Total Volume	Export	Import	Net Balance	Total Volume
2000	14.2	18.1	-3.9	32.3	22.2	17.3	4.8	39.5	16.5	20.2	-3.7	36.7
2001	14.5	17.4	-2.9	31.9	23.2	18.4	4.8	41.6	16.7	21.0	-4.3	37.7
2002	19.5	23.2	-3.7	42.8	31.2	23.6	7.6	54.8	21.9	28.0	-6.1	49.9
2003	29.1	30.6	-1.5	59.6	47.3	30.9	16.4	78.3	30.9	34.2	-3.3	65.1
2004	41.4	47.7	-6.4	89.1	63.0	42.9	20.1	105.9	41.6	48.4	-6.8	90.0
2005	52.3	61.1	-8.9	113.4	75.0	55.4	19.6	130.4	52.7	63.0	-10.3	115.7
2006	65.0	75.0	-9.9	139.7	89.5	69.5	20.0	159.0	66.7	78.7	-11.9	145.4
2007	77.9	93.2	-15.2	171.1	108.4	94.1	14.2	202.5	79.1	98.0	-18.9	177.1
2008	87.6	109.3	-21.7	196.9	117.0	114.3	2.7	231.3	88.7	113.2	-24.4	201.9
2009	81.6	96.6	-15.0	178.2	106.7	106.3	0.4	213.0	82.4	97.5	-15.1	179.9
2010	118.5	117.7	0.8	236.2	154.7	154.7	16.5	292.9	113.7	127.2	-13.5	240.9
2011	142.5	147.1	-4.6	289.7	193.0	193.0	22.9	363.1	142.5	157.1	-14.6	299.6
2012	141.9	177.6	-35.7	319.5	195.9	195.9	-8.4	400.1	141.9	178.7	-36.8	320.6
2013	-	-	-	-	-	-	-	-	153.2	205.0	-51.8	358.2

Source: Source: Nonoy Oplas, "Government and Taxes," March 20, 2015, <http://funwithgovernment. blogspot.tw/2015/03/china-asean-3-trade-and-investment.html>.

two-way trade was U.S.$443.6 billion.[18] On non-financial direct investment, China invested U.S.$5.74 billion in 2013 in ASEAN;[19] it grew 30% compared with the previous year. Until July 2014, the two-way investment has accumulated U.S.$120 billion.[20] Among the ASEAN member countries,

18 Ministry of Commerce, People's Republic of China,"*China, ASEAN Agree to Launch Negotiations on Upgrading FTA*," August 29, 2014, <http://english.mofcom.gov.cn/article/ newsrelease/significantnews/201408/20140800714706.shtml>.

19 "The 11th China-ASEAN Expo Background Information," *China-ASEAN EXPO Secretariat*, July 22, 2014, <http://eng.caexpo.org/notice/t20140722_109767.html>.

20 Li Keqiang, "Jointly open a brighter future for China-ASEAN relations," *The Philippine*

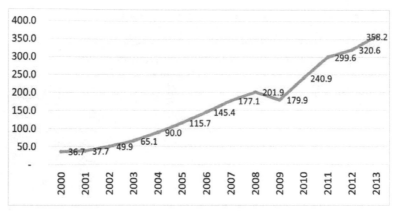

**Figure1: Growth in Volume of China-ASEAN Bilateral Trade (2000-2013)
(In U.S.$ billions)**

Source: Nonoy Oplas, "Government and Taxes," March 20, 2015. <http://funwithgovernment.blogspot.
tw/2015/03/china-asean-3-trade-and-investment.html>.

Singapore, Laos, and Cambodia have received the most Chinese capital. Viewing the increase of their bilateral trade, Chinese Premier Li Keqiang hence pledged to double trade and investment by 2020.[21]

According to Dr. Tang Zhimin, Dean of International College and Director of China-ASEAN Studies Centre, Panyapiwat Institute of Management, the reasons for the rapid growth of China-ASEAN bilateral trade are as following: (1) the reduction of trade barriers after the establishment of the CAFTA (ASEAN plus 1 FTAs); (2) the transfer of some supply chains from China to ASEAN for exports to Western markets; (3) China's growing demand for raw materials from ASEAN; (4) the increase of economic productivity of China and ASEAN resulting in the demand for

Star, November 11, 2014, <http://www.philstar.com/letters-editor/2014/11/11/1390363/
jointly-open-brighter-future-china-asean-relations>.

21 Zhou Xiaoyang, "The Diamond Decade," *Beijing Review*, No. 38, September 19, 2013,
<http://www.bjreview.com.cn/Cover_Stories_Series_2013/2013-09/16/content_572467.
htm>.

each other's products.[22] For the ASEAN countries, not just the huge potential of China's market but also Chinese capital and technology all attract them to develop relations with China. However, since they still have serious and long-term territorial disputes and conflicts with China, in addition to maintaining a stable relationship with China, ASEAN also clearly appreciate the importance for working closely with the United States and Japan. This therefore not only can balance the potential threats from China but also can balance the influence of the United States and Japan to deeply intervene in Asia-Pacific affairs

III. Strategic Importance of ASEAN to the U.S. Asia-Pacific Policy

ASEAN has played an important role not just on China's political operation, but also on China's military deployment and economic development. However, ASEAN has also occupied a very important strategic position on U.S. Asia policy. Since Hillary Clinton, the-Secretary of State announced that the United States was back and that it intended to broaden and deepen its partnership in the Asia-Pacific region when she visited Thailand in July 2009. She then signed the "Treaty of Amity and Cooperation in Southeast Asia" and proclaimed that Americans would continue their commitment to its Asia allies.[23] This therefore has increased the importance of the role ASEAN played on U.S. Asia-Pacific policy. Whether "returning to", "pivot to" or "rebalancing" Asia, the United States has adjusted and shifted the main focus of its foreign policy to Asia-Pacific by means of actively participating regional affairs, enhance the two-way trade and conducting military maneuvers with Asian countries. Not

---

22 韓碩，〈中國東盟雙邊貿易快速增長拉動亞洲內需〉，《人民日報》，2013 年 8 月 26 日，<http://finance.sina.com.cn/china/20130826/070716558368.shtml>。

23 "U.S. 'is back' is Asia, Secretary of State Hillary Clinton declares," *The Daily News*, July 21, 2009, <http://www.nydailynews.com/news/world/u-s-back-asia-secretary-state-hillary-clinton-declares-article-1.429381>.

just President Barack Obama but also many high-level U.S. officials have intensively and frequently visited Asian countries hence proposed to resolve regional affairs by means of multilateral regimes.

In fact, the U.S. "return to Asia Pacific" Strategy can be explained from economic, military and political perspectives. After the global financial and economic recession in 2008, American witnessed a decrease of it economic power and growth rate; hence realised the importance of economic security. From 2001 to 2007, the average annual economic growth rate of the United States was about 2.48%.[24] The situation became worse and worse especially after the subprime mortgage crisis. According to Table 3 and 4, from 2008 to 2011, its average economic growth rate was 0.3% and the unemployment rate reached 9% in 2011 from 4% in 2000. However, compare with the recession the United States faced, Asian countries (excluding Japan who was already a developed country) have achieved impressive economic growth; the average rate of economic growth was 8.1%. [25] The region therefore has become an important area and major source for U.S. economic interests. By means of economic and trade cooperation with ASEAN, the United States expects to expand and explore Asian market hence increase its exports to the region and improve its unemployed rate.

Table 3: GDP-Real Growth Rate of the United States (from 2001-2011)

Year	2001	2002	2003	2004	2005	2006	2007	2008	2009	2010	2011
Percentage (%)	0.3	2.45	3.1	4.4	3.2	3.2	2	1.1	-2.6	2.8	1.7

Source: Index Mundi. <http://www.indexmundi.com/g/g.aspx?v=66&c=us&l=en>.

---

24 See Accounting and Statistics , Executive Yuan, R.O.C., *Directorate-General of Budget*, <http://www.dgbas.gov.tw/ct.asp?xItem=13213&CtNode=3504&mp=1>.

25 About the economic growth rates of the United States and the world, can see "World Economic Outlook: Growth Resuming, Dangers Remain," *International Monetary Funds*, 2012, <http://www.imf.org/external/pubs/ft/weo/2012/01/pdf/tables.pdf>.

Table 4: Unemployment Rate of the United States (from 2000-2011)

Year	2000	2002	2003	2004	2005	2006	2007	2008	2009	2010	2011
Percentage (%)	4	5.8	6	5.5	5.1	4.8	4.6	7.2	9.3	9.7	9

Source: Index Mundi. <http://www.indexmundi.com/g/g.aspx?v=74&c=us&l=en>.

On military strategy, due to the occurrence of the 911 incident, the U.S. foreign policy shifted to the Middle East hence ignored the region of Asia-Pacific. To adjust its military deployment after the withdrawal of U.S. military forces from Iraq and Afghanistan and to response to the rise of China, the U.S. Department of Defense released the Quadrennial Defense Review Report (QDR) in 2010.[26] Just like the National Security Strategy of the United States of America issued by the White House in 2010,[27] the documents all indicated that to maintain U.S. military predominance in the world, the United States should employ a wide range of diplomatic, economic tools and international regimes, these "non-military tools" to protect U.S. national security. The United States should adopt a policy of "Engagement" to emphasise economic security and to enhance its relations with its allies. Hillary Clinton therefore proposed new ideas such as "forward-deployed diplomacy".[28] By means of intensive and close contacts and visits by high-level U.S. officials to Asia and active participation in Asia-Pacific regional affairs, the United States has enhanced its cooperation with Asian countries. For Americans, this can promote the establishment of "America's Pacific Century".[29]

---

26 The U.S. Department of Defense, *"The Quadrennial Defense Review Report 2010,"* 2010, <http://www.defense.gov/qdr/qdr%20as%20of%2029jan10%201600.PDF>.

27 The U.S. White House, *The National Security Strategy of the United States of America 2010*, <htttp://www.whitehouse.gov/sites/default/files/rss_reviewer/national_security_strategy.pdf>.

28 Hillary Clinton, *"America's Engagement in the Asia-Pacific,"* The U.S. Department of States, October 28, 2010, <http://www.state.gov/secretary/20092013clinton/rm/2010/10/150141.htm?goMobile=0>.

29 Hillary Clinton, "America's Pacific Century," *Foreign Policy*, October 11, 2011, <http://

Making good on the United States' commitment to its Asian partners will require the U.S. forces to continue to remain in Asia. The United States therefore adjusted its military deployment in Asia to enhance bilateral military cooperation with its allies. For instance, to strengthen military presence in Guam and Hawaii, to increase the number of troops in Japan and South Korea, as well as the signing of a military agreement with Australia, and to strengthen military cooperation with its traditional allies in the region. It is clear that the United States wants to adjust its military deployment in East Asia and Pacific region after the cut of the defense budget. By doing this, the United States can ask its allies to share the burden of regional security, namely they cannot just heavily depend on the U.S. forces. Therefore, strengthening its military cooperation with Japan, Korea, the Philippines, Thailand, and Australia, its traditional allies while expanding and developing new partnerships with Vietnam, Indonesia, Singapore, Malaysia, and New Zealand, these non-traditional military allies, are one of the major objectives for the United States to return to Asia.

On regional order, the United States hoped to develop a multilateral approach through multilateral mechanism and regimes to ensure the connection between the Asia-Pacific and international frameworks. This hence could protect Americans' interests in this area. On the development of free trade and economic relations, the United States promoted the "Trans-Pacific Strategic Economic Partnership Agreement (TPP)" to enhance its relations with the Asia-Pacific region. In order to achieve its purpose to return to Asia, Secretary of State Hillary Clinton actively participated and joined many times the meetings of APEC, ASEAN, ASEAN Defense Ministerial Meeting Plus (ADMM Plus), EAS, ARF and other East Asian regional organisations. This clearly indicates that the United States wants to take back the right of speech and show absolute leadership in this region. That is to say that the basic tenets of the United States return-to-Asia policy

---

www.foreignpolicy.com/articles/2011/10/11/americas_pacific_century>.

is to shape the economy of Asia-Pacific, change regional security structure, support the system and value of democracy, and spread universal values. Therefore, applying the strategy of "selective engagement" can effectively decrease the cost and risk for intervening in regional affairs.

After examining and analysing the reasons and background for the U.S.'s "Return to Asia-Pacific" Strategy, this paper considers that it should not be only considered for counterbalancing or containing the rise of China. For the United States, "Returning to Asia" not just can balance its military expenditure and spending but can also save its unemployment rate and improve domestic economic situation by means of sharing excessive burdens to Asian countries. This can also help to maintain U.S. military presence in this region while avoiding provoking China. For Asian countries, they will continue to rely on the United States on regional security by means of political and military cooperation while maintaining close trade and economic contacts with China. For China, it is of importance to continuously deepen its economic reforms by means of economic cooperation with its neighbors while actively participating in regional affairs and eventually assume the role of leader in Asia-Pacific. That is, in the short term, the United States will still maintain a relationship of cooperation and competition with China; and vice versa.

IV. Some Reflections on China's Strategic Arrangement and Layout in Asia-Pacific Region

When Chinese President, Xi Jinping took office in March 2013, on the relations with ASEA, he greatly proposed an "amicable, secure and prosperous neighborhood" policy and a "new security concept for Asia".[30]

---

30 When giving a keynote speech on a new Asian approach to security at the Conference on Interaction and Confidence Building Measures in Asia (CICA) Summit of in May 2014, Chinese President Xi Jinping called for a common, comprehensive, cooperative and sustainable security strategy for Asia. He claimed that Asia's security problems should be

He therefore promoted the establishment of an Asian-Pacific Free Trade Zone and Asia-Pacific innovation development and economic reform by means of strengthening links and infrastructure. Xi therefore suggested the strategic concept of "One Belt and One Road" (OBOR).[31] "One Belt" refers to the network of overland corridors that China is developing; that is to say, the new roads and rail links from its eastern part to far-flung regions in western and southwestern parts. By building this corridor, China can connect its distant frontiers to the central parts with highways, railroads and pipelines and eventually extend them all across the Eurasian landmass. On the proposal of "One Road", namely the "21st century maritime silk road", China wants to build maritime infrastructure throughout the Indo-Pacific, including new ports and special economic zones around this region. Figure 1 showed the routes of the OBOR. Beijing announced a fund of U.S.$500 million to promote this "maritime silk road" in Southeast Asia.[32] By means of the initiative, China not only can boost regional trade with Asian countries under Beijing's leadership, but also can smartly connect Xi's "Chinese Dream" with that of "Asia-Pacific Dream". According to Professor Tang Zhimin, the shift of China's ASEAN policy will happen in several aspects, Beijing will focus on promoting China-ASEAN cooperation under the initiatives of One Belt and One Road; forging bilateral and multilateral FTAs; adjusting its role to a major exporter of technologies and capital, and also to an important party in the global rule-making process.[33]

---

solved by Asians themselves only by cooperation and oppose the arbitrary use of force or threats. On Xi's new Asian security concept, can see "China Focus: China's Xi proposes security concept for Asia," *Xinhua Net*, May 21, 2014, <http://news.xinhuanet.com/english/china/2014-05/21/c_133351210.htm>.

31 Chinese President Xi Jinping suggested in 2013 the initiative of OBOR, a Chinese framework for organising multinational economic development mainly in Eurasia by the land-based "Silk Road Economic Belt" (SREB) and oceangoing "Maritime Silk Road" (MSR).

32 "China Takeaway: One Belt, One Road," *The Indian Express*, August 13, 2014, <http://indianexpress.com/article/opinion/columns/chinese-takeaway-one-belt-one-road/>.

33 "China's bid to further opening up benefits world," *China Daily*, March 16, 2015. <http:///usa.chinadaily.com.cn/business/2015-03/16/content_19819642.htm>.

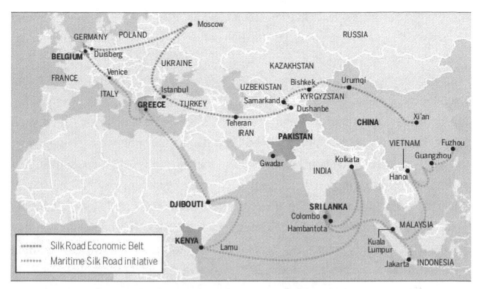

Figure 2: The Routes of the OBOR

Source: "One Belt, One Road," Asia Pacific Intellectual Capital Centre, February 25, 2015, <http://www.slideshare.net/AlanLung/st-20141213-p1blurbs13901917>.

This hence creates a shared destiny in the Asia-Pacific region and that the importance of ASEAN and the role it can play in China's new foreign policy therefore has greatly increased.

To fulfill its plan of One Belt and One Road, Beijing then proposed an Asian infrastructure investment bank (AIIB) in October 2013 when Xi met Indonesian President Susilo Bambang Yudhoyono. The AIIB then was established in 2014 to finance infrastructure projects in the Asia-Pacific Region with headquarters in Beijing. The initial subscribed capital of AIIB is U.S.$50 billion and will be increased to U.S.$100 billion. The AIIB will provide financing for roads, railways, airports and other infrastructure projects in Asia. It is expected to be established by the end of this year. Now there are 57 Prospective Founding Members (PFM) from five continents joining the AIIB.[34] Even in the beginning, the United States tried to

---

34 Sweden, Israel, South Africa, Iceland, Portugal and Poland were all included as founding

dissuade its allies such as the United Kingdom, South Korea, Australia and Japan, etc., not to join the AIIB until clearly appreciate its operation, aims and rules. However, many countries have already applied to join it. For Americans, the Washington-based World Bank and the Manila-based Asian Development Bank (ADB) already can provide over U.S.$383 billion to this region, the AIIB capital is small. For the United States, it seriously worried about the influence of Beijing in the region will be enhanced by means of the establishment of the AIIB. For China, being the world's second largest economy, it strongly demands more rights to speak; however, whether in ADB, the World Bank, or the International Monetary Fund (IMF), China's voice have not be heard easily. No matter what kind of Chinese motivations might be, it is noteworthy that even countries that have disputes with China on its military expansion in the East and South China seas are also willing to join the AIIB. This clearly demonstrates that economic interests are obviously of paramount importance. Figure 3 showed the members of ADB and AIIB in different colors.

Many scholars in the field of International Relations claim that China's strategic layout in Southeast Asia can be considered as an arrangement to oppose the intervention of the United States in the region of Asia-Pacific, especially after the high profile of the announcement of the U.S. returning to Asia. This paper considers that the design of China's ASEAN policy can be explained from some perspectives. It cannot be only considered as China's containment of U.S. influence in this region, or the Chinese version of "rebalancing policy to Asia" although this is one of the considerations. The major reason can be explained from the neoliberal approach suggested by Robert Keohane and Joseph Nye. To clearly explain their ideas and to compare them with the realist ideal type of world politics,[35] Keohane and

---

members of the AIIB. See "$50bn Asian infrastructure bank approves 57 founding members," *Reuters*, April 15, 2015, <http://rt.com/business/249873-aiib-countries-membership-ministry/>.

35 For political Realists, international politics is a struggle for power. They suggest three

Nye suggest the idea of "complex interdependence",[36] which includes three main characteristics:

> "multiple channels connect societies; the agenda of interstate relationships consists of multiple issues that are not arranged in a clear or consistent hierarchy; and military force is not used by governments towards other governments within the region, or on the issues."[37]

Keohane and Nye consider that the ideal type of complex interdependence increasingly reflects the reality of many situations in the world. They intend to establish a method to understand not only world politics but also the model of institutionalised international cooperation while reserving some realist assumptions regarding the effect of power and interests in world politics. After the rise of China, it certainly will seek a position that matches its status as being the second largest economy in the world. This paper considers that China has tried to develop complex interdependent relations with other countries, and this will be helpful for China to take the leadership in the future. To establish its influence in the world, China has smartly learned from the Western experience; that is to say, enhancing its relations with other countries by economic and trade cooperation, providing economic aid to developing countries, creating and building Chinese-led international or regional regimes, and developing relations with countries with abundant resources. Since the rise of its economic power, now China has much more bargaining chips that can be

---

assumptions about world politics: first, states as coherent units are the dominant actors in world politics; second, force is a usable and effective instrument of policy; and third, a hierarchy of issues in world politics. See Robert O. Keohane and Joseph S. Nye, *Power and Interdependence*, 3rd ed. (U.S.A: Longman, 2001), p. 20.

36 Keohane and Nye insist that 'complex interdependence' is an ideal type rather than an accurate description of world politics or a forecast of trends. They did not pursue complex interdependence as a theory, but as a thought experiment about what politics may look like if the basic assumptions of Realism were reversed. See Robert O. Keohane and Nye, *Power and Interdependence* (London: Pearson, 2001), p. 275.

37 Ibid, p. 21.

used as tools of foreign policy.[38] Facing the decrease of U.S. economic power, China now apparently has occupied a better position. Therefore, to maintain regional peace, the United States should search for cooperation with China while maintaining its military predominance. That is, it should keep this relationship of cooperation and competition with China.

Viewing close contacts and exchanges between China and ASEAN, the relationship of cooperation and competition between the United States and China in this region, this paper considers that Taiwan should have some strategic considerations as well. Perhaps this can be thought from two perspectives, namely in terms of economy and politics. On economic level, Taiwan should enhance its trade and economic cooperation with ASEAN. On their paper "An Analysis of the Evolving ASEAN-China Trade Linkages", Kevin Chua, Ronald U Mendoza and Monica Melchor used many materials and data to examine if China and ASEAN are strategic partners or competitors. According to their research, although bilateral trade between China and ASEAN was sharply increased, the two are also competing in the exports of major goods to similar trade destinations.

This means that they have a relationship of cooperation with competition, it undoubtedly give some spaces for the third country to utilise and manipulate. Now China is Taiwan's largest trading partner while ASEAN ranked second, this means that both of them are of importance to the development of Taiwan's trade and economy. However, bilateral trade between Taiwan and ASEAN is closer to complementary; this means that Taiwan does not need to compete with the ASEAN member countries. Conversely, Taiwan should work closely with ASEAN by means of signing the FTA and actively joining regional affairs. On political considerations, there are serious disputes and conflicts on territory between China and

---

38 See Kevin Chua, Ronald U Mendoza and Monica Melchor, "An Analysis of the Evolving ASEAN-China Trade Linkages," *Asian institute of management policy center*, <https://phileconsoc.files.wordpress.com/2014/11/asean-china-trade-linkages.pptx>.

Card-carrying members

- ADB members and AIIB prospective founding members
- ADB members but not AIIB prospective founding members
- AIIB prospective founding members but not ADB members

SCMP

Figure 3: Members of ADB and AIIB

Source: "57 nations approved as founder members of China-led AIIB," *South China Morning Post*, April 15, 2015, <http://www.scmp.com/news/china/diplomacy-defence/article/1766970/57-nations-approved-founder-members-china-led-aiib>.

ASEAN, and a long term alliance relationship between the United States and ASEAN in Asia-Pacific region. While searching for a peaceful solution to territorial disputes, Taiwan should work together with ASEAN and the U.S.A to develop its own policy. The most important is that facing the integration of Asia economies, Taiwan should work closely with ASEAN; this not only can decrease and diversify its investment risks but also can help to balance its high trade dependency on China that has already reached up to 40%.

V. Conclusions

After examining the relations between ASEAN and China, and the role ASEAN played in U.S. Asia-Pacific policy, one can clearly appreciate that for China, on military security, ASEAN is not only a breakthrough to oppose the United States' returning to Asia but also the foundation of a Chinese version of the "Asia-Pacific rebalancing strategy". On China's economic development and plans to build the "21st Century Maritime Silk Road", and the upgraded version of "China-ASEAN Free Trade Area", ASEAN also occupies a very critical and important strategic position. Therefore, China must maintain its close and intensive contacts with ASEAN by means of cooperation on construction of infrastructure and links of communication and traffic to continuously participate in Asia-Pacific affairs hence maintain the rights of speak and leadership in this region. This is critical for China to break through the alliance and cooperation between the United States and Japan on the search for power in this region and guarantee a stable environment for China's national development.

When Xi took office in March 2013, he suggested a series of new foreign policies and strategies. For instance, he promoted an "amicable, secure and prosperous neighborhood" policy with China's neighboring countries; proposed a "new model of great power relationship" with the United States; proposed a "new security concept for Asia"; proposed an international order for peaceful coexistence for states by shared prosperity, mutual tolerance, and sustainable development. As Xi's Chinese Dream has deep connection with the Asian-Pacific Dream he proposed, he therefore called upon the governments of ASEAN to cooperate with China to develop this region together. Whether it is involved in multilateral dialogue mechanism in East Asia, promote its "good-neighborly diplomacy" and the Regional Comprehensive Economic Partnership (RCEP), China wants to enhance its economic cooperation and integration with Southeast Asian countries hence establish a common destiny for China and ASEAN. These are all Chinese foreign strategies to fulfill its national development. Therefore, ASEAN played a critical role on Beijing's grad strategy,.

After establishing a "good-neighborly and mutual-trust partnership" with ASEAN in 1997, and "Strategic Partnership for Peace and Prosperity" in 2003, China was also the first country to sign the "Treaty of Amity and Cooperation in Southeast Asia" (TAC) with ASEAN in 2003. After the launch of ASEAN plus three in 2010, the two-way trade between ASEAN and China has quickly and greatly increased. For instance, in 2000, the bilateral trade between China and ASEAN were U.S.$39.52 billion; it then quickly rose to U.S.$400 billion in 2012. The bilateral trade grew 10 times. Now China is the largest trading partner of ASEAN, and it was China's third trading partner. This indicates that even the United States is promoting the TPP in this region; its effectiveness cannot be compared with what China has done here. Perhaps, the bargaining chips the United States can utilise are the territorial disputes in East and South China Seas and the increase military expenditure and spending of China. However, for the ASEAN countries, they will continue to smartly seek for cooperation with global powers without taking any sides.

In Xi's "Four Strategies" for China's national development; that is to say, democracy, the rule of law, economics, and a strong military; although the last strategy is designed for ruling the nation, it has led to increasing concerns of ASEAN about China's military expansion in the South China Seas. This hence caused dilemma for ASEAN. For the ASEAN countries, in terms of economic development, it is completely unlikely to exclude China; however, on regional security, military and politics, they greatly depend on the support and protection of the United States. There is no doubt that ASEAN will continue to seek cooperation with China and the United States and other regional powers at the same time, and find the best way for their own interests and national development. That is to say, they will continuously adopt this kind of balance policy and strategies. Taiwan should learn the experience and lessons from ASEAN to see how to cooperate economically with China while maintaining a stable cross-Strait relationship and continuously develop a good relationship with the United States, and not to take any sides.